Shadows of Doubt

Shadows of Doubt

Stereotypes, Crime, and the Pursuit of Justice

Brendan O'Flaherty
Rajiv Sethi

 Harvard University Press

Cambridge, Massachusetts

London, England

2019

First printing

Design by Dean Bornstein

Library of Congress Cataloging-in-Publication Data

Names: O'Flaherty, Brendan, author. | Sethi, Rajiv, 1963– author.
Title: Shadows of doubt : stereotypes, crime, and the pursuit of justice /
    Brendan O'Flaherty, Rajiv Sethi.
Description: Cambridge, Massachusetts : Harvard University Press, 2019. |
    Includes bibliographical references and index.
Identifiers: LCCN 2018047862 | ISBN 9780674976597 (alk. paper)
Subjects: LCSH: Discrimination in criminal justice administration—United
    States. | Stereotypes (Social psychology)—United States. |
    Discrimination—United States. | Discrimination in law enforcement—
    United States.
Classification: LCC HV9950 .O25 2019 | DDC 364.97308—dc23
LC record available at https://lccn.loc.gov/2018047862

In memory of
Marjorie Miller and Patrick J. Gallagher

Contents

Preface

Crime and punishment are both accompanied by a great deal of uncertainty. Offenders often decide on targets without knowing whether their victims will resist or retaliate. Potential victims make guesses about how to avoid becoming targets, and must quickly choose how to respond if they guess wrong. Witnesses need to consider the consequences for their own safety and social relations if they cooperate with law enforcement officials. Police officers make judgments about the likelihood of contraband recovery when deciding on a stop or search, and about the danger to themselves and others when contemplating the use of force. Prosecutors and defense attorneys wonder about the inclinations of potential jurors when choosing whom to strike from the jury pool. Jurors make up their minds about whether laws were broken without ever hearing complete stories. And judges and parole boards are often expected to estimate what crimes a defendant might commit in the future if permitted to be free. All of these decisions are made deep in the shadows of doubt.

Moreover, people are aware that others are also groping for answers as they confront their own doubts, and take this into account when interacting with strangers. The motorist who is pulled over must think about what the officer might be thinking and attempt to react in ways that keep the interaction brief and safe. And the officer must interpret the driver's behavior with this mental process in mind. Mutual uncertainty can lead groups of people to do things that they would never do if they confronted their doubts alone.

When thinking about crime and punishment in modern America, one cannot escape the question of race. Americans draw many inferences from bodily features like skin color, hair texture, and eye shape that are markers of race today, and they know that everyone else around them is also drawing inferences from these features in predictable ways.

To illustrate this welter of uncertainty, consider the following anecdote related by the philosopher Elizabeth Anderson:

> One late night in 2007 I was driving in Detroit when my oil light came on. I pulled into the nearest gas station to investigate when a young black man approached me to offer help. "Don't worry, I'm not here to rob you," he said, holding up his hands, palms flat at face level, gesturing his innocence. "Do you need some help with your car?" I thanked him for his offer and told him I wasn't sure how much oil I needed. He read the dip stick, told me the car needed two quarts, and offered to do the job for free. From the look on his face when I paid him anyway, it was clear that he needed the cash.[1]

This young man knew that he was not going to rob the woman in the car, but he also knew that the woman was probably afraid that he might do so. His inference was based on beliefs about how she might perceive and interpret his appearance. He also thought that his acknowledgment of this probable fact, and the accompanying ritual, might put her mind at ease. And he was right. She understood his ritual because she knew that he believed that she was probably afraid. As a consequence, two strangers navigated in the shadows of doubt in ways that led them both to benefit.

If mutual uncertainty were not at play, this would be an uncomplicated story about the level of oil in a car. It had nothing to do with crime—no one wanted or tried to commit a crime, and no crime was committed or prevented. And automotive maintenance has nothing essential to do with race either. Yet, because this incident occurred in Detroit in 2007, both parties reacted to their doubts with elaborate inferences about race and crime, and the transaction could have broken down in many different ways. In fact, even though both parties had good intentions and everything worked out well in the end, Anderson argues that the young man was nevertheless harmed: "The harm consists in the fact that he walks under a cloud of suspicion in unstructured encounters with strangers. To gain access to cooperative interactions, he must assume the burdens of dispelling this cloud, of protesting and proving his innocence of imagined crimes."

Given the history of criminal justice in the United Sates, such clouds hang over all manner of interactions. If both the driver and the officer at a traffic stop are white, the driver might worry about whether any objects in the vehicle might arouse suspicion and lead to a search. If the driver is black he may wonder, in addition, whether race played a role in the stop itself. More ominously, he might wonder if the officer gained pleasure from prolonging the stop or from finding a pretext for an invasive search. And the officer's awareness of these concerns could affect his behavior, too, perhaps even more so if he considers the fears groundless.

This book is about how people confront these shadows of doubt, and about what the implications are for crime and criminal justice. We investigate how crimes are committed, who is victimized, how law enforcement officials respond, and how justice might be pursued in better ways.

Many books about crime and punishment have been written; what makes this one different is our emphasis on information and beliefs and on the interplay between the beliefs of many different people. Put simply, the book is about the doubts that faced the philosopher and the young man who assisted her late that night in Detroit, and the countless other situations in which similar uncertainties arise.

INTRODUCTION

Daily life is full of encounters between people who know very little about each other. Taxi drivers interact with riders, for example, as do servers with diners, hotel staff with guests, doctors with patients, and teachers with students. Even when interactions are repeated—as in the latter two cases—knowledge of others is narrowly circumscribed. After all, medical histories and academic records can tell us only so much about a person.

In managing such encounters, people often rely on beliefs formed on the flimsiest of evidence, such as race, ethnicity, gender, build, accents, tattoos, and piercings. Whether consciously or unconsciously, we attribute to individuals certain characteristics of the groups to which we imagine they belong. We stereotype.

For instance, a cab driver may use racial or ethnic markers as a guide to a rider's likely destination, and decide to bypass one person in favor of another. A server may similarly make judgments about the likely tipping behavior of a diner, and choose a level of attentiveness to match.

Stereotypes affect behavior both directly, by influencing the actions of those who hold and act on them, and indirectly, by influencing those who anticipate or expect them. People may avoid an interaction if they suspect that they will be harmfully stereotyped, or they may actively seek out such interactions if the stereotype operates in their favor. In fact, we stereotype about stereotypes, attributing to individuals the beliefs that are common among members of the groups to which we assign them.

In many instances, stereotypes cause interactions to play out in ways that make them self-fulfilling. The server who provides poor service expecting a small tip is likely to receive exactly that, even if the very same customer would have been generous in rewarding good service.

This book is about how stereotypes affect interactions connected to crime and the criminal justice system. Many of the relevant interactions here are not routine; they arise only under unexpected contingencies. These include interactions between victims and offenders, buyers and sellers of contraband, parties to a dispute, police officers and suspects, prosecutors and witnesses, and judges and defendants. In all such cases, decisions must be made under conditions of limited information, time pressure, and significant consequences for the well-being of one or more parties involved. Stereotypes loom especially large in such instances.

Without examining the role of stereotypes at the level of fine-grained interactions, we believe that it is impossible to make sense of crime and punishment in the United States.

Consider the following facts.

We are by far the most punitive society in the economically advanced world, with Russia a distant second. It wasn't always this way: before the 1970s the incarceration rate was relatively stable and within the bounds of international norms. Then began a steady and inexorable rise such that by the peak in 2008 we had seen a fourfold increase in the rate of confinement. There has been a modest decline since then.

Crime, meanwhile, rose sharply in the 1960s and 1970s, peaked in the early 1990s, and declined steadily over the next two decades. By 2013, across all major categories, including robbery, homicide, burglary, and theft, crime had fallen to levels not seen in five decades. There has been an uptick in homicide since then, with especially large increases in some cities. Whether this represents a brief interruption or a longer-term reversal of the trend toward lower crime remains to be seen.

The population behind bars is largely young and male, with fewer years of schooling than in the country as a whole. It is also disproportionately black and—to a lesser extent—Hispanic. In 2010, for example, there were about 450 white men imprisoned per 100,000 in the population. The corresponding figures for Hispanics and blacks were 1,250 and 3,100, respectively.

These racial and ethnic disparities far exceed those on many other dimensions of inequality, such as income and years of schooling. They also vastly exceed differences across groups in such social indicators as single parenthood.

Not surprisingly, disparities in incarceration rates mirror differences across groups in rates of arrest. But these differences vary sharply depending on the type of crime. Among crimes primarily motivated by the acquisition of property, the proportion of arrestees who are black is twice as high for robbery as it is for burglary or theft. Similarly, arrestees charged with homicide are significantly more likely to be black than arrestees for arson, rape, and aggravated assault.

Understanding such variations across crimes requires us to consider the role that stereotypes play in affecting face-to-face interactions, such as those typically involved in robbery and homicide. Crimes such as burglary and larceny are fundamentally different because they do not generally involve personal contact, and thus stereotypes do not come into play in the same way.

In the case of robbery, victims and offenders usually do not know anything about each other when the interaction is initiated. They do, however, observe (or think they observe) a number of physical attributes, including race, sex, build, and age. Offenders use these cues when selecting a victim, and thus some types of victims are targeted more often than others. Furthermore, victim resistance depends on the observable attributes of offenders, making robbery more lucrative for those who expect to face less resistance.

In general, being feared is profitable for offenders, because they face less resistance. Being feared also benefits potential victims, because they are confronted less often. A number of patterns in the data on robbery can be understood once such effects are taken into account. Among these are white offenders' almost complete avoidance of black victims, and black offenders' attraction to white victims.

Next consider homicide, which is the only serious crime that can be motivated by preemption—people sometimes kill simply to avoid being killed. In fact, a significant fraction of killings arise from escalating disputes involving strangers or casual acquaintances. Under such conditions, beliefs about the likelihood of being killed are important determinants of preemptive killing. But these beliefs are themselves shaped by stereotypes.

Those who believe that they can be killed with impunity have the strongest incentive to kill preemptively. This belief implies that in areas with low homicide clearance rates—where most homicides remain unsolved—the rate of preemptive killing will be especially high. Furthermore, those belonging to a group whose members have historically been killed with impunity will have the most to fear. They will be more likely to take preemptive action, which will also make them more feared, and indeed more likely to be killed preemptively. These cascading beliefs can result in very high homicide rates in some communities. They can also give rise to sharp fluctuations in homicide rates across time and space, as changes in the level of fear become self-fulfilling through the logic of preemption and retaliation.

Stereotypes also affect the actions of law enforcement officials, the elected representatives who establish the framework within which they work, and the voters who elect these representatives. It is not possible to adequately explain or effectively change what cops on the street do without thinking about those who pay them, train them, and give them orders, both directly and indirectly.

Consider police stops. The legal basis for such stops is reasonable suspicion, which is less demanding than probable cause, the standard for more intrusive searches and seizures. Officers have considerable discretion in deciding what constitutes suspicious behavior, and stereotypes can again come into play in these determinations.

One way to think about whether the same standard of reasonable suspicion is being applied across different groups is to look at the rate at which contraband is recovered. The available evidence using this method suggests considerable racial and ethnic profiling in both traffic and pedestrian stops. That is, it suggests that some groups are viewed as more suspicious independently of their actions at the time of contact with law enforcement agents. As a result, large numbers of innocent members of such groups are targeted for stops and searches.

One interpretation of this evidence is that officers on the ground have discriminatory motives when they select motorists and pedestrians to stop. But it is also important to consider whether the operations that officers have been tasked to perform are discriminatory in effect, even when they are executed without bias. In the language of lawyers, there is a distinction between disparate impact (whether the policies disproportionately burden some groups without being necessary to advance the public good) and disparate treatment (individual officers treat members of some groups differently from others during encounters, without good reason).

Whether disproportionate targeting results from discriminatory treatment or discriminatory impact, it has consequences for general attitudes toward law enforcement in the affected communities. In particular, it results in lower rates of witness cooperation. The unwillingness of witnesses to come forward contributes directly to low clearance rates for homicide, greater killing with impunity, and greater preemptive killing. Thus, stereotypes that sustain bias in police stops for minor infractions can increase both the incidence of homicide and the extent to which killers are brought to justice.

Yet another factor that affects witness cooperation is the degree to which multiple witnesses to a crime believe that others will step forward to corroborate their testimony. In the absence of such corroboration, convicting defendants becomes more difficult. Low conviction rates further stoke fears of retaliation among witnesses, making them even less inclined to testify. Just as high rates of homicide perpetuate themselves through preemptive killing in a climate of fear, low rates of witness cooperation sustain themselves in a climate of collective silence. And sometimes the courage of a single witness can open the door for others to come forward, as several celebrities accused of serial sexual assault have recently discovered.

Stereotypes are also implicated in homicides that involve police. This is one domain in which preemptive action based on a fear of violence is especially salient. About fifty officers are killed feloniously in the line of duty every year in the United States, and many more suffer nonfatal injuries. Policing is dangerous business. But the number of civilians killed by police is much higher, exceeding a thousand annually in recent years. A significant fraction of those killed are armed and dangerous, but there are also several hundred unarmed victims of police homicide every year.

The question of whether racial bias is implicated in some of these killings is now at the forefront of public debate and animates the Black Lives Matter movement. The increasing availability of video evidence has brought to light a number of cases in which the officers in question appear to be acting with unwarranted fear, in apparent reaction to the fact that they are interacting with a black male. This may be called the fear hypothesis.

Yet, in the nation as a whole, the rate at which black civilians are victims of police shootings is roughly on par with the arrest rates they face. This has led some to argue that the likelihood of any given encounter resulting in a fatal shooting does not vary significantly across groups, and that the focus should be on the frequency of encounters rather than excessive fear or other biases that emerge during encounters. This may be called the contact hypothesis. We try to reconcile these two seemingly conflicting pieces of evidence by closely examining geographic variation in the incidence of police homicides, and in doing so we find staggering differences across locations in the incidence of lethal force.

As with police stops, we study disparate impact as well as disparate treatment, because the well-being of disadvantaged groups can be severely harmed even by policies that are facially neutral and implemented without bias. With police homicides, moreover, determining conclusively whether disparate treatment was implicated in any particular case is almost impossible. That gives us another reason to focus on disparate impact—to study police policies and training methods, for instance, rather than the hearts and minds of individual cops on the beat.

Just as police officers hold stereotypes that can shape assessments of reasonable suspicion, jurors hold stereotypes that can shape assessments of guilt. Awareness of this fact influences the decisions of prosecutors and defense attorneys during the process of jury selection and in requests for changes of venue. Similarly, the beliefs of judges regarding defendants awaiting trial can be affected by stereotypes, thus influencing their decisions regarding bail.

Finally, consider mass incarceration. Recent efforts at decarceration have started to reverse the swelling of prison populations, but levels of incarceration in the United States still lie well outside historical and international norms. One possible reason is that the incentive-based and strategic mechanisms that we highlight throughout this book are not apparent to most observers. Instead, there is a tendency to view those in prison as deserving of their fate, and as immutably so depraved that they should not be allowed to mingle with innocent people.

This interpretation of criminal offenders as depraved and unworthy is tied to the stereotypes and stigma that have historically attached to African Americans. That is, the indifference to mass incarceration is itself tied to stereotypes held by the general public about those who are most at risk of prison entry.

In the chapters that follow we consider all these phenomena—victimization, offending, police stops, the use of force, witness cooperation, jury selection, bail setting, and punishment—with an emphasis on the role of beliefs and information in shaping encounters and determining outcomes. The common thread running through the book is the role of stereotypes, and so we start with an overview of what psychology teaches us about the formation of beliefs and the processing of information, and what economics teaches us about the resulting incentives and behavior.

Our main task in this book is to reveal the underlying incentives and strategic calculations that give rise to patterns of criminal offending, witness cooperation, and public action. The goal is to show that we can understand our world without appealing to deep and unchanging group characteristics. The policy implications that flow from this analysis are the topic of the Conclusion, which deals with hope, humanization, forgiveness, and doubt.

We make many references in the book to race and ethnicity, and it is worth clarifying at the outset what we mean by these terms. They refer to socially constructed categories into which people place themselves and others, based on physical and cultural cues. Being socially constructed makes them no less real; as philosopher Paul Taylor points out, money is also a social construct but most of us manage to take it very seriously.[1] In the United States Census, race and ethnicity are cross-cutting categories; people can self-identify as white or black or Asian or Native American (by race) and Hispanic or non-Hispanic (by ethnicity).[2] While the categories themselves are historical creations, they reproduce themselves because people are attentive to them. As Glenn Loury has observed, the concept of race itself would cease to exist "unless, on a daily basis and in regard to their most intimate affairs, people paid assiduous attention to the boundaries separating themselves from racially distinct others."[3] These are not innocent distinctions—they carry particular social meanings, about which we will have more to say in subsequent chapters.

Although the United States is an increasingly multiracial and multiethnic society, in many sections of this book we focus on interactions involving blacks and whites. For this we offer two rationales.

The first is historical significance. Questions about how white and black Americans relate to each other have been the dominant issues in the country's history, with the Civil War being a defining event. As Paul Taylor puts it: "Simultaneously despised and essential, alien and intimate, African Americans were made a part of the country in ways that Indian wars and Asian exclusion acts made impossible for those populations."[4]

The second rationale is practicality. Much more has been written about blacks and whites in the United States than about any other groups, and so collectively we know more and have better data. Hispanics, in particular, are not recorded the same way everywhere: ethnicity in the U.S. Census, for instance, is self-assessed, but for many criminal justice purposes, the person making the determination about ethnicity—an arresting officer, a victim, a corrections officer, a medical examiner—is not the person who is being arrested, or someone who knows that person well, or even someone who knows the federal definitions or cares about implementing them. Data about blacks and whites are not perfect either, but the inconsistencies are less extreme.

Although much of our evidence is limited to the data collection protocols in the United States, the theoretical arguments are quite general and, with suitable adaptation, can be used to shed light on crime and punishment in other divided societies. The particularities of identity may differ—with caste, ethnicity, or religion defining lines of cleavage—but there are many commonalities in the manner in which stereotypes determine patterns of interaction. We believe that the framework developed here is versatile enough to find broad application.

chapter 1

STEREOTYPES

In October 2016, Tamika Cross was on a Delta flight from Detroit to Minneapolis when she heard a scream for help from a woman whose husband had become unresponsive. Cross, who is a doctor, rose to assist but, according to her account, was initially prevented from doing so by a flight attendant because the flight crew was looking for "actual physicians or nurses or some type of medical personnel."[1] Cross is young, black, and female, and it appears that in the eyes of the flight attendant seeking a trained physician, she just didn't look the part. She didn't fit the stereotype.

Cross published her version of the events online on October 9, and the post promptly went viral. Several prominent news outlets, including the *Washington Post* and the *New York Times*, reported the story on October 14. The airline released a statement on that same date, pledging a thorough investigation but also claiming that a request for medical identification was consistent with the training received by its staff. On October 20, the *Washington Post* published a piece by a physician, Pamela Wible, featuring broadly similar accounts by six other female doctors.[2]

In their book *Blindspot*, Mahzarin Banaji and Anthony Greenwald use the following popular riddle to illustrate the phenomenon that appears to be at work here.[3] A man and his son are involved in a terrible car crash. The father dies instantly and the son is rushed to the nearest hospital in critical condition. The attending surgeon walks into the operating room and exclaims: "I can't operate on this boy; he's my son." How could this be?

Many people hearing this for the first time are stumped. Some guess that either the surgeon or the man who died is the boy's stepfather. Others think that the boy's parents are a same-sex couple. But few people come up with what in retrospect seems like the most obvious answer: the surgeon is the boy's mother.

People can have varying degrees of self-awareness about the content of the stereotypes they hold and the effects that their expressions of these beliefs have on others. But the act of stereotyping itself cannot be entirely escaped. Even if we are fully committed to judging others by the content of their character, we cannot avoid making inferences based on visual cues.[4]

This is because stereotyping is an instance of what the psychologist Jerome Bruner called "going beyond the information given." The capacity for *equivalence grouping*—assigning objects to categories and making inferences about their specific attributes based on what we think we know about the category in general—is part of the cognitive machinery that allows us to deal with novelty in everyday life. As Bruner put it: "If we were to respond to each event as unique and to learn anew what to do about it or even what to call it, we would soon be swamped by the complexity of our environment."[5]

Along similar lines, Walter Lippmann argued in his 1922 book *Public Opinion:* "Were there no practical uniformities in the environment, there would be no economy and only error in the human habit of accepting foresight for sight. But there are uniformities sufficiently accurate, and the need of economizing attention is so inevitable, that the abandonment of all stereotypes for a wholly innocent approach to experience would impoverish human life."[6]

Just because stereotyping is cognitively inescapable, however, does not mean that stereotypes are generally accurate: we also have cognitive mechanisms in place that make stereotypes resistant to change in the face of conflicting evidence. This is especially the case when stereotypes are laden with emotional content and thus form the basis for prejudice.

In his 1954 book *The Nature of Prejudice,* Gordon Allport argued that a prejudice, "unlike a simple misconception, is actively resistant to all evidence that would unseat it. . . . We selectively admit new evidence to a category if it confirms us in our previous belief. . . . But if we find evidence that is contrary to our preconception, we are likely to grow resistant." Some categories may lack "even a kernel of truth . . . , for they can be composed wholly of hearsay evidence, emotional projections, and fantasy."[7]

Or, as Walter Lippmann put it: "For the most part we do not first see, and then define, we define first and then see. . . . What is alien will be rejected, what is different will fall upon unseeing eyes. . . . For when a system of stereotypes is well fixed, our attention is called to those facts which support it, and diverted from those which contradict. . . . Except where we deliberately keep prejudice in suspense, we do not study a man and judge him to be bad. We see a bad man. We see a dewy morn, a blushing maiden, a sainted priest, a humorless Englishman, a dangerous Red, a carefree bohemian, a lazy Hindu, a wily Oriental, a dreaming Slav, a volatile Irishman, a greedy Jew, a 100% American."[8]

Self-Reports

Early research into the content of stereotypes relied on self-reports: researchers simply asked individuals to assign adjectives to groups.

In one influential study, published in 1933, Daniel Katz and Kenneth Braly elicited the beliefs of a hundred Princeton undergraduates about ten different groups defined by race, religion, and national origin.[9] The students were all white men; Princeton did not knowingly admit African Americans to its undergraduate program until 1942, and no women were admitted until 1969.

The authors presented the respondents with a list of eighty-four adjectives and, for each group, asked them to select words that adequately characterized its members. Some groups were viewed favorably: Germans were thought to be scientifically minded and industrious, and the English sportsmanlike and intelligent. But the subjects held deeply negative stereotypes about others: Jews were described as shrewd and mercenary, Turks as cruel, and the Chinese as superstitious and sly. Americans were said to be industrious and intelligent, but this (implicitly) referred only to white Americans; "Negroes" were described as superstitious and lazy.

This study has been replicated several times, allowing for changes in beliefs about groups to be tracked.[10] The belief that African Americans are superstitious was reported by 84 percent of respondents in the original study, and this fell to 41 percent by 1951 and 13 percent by 1969. By 2001, among white respondents, it was less than 2 percent. Along similar lines, the belief that African Americans are lazy was reported by three-fourths of respondents in the initial study, and this fell to 31 percent by 1951, 26 percent by 1969, and 12 percent (among white respondents) by 2001.

But just as old stereotypes faded, new ones emerged. By 1951, musical had replaced lazy as the second most frequently selected adjective when describing African Americans (while superstitious remained the most frequently selected). By 1969, musical was at the top of the list, followed by happy-go-lucky. Musical continued to be chosen with high frequency even in 2001, but certain words that had rarely been selected, if at all, in the earlier studies had become quite popular by then. These newly emergent descriptors included loud, loyal to family ties, aggressive, quick-tempered, and rude.[11]

Echoing the earlier assessment of Lippmann, Katz and Braly argued that individuals tend to neglect evidence that conflicts with existing stereotypes, while stereotype-confirming evidence takes on heightened salience: "By thus omitting cases which contradict the stereotype, the individual becomes convinced from association with a race that its members are just the kind of people he always thought they were. In this manner almost any characteristic can become attached to any race and stick there with scarcely any factual basis."[12]

The survey-based method has a significant disadvantage as a means of eliciting the content of stereotypes, since it depends on the willingness of respondents to declare their beliefs sincerely. They may not do so if they feel that openly expressing those beliefs would be frowned on, a phenomenon referred to as *impression management.*[13] Pollsters forecasting elections and social scientists investigating attitudes toward such matters as residential segregation and antimiscegenation laws routinely face this problem. Greater acceptance of intermarriage and integration in self-reports may arise, in part, because a declaration of opposition violates norms of tolerance that have taken root over recent decades.[14]

Furthermore, even if one could be confident that survey-based responses are entirely sincere, it remains possible that the associations between groups and traits that people report are those that align with their explicit normative commitments. They may in fact hold quite different associations in their minds, without being aware of it. But how can one detect the existence of such implicit beliefs if the subjects holding them are themselves in the dark? The key innovation that allowed researchers to investigate such beliefs was the implicit association test.

Implicit Associations

Over the past two decades, psychologists have developed methods for uncovering implicit beliefs by measuring response times on carefully designed tasks instead of relying on self-reports. The findings from these experiments do indeed reveal a divergence between explicit and implicit beliefs. As Banaji and Greenwald put it, these implicit association tests (IATs) hold up "a mirror in which many see a reflection that they do not recognize."[15]

The methodology is versatile enough to detect the relative strength of association between any set of categories. For instance, it can uncover the degree to which professional careers are more strongly associated with men than women, or the extent to which words that evoke pleasant sensations are more strongly associated with whites than blacks. The latter test is known as the Race IAT.

The basic structure of the Race IAT is as follows. Each subject is given four tasks (though not necessarily in the following sequence). The first task involves viewing a sequence of faces and classifying each face as either white or black—for instance, by pressing one of two keys on a keyboard. The second task involves classifying words (such as "sunshine" or "vomit") as either pleasant or unpleasant. The third task requires subjects to view stimuli that could be either words or images of faces. The subject presses one key if the image is either a white face or a pleasant word, and presses the other key if the image is either a black face or an unpleasant word. And finally, the fourth task reverses the association, by pairing images of black faces with pleasant words and images of white faces with unpleasant words.

These are relatively simple tasks, which few people have difficulty completing. But there are significant differences in the speed with which people perform them. For instance, about 80 percent of white subjects can perform the third task faster than the fourth.

One interpretation is that the association of images of white faces with pleasant-sounding words is already entrenched, and thus it imposes a smaller cognitive load. By the same token, those with negative implicit responses to images of black faces find the fourth task more time-consuming because they must overcome this association.

Experimenters often refer to the third task as the *congruent block,* and the fourth as the *incongruent block.*[16] The terminology reflects the finding that a clear majority of white respondents complete the third task more rapidly than the fourth. One might imagine that the situation would be fully reversed for black respondents, but this is not the case; about 35 percent of black respondents also complete the third task at greater speed. It appears that the bias is toward a socially dominant group rather than simply a parochial positive association for members of one's own group.

Over the past couple of decades, a wide range of such tests have been administered to millions of participants online and in experimental laboratories. They are versatile enough to elicit information on positive or negative sentiments associated with groups defined by race, ethnicity, religion, gender, age, and just about any other common mode of classification. Furthermore, the same design may be used to explore many other kinds of associations: instead of pleasant or unpleasant words, one could use words or images associated with professional careers versus those associated with child care or work within the home, or just about any other set of dichotomous traits.[17]

Most relevant for our purposes is the Race–Weapons IAT, which uses images of objects rather than pleasant or unpleasant words. The objects are either weapons such as swords, cannons, or battle-axes, or harmless everyday objects such as phones, cameras, or calculators. The set of weapons is deliberately chosen to be archaic and not in contemporary use. The tasks involve classifications of images (black or white faces) and objects (weapons or harmless objects). One block pairs black faces with weapons and white faces with harmless objects; the other block reverses this association.

Response times are faster, on average, for the task that pairs black faces with weapons and white faces with harmless objects than the reverse. This effect is strongest for white and Asian respondents, and least strong for black respondents, but all groups reveal broadly similar patterns of association.[18] It appears that the association of black faces with images of weapons is cognitively less demanding today than the association of white faces with weapons.

Snap Judgments

Could such associations result in systematic errors when snap judgments must be made? The possibility has been explored in a series of experiments involving video games designed to simulate interactions between police officers and suspects who may be armed.

In one such experiment, subjects were confronted with images of individuals holding either firearms or harmless objects, and tasked with "shooting" those with guns by pressing a button with one hand, and "not shooting" those with harmless objects by pressing a different button with the other hand.[19] The images were all of black or white males. Note that errors could be of two types: shooting a target with a benign object, or failing to shoot one with a firearm.

The researchers collected response times and error rates for two different time pressure conditions. When time pressure was not intense, error rates were low for all combinations of target identity and object held, but experimental subjects were quicker to shoot armed targets if they were black, and quicker to "not shoot" harmless targets if they were white. Under intense time pressure, it was error rates rather than reaction times that revealed a difference: unarmed targets were more likely to be erroneously shot if they were black, while armed targets were more likely to be erroneously "not shot" if they were white.

In attempting to understand the mechanisms giving rise to this "shooting bias" in reaction times and error rates, the authors collected individual information from subjects using questionnaires. They found that simple awareness of a cultural stereotype linking African Americans to violence was a predictor of the extent of bias, regardless of whether a subject personally endorsed the stereotype. Furthermore, greater prior contact with African Americans (for instance, in high school) resulted in greater shooting bias. The authors also found that using a separate sample of subjects drawn from the community resulted in no significant difference between black and white subjects in the degree of shooting bias.

Broadly similar results have been found in many other studies.[20] In one case, subjects were simply asked to identify items as guns or harmless objects; but before they made their choice, they were briefly shown an image of either a black or a white human face. When the image was of a black face, subjects identified guns faster (when given ample time) and falsely identified harmless objects as guns more often (when time pressure was intense).[21] In another study, subjects were asked to "shoot" targets on a screen (by clicking with a mouse) if they were armed civilians, to mark them as safe (by pressing the space bar) if they were armed police officers, and to take no action if they held harmless objects. Subjects had greater difficulty distinguishing weapons from harmless objects when the target was black, and civilians holding harmless objects were mistakenly shot more often if they were black.[22]

How should the findings of such laboratory experiments be interpreted? As a guide to understanding the behavior of police officers in the field, the findings suffer from at least three deficiencies. First, the populations from which the experimental subjects are drawn are not representative of those from which officers are typically recruited. Second, the subjects have not been through the selection and training required of officers. And third, scenarios involving mouse clicks and keystrokes in response to static images may not effectively mimic conditions faced by officers in the field.

A group of researchers at Washington State University has raised these objections, arguing that there is a countervailing effect that could induce officers to be slower in responding with lethal force to black suspects believed to be armed, in anticipation of the greater public scrutiny that such actions would entail.[23] To test for this effect they used a subject pool composed of active-duty officers from the Spokane Police Department and simulators akin to those employed routinely in police training. Subjects were confronted with unfolding scenarios—such as vehicle stops or domestic disturbances—that could conceivably result in contact with an armed suspect. Suspects were either black or white and were played by trained actors following tightly scripted instructions. Paired scenarios were designed to differ only with respect to the suspect's race, holding all other aspects of the interaction as close to constant as possible.

The findings of this study are quite different from those using civilian subjects with more schematic representations of interactions with potential suspects. In particular, the officers were slower to shoot armed suspects if they were black, and more likely to shoot unarmed suspects if they were white. This is despite the fact that more than three-quarters of the officers in the study had moderate to strong associations of blacks with weapons on an IAT.

As we shall see in Chapter 8, there is enormous geographic variation in both the overall rates at which police kill civilians and the extent to which victimization rates involve racial disparities. It is important, therefore, not to draw national implications from location-specific studies. Nevertheless, the Spokane study does suggest that experimental subjects drawn from the general civilian population may act quite differently from trained police officers, even if the level of implicit bias does not vary much across these pools.

While a patchwork of experiments with a variety of protocols and subject pools have been conducted, no clear and consistent conclusion has emerged as yet on the manner in which stereotypes condition the responses of civilians and officers to dangerous situations. It is possible that the level of perceived danger is greater in interactions with black suspects, but that police training and public pressure can lower the use of lethal force in such situations. There may well be considerable heterogeneity both within and across police departments in the quickness with which lethal force is used, and the extent of its use in situations that turn out to be objectively unthreatening. We return to these issues in Chapter 8.

Interracial Contact

Psychologists have examined the impact of interracial contact on cognitive functioning in laboratory settings. One approach involves the random assignment of individuals to experimenters with whom they have an "interview-like interaction," after which their performance on a cognitively demanding task is measured. Those assigned to own-group partners tend to perform significantly better on the challenging task than those assigned to partners from different groups. Reviewing these findings, Jennifer Richeson and Nicole Shelton conclude that "interracial contact continues to be awkward, if not stressful, for many," to the point that "individuals often exit interracial interactions feeling drained both cognitively and emotionally."[24]

Members of all groups experience cognitive impairment as a result of interracial interactions, but for very different reasons: "White participants in interracial interactions are often concerned about

appearing prejudiced, whereas racial minorities are often concerned about being the target of prejudice and / or about confirming
negative group stereotypes."[25] Furthermore, those who exhibit a
higher degree of bias on IATs tend to suffer the highest levels of cognitive impairment. These findings are consistent with results from brain
imaging studies, which reveal activity in regions associated with executive control among whites after exposure to unfamiliar black faces.[26]

This cognitive impairment would create incentives for the avoidance of interracial contact, leading to social segregation. But with
crime and the justice system, contact is rarely voluntary. Victims don't
choose among offenders, judges and jurors don't select defendants,
and civilians don't decide which police officers will stop and search
them. On the other hand, offenders do sometimes select victims,
prosecutors and defense attorneys can strike jurors from the jury pool,
and officers often decide which motorists or pedestrians they will stop.
Such interactions—which are the topic of subsequent chapters—
follow trajectories that are very sensitive to the identities of the
parties involved.

Incentives

Psychologists have approached stereotypes with an open mind—
allowing for the possibility that they may be untethered from any
underlying reality, with a wide gulf between explicit and implicit
beliefs. And they have recognized and explored the possibility that beliefs affect behavior quite differently under severe time constraints
than they do in situations that allow for thoughtful reflection.

Economists have taken a different approach in their study of stereotypes. In keeping with the standard model of rational choice,
beliefs in economic theory are assumed to be based on probabilistic

reasoning applied in a detached manner to the available evidence. Economic models of stereotypes generally assume not just a "kernel of truth" but accuracy of beliefs relative to the distribution of characteristics in the population. But these characteristics are not taken to be constant; they depend on beliefs generated through the incentive effects of stereotypes. In other words, the distribution of characteristics in a population is determined jointly with beliefs about these characteristics.

Since beliefs have incentive effects, individuals may act in ways that confirm a stereotype, even if they would act quite differently in the absence of the stereotype. Recall our example of the server who stereotypes a customer as being unlikely to tip generously, and provides poor service in response. A generous tip under these circumstances is indeed unlikely, so the stereotype will tend to be confirmed. But that does not mean that the stereotype had any factual basis to begin with—the very same customer might have been extremely generous in rewarding good service. The systematic exploration of such interactions between beliefs and behavior is the key contribution made by economists to the analysis of stereotypes.[27]

Consider, for instance, the situation of employers and employees in the labor market. If black applicants are stereotyped as being less productive than whites with similar credentials, they will need to perform at higher levels during the screening process in order to be hired. But performance during the screening process depends on costly prior investments made in education and skills. Being required to meet a higher performance threshold in order to be hired makes these investments less worthwhile, since any given level of investment is less likely to result in employment. The rational response for members of negatively stereotyped groups may sometimes be to invest at lower rates, thus fulfilling the stereotype that they are indeed less productive.[28]

In *The Anatomy of Racial Inequality,* Glenn Loury considers a thought experiment that illustrates the process at work here. Suppose that taxi drivers in a city believe, for whatever reason, that black passengers are more likely to attempt robbery than otherwise similar white passengers. The drivers' resulting avoidance of black passengers will increase wait times for members of this group and lead those who simply want to get from one place to another to choose alternative modes of transport. Those actually wanting to rob drivers will continue to hail cabs, with the consequence that among those hailing cabs, members of the stereotyped group will indeed be more likely to attempt robbery. This will be the case even if in the absence of the stereotype, the proportion of robbery offenders in the two groups would be precisely the same.

The point here is not that differences across groups in criminal offending arise only as a result of stereotypes, but that stereotypes can give rise to incentive effects that cause any existing differences to be amplified. Moreover, these incentive effects operate in a stealthy manner, invisible to most observers. As a result, incentive-driven phenomena can be interpreted as reflecting deep and immutable characteristics of a group. We return to this point in Chapter 11 when considering public tolerance for mass incarceration.

The economic approach to stereotypes, being based on rational deliberation and statistical inference, has some obvious limitations. But the focus on incentives is extremely valuable in understanding the behavior of individuals who anticipate being stereotyped. Such individuals will avoid some interactions and seek out others, in a manner that could well be based on sound and deliberative reasoning.

In fact, an incentive-based analysis of stereotypes could be even more useful in shedding light on crime and criminal justice issues than it is in the more traditional domain of application to labor markets. Employers can get detailed and specific information on applicants through letters of recommendation, transcripts, and job interviews. In many interactions involving crime and criminal justice, no such information is available. A robbery victim cannot consult an offender's prior victims before deciding whether or not to resist, and an offender likewise cannot seek information from those who have previously confronted the potential victim. Similarly, police officers, prosecutors, jurors, witnesses, and defendants must all make decisions with enormous consequences in the face of time constraints and very limited information. These are settings in which an analysis of the incentive effects of stereotypes can be very fruitful.

Location Stereotypes

People aren't the only things that are the subject of stereotypes. Dogs (Labrador retrievers are loving, and pit bulls are fierce) and cuisine (Indian food is spicy, and British food is bland) are both subjects of generalizations that don't always apply. To some extent, stereotypes about nonhumans can also be self-confirming: the affection you show because you think of your puppy as lovable may be repaid, and if you believe deeply enough that glucosamine can relieve your arthritis, taking it can make you feel better. Beliefs about natural phenomena can also be *disconfirming:* if enough people believe that climate change is neither serious nor anthropogenic and therefore continue to emit copious amounts of greenhouse gases, climate change will be even more serious and more closely tied to human activity.

For discussions of crime, beliefs about locations are probably the most important kind of stereotype that does not have to do with humans. Some places are viewed as dangerous and others safe, and how people think about places influences who goes there and who does not. Individuals contemplating burglary or theft can make many inferences about property without seeing the owner—for instance, from the location of a home or the make and model of a parked car. Similarly, bumper stickers on vehicles and political signs in front yards can also shift and shape stereotypes.

In a notable 1989 paper, the criminologists Lawrence Sherman, Patrick Gartin, and Michael Buerger examined the precise location of every call for police service in Minneapolis in 1986—down to the level of an address or an intersection.[29] Crime locations were highly concentrated: out of 115,000 places in the city, about 40 percent had no calls, and most of the rest had only one. But 3.3 percent of places had more than fifteen calls in the year, and those places accounted for half of all calls.

Some places have more crime because they have more people: for instance, the bus depot had the second-highest number of calls for predatory crime (twenty-eight in the year). Other places may have a lot of crime because their physical configuration makes crime easy— the authors report that in Birmingham, England, pedestrian tunnels accounted for 13 percent of criminal attacks on persons. But there are also some hot spots that are quite ordinary in both population density and physical configuration. For instance, Moby Dick's Bar was tied for sixth on the list with twenty-five predatory crime calls in the year.

Think about a place like Moby Dick's Bar. Why would anyone go there when it's known to be so dangerous? The people who went to Moby Dick's in its heyday were unusual—people looking for excitement, people looking for fights, and people looking for the deals and action not found in more sedate bars. Thus the stereotype about Moby Dick's became a stereotype about the people who went there, and it became self-confirming.

Larger areas can also be stereotyped. Consider the word "ghetto." Originally the word as a noun referred to sections of sixteenth- and seventeenth-century European cities where Jews, including wealthy ones, were compelled to live. Traditional ghettoes had largely disappeared by the early twentieth century, but the Nazis revived them as way stations for concentration camps in cities under their control. In the United States, by the 1960s the word had come to refer to the black neighborhoods in cities and was used matter-of-factly in public discourse. An *Ebony* magazine editorial in 1966, for instance, said that "something must be done, and done soon, to build a strong and stable family structure among Negro ghetto dwellers."[30] By the 1990s, however, the word as a noun had come to describe a neighborhood of desperation, drugs, danger, and excitement, all of which are captured in Busta Rhymes's 2006 song "In the Ghetto." Now "ghetto" has become an adjective and adverb referring to anything low class, disreputable, jury-rigged: being ghetto, acting ghetto, ghetto-fabulous. It can be used as an insult (or a boast).

Being in a neighborhood that could be labeled a ghetto implies a heightened sense of danger and criminality, and so people act differently there and expect others to act differently toward them too. In particular, they expect both the police and witnesses to act differently. Indeed, police use of force is highly variable across space—in what they perceive as ghettoes, officers use more force, holding other conditions constant.[31] Such differences have an impact on who lives there and how hard some families try to live elsewhere. We revisit these issues at various points in the book.

Essentialism

People hold stereotypes for many different reasons. Sometimes the reason is simple repetition: if you observe that when you have waited a long time for a subway train, several trains often arrive quickly together, you may start to expect a bunch of trains whenever you've been waiting a long time. This belief does not require any knowledge or theory of subway system operation. Expecting empirical regularities to hold without understanding them is common and essentially un-avoidable. As Walter Lippmann and Jerome Bruner explained generations ago, this is part of the mental infrastructure that we use to negotiate a complex world.

But you may also develop a theory about how subway systems operate to explain why the bunching occurs, and this could lead you to adopt other beliefs that were not previously held. The economist William Vickrey's theory of bus and subway gregariousness, for instance, is based on changes in loading times as the lead train slows and the trains behind it speed up. This gives rise to the prediction that bunching should be less common in off-peak hours. Some theories turn out to be productive in this way (the germ theory of disease, for instance), while others do not (the miasma theory of disease).

When trying to impose structure on the empirical regularities they observe, people often adopt theories that are *essentialist*. Essentialism is the view that "categories have a deep and unobservable reality, that this reality or 'essence' gives rise to surface features of category members . . . that it is unchanging and unchangeable by human interference, and that it has a 'natural' basis."[32] In Western philosophy, essentialism dates back to Plato and Aristotle, and some developmental psychologists argue that most humans are intuitive essentialists.[33]

Racial essentialism is the theory that there exist distinct human groupings, each with its own essence that is passed down from generation to generation. It is an element of what philosophers label racial naturalism: "the division of humanity into a small number of groups based on five criteria: (1) Races reflect some type of biological foundation. . . . (2) This biological foundation generates discrete racial groupings. . . . (3) This biological foundation is inherited from generation to generation. . . . (4) Genealogical investigation should identify each race's geographical origin. . . . and (5) This inherited racial biological foundation manifests itself primarily in physical phenotypes . . . and perhaps also behavioral phenotypes."[34]

To illustrate, suppose that through repeated observation you come to believe that people with straight black hair and epicanthic folds (which produce the eye shape often found among people in Central and East Asia) are more likely than other humans to be adept at using chopsticks and to speak Korean. Your development of this stereotype is not attached to any particular causal theory. An essentialist theory would impose a causal connection on the observed traits—for instance, by attributing them to a common source, an essence of being East Asian. Such a theory would make it hard for you to imagine a world in which the correlation does not hold—one in which blond Scandinavians have greater facility with chopsticks than native speakers of Korean, for example.[35]

Few people hold essentialist views about language fluency or skill with eating implements. But when it comes to crime, essentialist interpretations of statistical correlations have a long and sordid history in the United States. In *The Condemnation of Blackness*, Khalil Muhammad documents the degree to which essentialist notions permeated popular discourse and scholarship on crime following publication of the 1890 census: "From the 1890s through the first four decades of the twentieth century, black criminality would become one of the most commonly cited and longest-lasting justifications for black inequality and mortality in the modern urban world."[36]

Muhammad points out that "European immigrants—the Irish and the Italians and the Polish, for example—gradually shed their criminal identities while blacks did not," and chronicles the efforts of black writers such as Kelly Miller, James Stemons, Ida B. Wells, and W. E. B. Du Bois to bring to light the "racial double standards in the urban crime discourse" of their time and to interpret the emerging statistical evidence in "universal and antiracist terms." Eventually, he argues, some prison reformers "began to see the inconsistency between a hopeful vision of white criminality as largely a symptom of industrial capitalism and a reason to intervene, and a pessimistic view of black criminality and the futility of reform."[37]

As Melvin Rogers has recently documented, many of the black abolitionists writing in the antebellum period treated "laws and institutions . . . as derivative of the characterological properties of the nation." Arguing that true liberty "requires not merely freedom from the arbitrary whim of particular agents or laws that limit arbitrary power, but a transformation of the system of cultural value in which blacks occupy a lower position of worth," these writers "desired a form of citizenship found not only in the law, but also in the heart."[38] That is, they desired freedom not only from slavery but from essentialist classification.

Modern biologists and philosophers of biology have not found essentialism a useful theory even for thinking about distinct animal species. The philosopher Philip Kitcher writes: "Biological taxa are not demarcated by essential differences; in general, there is no analogue of atomic number, no genetic feature, say, that separates one species of mosquito or mushroom from another; there are occasional exceptions . . . but these are relatively rare." In practice, taxonomists do not think of the work of dividing plants and animals into different species as "finding the fence-posts our concepts must respect," but rather as finding the divisions that are useful for whatever task is at hand. "There is a nondenumerable infinity of possible accurate maps we could draw for our planet; the ones we draw, and the boundaries they introduce, depend on our evolving purposes."[39]

Obviously, then, modern scientists do not find essentialism a useful theory for thinking about human variation either. There are no races in the sense of racial naturalism. There are no sharp divisions or immutable traits or necessary characteristics. Of course, there are correlations with salient superficial characteristics, and these correlations can form the basis of stereotypes. But there is no "essence" that simultaneously produces all the correlated traits; these traits are not tied to any common cause.

Yet racial essentialism is not dead in the minds of many modern Americans. For instance, one of us has been present at heated discussions involving educated residents of Newark of diverse backgrounds about whether Effa Manley, the owner of the Newark Eagles baseball team in the Negro Leagues and the first woman inducted into the Baseball Hall of Fame, was "really black" or "really white." Because there are no racial essences, no one is really white or really black, and Effa Manley was who she was (in defiance of many stereotypes).

Psychologists have found that people who have higher degrees of essentialist beliefs hold on to stereotypes more firmly than those who do not have such beliefs, even when other predispositions are kept constant.[40] Members of all identity groups (including those defined by gender and sexual orientation) in the United States hold essentialist beliefs, and they can often be of considerable comfort, reassurance, and pride, especially to those on whom the dominant society looks down. But essentialist beliefs can also form the basis for contempt, loathing, and stigma.

Stigma

Essentialism as a way of looking at the world is closely linked to racial stigma. They are, however, distinct intellectual habits: one can be a racial essentialist without indulging in racial stigma. People proud of their heritage may sometimes hold essentialist beliefs without stigmatizing others, and even Du Bois expressed essentialist ideas in some of his early writing.[41] But racial stigma is almost always accompanied by racial essentialism. While essentialism is a belief about how the world works, stigma is about which beliefs should be revised in light of surprising evidence.

In his 1953 essay entitled "Two Dogmas of Empiricism," the philosopher Willard V. O. Quine observed that "our statements about the external world face the tribunal of sense experience not individually but only as a corporate body."[42] That is, we seldom get information that pertains to a single proposition in isolation; stereotypes can never be decisively disconfirmed, because nature never presents us with a clean test. Anytime we see something that surprises us we have a choice of which of our beliefs to discard.

Imagine that you step on a scale and see that you weigh ten pounds less than you thought you did. You are surprised and will have to revise your beliefs about something. Maybe you think that the scale is broken, that you have been exercising diligently, that your diet is working, or that you are quite ill. You may entertain all of these possibilities at the same time. You may even think that the laws of gravity are weakening in ways that make all objects appear lighter. Not only do you need to have beliefs, but you also need to have a hierarchy in which to arrange them so that you know which to discard and which to retain when something unexpected happens. In this example, most individuals do not entertain the possibility that the laws of gravity are weakening. The idea that gravity is not an exhaustible resource is so fundamental to our thinking that we don't question it; we don't even realize that we believe it.

Racial stigma refers to such hierarchies of beliefs. For a person who holds to racial stigma, the belief in the inferiority of African Americans is high in the hierarchy, like the inexhaustibility of gravity for most of us, and thus is resistant to change when confronted with surprising evidence. Glenn Loury defines racial stigma as "an entrenched if inchoate presumption of inferiority, or moral inadequacy, or unfitness for intimacy, of intellectual incapacity, harbored by observing agents when they regard race-marked subjects."[43] Deep-seated beliefs about the essential character of groups, he argues, determine what we find curious and puzzling and what we take to be normal or routine:

> Racially biased social cognitions . . . cause some situations to appear anomalous, disquieting, contrary to expectation, worthy of further investigation, inconsistent with the natural order of things—while other situations appear normal, about right, in keeping with what one might expect, consistent with the social world as we know it. These cognitive distinctions tend to be drawn to the detriment of millions of racially stigmatized citizens . . . because of the taint of dishonor that is part and parcel of the social meaning of race in the United States.[44]

Having emerged from the dishonor of slavery, racial stigma "remains yet to be fully eradicated."

Around the time of World War II, in his study of the Jim Crow South, the economist Gunnar Myrdal also observed the operation of racial stigma attached to essentialist reasoning: "The stereotypes are ideological fragments which have been coined and sanctioned. They are abstract and unqualified, as popular thinking tends to be. . . . In addition, they are loaded with pretension to deep insight. It is because of this emotional charge that they can serve to block accurate observation in everyday living and detached thinking. They are treated as magical formulas. It is amazing to see the stern look of even educated people when they repeat these trite and worn banalities, inherited through the generations, as if they were pointing out something new and tremendously important, and also to watch their consternation and confusion when one tries to disturb their conventional thought-ways with 'outlandish' questions."[45]

Hidden from Whom?

The subtitle of *Blindspot—Hidden Biases of Good People*—reflects the fact that explicit and implicit beliefs can diverge significantly, and egalitarian commitments can reside alongside implicit biases in the same mind. But while implicit biases may be hidden from those who harbor them, they are not hidden from those who experience their behavioral expression.

Those who are negatively stereotyped can suffer harms that range from mild annoyance to bodily injury or death. This happens regardless of whether the stereotype is based on statistical generalizations about groups or arises from implicit or explicit biases that overwhelm rational thought.

Trayvon Martin was a seventeen-year-old high school junior staying with relatives in a Florida gated community when he was suspected of being a burglar, pursued, and eventually shot and killed by neighborhood watch coordinator George Zimmerman. A struggle ensued before the fatal shot was fired, and Zimmerman claimed that he acted in self-defense, fearing for his life. He was eventually charged with second-degree murder and acquitted at trial.

The affidavit of probable cause filed by the state attorney in bringing the murder charge against Zimmerman vividly illustrates the role that stereotypes played in the case:

> On Sunday February 26, 2012, Trayvon Martin was temporarily living at the Retreat at Twin Lakes, a gated community in Sanford, Seminole County, Florida. That evening Martin walked to a nearby

7–11 store where he purchased a can of iced tea and a bag of skittles. Martin then walked back to and entered the gated community and was on his way back to the townhouse where he was living when he was profiled by George Zimmerman. Martin was unarmed and was not committing a crime.

Zimmerman who also lived in the gated community, and was driving his vehicle observed Martin and assumed Martin was a criminal. Zimmerman felt Martin did not belong in the gated community and called the police. . . . The police dispatcher informed Zimmerman that an officer was on the way and to wait for the officer.

During the recorded call Zimmerman made reference to people he felt had committed and gotten away with break-ins in his neighborhood. Later while talking about Martin, Zimmerman stated "these assholes, they always get away" and also said "these fucking punks."

During this time, Martin was on the phone with a friend and described to her what was happening. The witness advised that Martin was scared because he was being followed through the complex by an unknown male and didn't know why. Martin attempted to run home but was followed by Zimmerman who didn't want the person he falsely assumed was going to commit a crime to get away before the police arrived.

Zimmerman got out of his vehicle and followed Martin. When the police dispatcher realized Zimmerman was pursuing Martin, he instructed Zimmerman not to do that and that the responding officer would meet him. Zimmerman disregarded the police dispatcher and continued to follow Martin who was trying to return to his home.

Zimmerman confronted Martin and a struggle ensued. Witnesses heard people arguing and what sounded like a struggle. . . . Zimmerman shot Martin in the chest. . . . Assistant Medical Examiner Dr. Bao performed an autopsy and determined that Martin died from the gunshot wound.[46]

It appears that Zimmerman was completely convinced that Martin was a burglar, and pursued him despite instructions from the police dispatcher to wait for assistance. But on what basis did he come to believe that a high school student holding a bottle of iced tea and a bag of Skittles was about to commit a felony? The question answers itself—Martin was a young black male in a hoodie. This is the only visible cue that could plausibly have given rise to the mistaken belief that he was a criminal trespasser.

Even when there is no physical harm, being negatively stereotyped can leave psychological scars. In an emotional speech on the floor of the United States Senate in July 2016, Senator Tim Scott of South Carolina recounted in deeply personal terms his own experience as a victim of stereotyping.[47] He described being refused entry to the Senate despite wearing the official pin, being tailed for no apparent reason, and being stopped for driving too nice a car. "Imagine the frustration, the irritation, the sense of a loss of dignity that accompanies each of those stops," he said. "There is absolutely nothing more frustrating, more damaging to your soul than when you know you're following the rules and being treated like you are not."

It is certainly true—for reasons discussed in subsequent chapters—that black men are significantly overrepresented among those incarcerated for violent felonies, especially robbery and homicide. But as Paul Butler observes in *Chokehold*, the fear that people exhibit in routine interactions is untethered from objective assessments of risk:

> The bottom line is that it is not crazy or racist for a person to think she is more likely to be the victim of a street crime perpetrated by an African American man than a man of another race. It is just that it is unlikely that either event will occur. The person who is at most risk from a black man is another black man, and even this risk is relatively low. For the most serious crimes—homicide and rape—whites are

much more likely to be victimized by white people they know than by black strangers.[48]

Why, then, are subjective fears so out of line with objective realities? The psychologists Daniel Kahneman and Amos Tversky have examined the degree to which people "follow the principles of probability theory in judging the likelihood of uncertain events," finding that "people replace the laws of chance by heuristics, which sometimes yield reasonable estimates and quite often do not."[49] Among these mental shortcuts is the *representativeness heuristic*, which induces individuals to assign higher probabilities to events that appear to be typical or representative. One consequence of this heuristic is the *conjunction fallacy*, which involves a violation of one of the most basic laws of probability: a more inclusive event cannot be less likely than an event that it subsumes. As an example, the likelihood that you will be hit by a vehicle while crossing the street in New York tomorrow cannot be smaller than the likelihood that you will be hit by a speeding taxi cab while crossing the street in New York tomorrow. Yet individuals consistently violate this principle.

In an experiment conducted in 1982, subjects were randomly assigned to two groups. Those in the first group were asked to assess the probability of 1,000 people drowning in a massive flood that would occur the following year somewhere in North America, while those in the second group were asked about the probability of 1,000 people drowning in a flood caused by an earthquake in California that would occur the following year. The latter event cannot possibly be more likely than the former, and yet was assessed to be considerably more likely.[50]

Probability assessments are affected by *imagined narratives:* if people can tell themselves a story about how an event may occur, they consider it to be much more likely. Stories of black male involvement in violent crime are ubiquitous, from news reports and social media to images from security cameras posted on walls. Coupled with the manner in which the human mind makes judgments under uncertainty, these stories and stimuli can result in beliefs that vastly inflate the true underlying risks.

Impression Management

As Elizabeth Anderson has pointed out, people who find themselves under "a cloud of suspicion in unstructured encounters with strangers" suffer genuine harm.[51] And the suspicion can be revealed in many ways, from facial expressions and visible tension to the locking of car doors and the crossing of streets. People react differently to this experience, sometimes taking elaborate steps to alter the perceptions of others. Paul Butler vividly describes the process as follows:

> Most of the time . . . people being afraid of you is aggravating, embarrassing, and dispiriting. You take steps to allay the fear. You look down on the elevator. You wear your college T-shirt, and conspicuously display your work ID. You love the Dodge Charger, but if you buy the Mini Cooper you won't get pulled over as much. You try not to care. But it comes to feel like you are apologizing for your existence. It eats you up inside because it is relentless. Every time you leave your home, you are the star of a bizarre security theater.[52]

The desire to signal—to separate oneself from a stereotype—is not confined to men. After an unsettling interaction with a neighbor in which she felt that she had been perceived as a threat, Gabrielle Union chose to wear mittens rather than gloves in the Chicago winter because "thugs don't wear mittens."[53]

The psychologist and *New York Times* writer Brent Staples was a graduate student at the University of Chicago in the 1970s when he noticed that he instilled fear in passers-by. His initial reaction was to try to put them at ease by shifting the stereotype:

> I became an expert in the language of fear. Couples locked arms and reached for each other's hand when they saw me. Some crossed to the other side of the street. People who were carrying on conversations went mute and stared straight ahead, as though avoiding my eyes would save them. . . . I tried to be innocuous but didn't know how. . . . I began to avoid people. I turned out of my way into side streets to spare them the sense that they were being stalked. . . . Out of nervousness, I began to whistle and discovered I was good at it. My whistle was pure and sweet—and also in tune. On the street at night, I whistled popular tunes from the Beatles and Vivaldi's "Four Seasons." The tension drained from people's bodies when they heard me. A few even smiled as they passed me in the dark.[54]

There is a twist in this poignant tale, to which we return in Chapter 3.

Summing Up

The stereotypes that people hold are not simple mirrors that passively and accurately reflect their experiences and observations. Though not completely untethered from those experiences, stereotypes can reflect both outworn theories and hierarchies of belief, which produce essentialism and stigma. They can arise ex nihilo if they provide incentives that make them self-confirming. They can be based on heuristics—shortcuts that sometimes lead to places where it makes no sense to go. But we cannot entirely escape them.

We have examined stereotypes because we want to understand how they affect crime and punishment. We now turn to a general discussion of crime so that we have the necessary background to see how the two phenomena, stereotypes and crime, are closely entwined.

chapter 2

CRIME

Defining crime is not easy. Some activities—such as blasphemy, sodomy, alcohol consumption, adultery, and abortion—have been crimes at various times and places while being permissible at others. Interracial marriage was a crime in parts of the United States until 1967, and the title of Trevor Noah's memoir, *Born a Crime*, reminds us that his Xhosa mother and Swiss / German father could not legally have "carnal intercourse" in South Africa at the time of his birth in 1984. The only consistently applicable definition of crime appears to be the set of activities that governments have decided to punish severely.

While this nominalist definition of crime is adequate for the descriptive and predictive parts of this book, it is inadequate for the prescriptive and policy-oriented parts. The reason is this: sometimes governments threaten to punish activities that should not be punished, and neglect activities that should be punished. Enforcing unjust laws cannot produce justice.

The problem is also one of interpretation: when they hear the word "crime," many people think "activities that *should* be punished severely"; and when they hear the word "criminals," they think "people who *should* be punished." To use the words this way requires an ethical theory of punishment.

There are many such theories, and we don't intend to sort them out in this book or to champion any particular one. Each has different implications about what activities should trigger punishment, how severe that punishment should be, and who should be punished—in other words, what should be crimes, and who should be deemed criminals.

These distinctions matter when we consider incarceration and its ancillaries, as we do later in the book. But in this chapter we focus on a set of activities that are considered intrinsically bad, or *mala in se* in legal doctrine, and are outlawed almost everywhere. In the United States, such activities include the so-called index crimes: murder, rape, robbery, assault, burglary, larceny, motor vehicle theft, and arson. For these crimes the Federal Bureau of Investigation (FBI) publishes detailed annual statistics, allowing us to track changes over time with reasonable consistency.

Appropriation and Destruction

The eight index crimes are typically divided into two groups: property crimes (burglary, larceny, motor vehicle theft, and arson) and violent crimes (murder, rape, robbery, and assault). However, for the purposes of this book, it is useful to adopt a somewhat different classification based on motive. We distinguish between *crimes of appropriation*, motivated primarily by the taking of property, and *crimes of destruction*, which result in bodily harm, loss of life, or damage to structures but do not typically involve an acquisitive motive. In the former class we place robbery, burglary, larceny, and motor vehicle theft; in the latter we have murder, rape, assault and arson.

The distinction is not watertight by any means: arson can be accompanied by fraudulent insurance claims, and murder can be motivated by the acceleration of a bequest. Nevertheless, this grouping allows us to see and understand certain patterns in the data more clearly than the traditional classification.

In the United States, robbery is defined as the act of "taking or attempting to take anything of value from the care, custody, or control of a person or persons by force or threat of force or violence and / or by putting the victim in fear."[1] This makes it unique among crimes of appropriation in that it routinely involves contact between victims and offenders. Burglary, larceny, and motor vehicle theft usually do not. Someone who steals your car while it is parked on the street at night has committed motor vehicle theft; someone who seizes your car from you while you are stopped at a traffic intersection (a carjacking) has committed robbery.

Robbery victims can usually describe the offenders to law enforcement officials or on victimization surveys, which is typically not the case with the other crimes of appropriation. Furthermore, it is only in the case of robbery that victims respond to the offender as the crime is in progress. As a result, stereotypes can influence the manner in which a robbery proceeds in ways that are not generally possible for burglary, larceny, or motor vehicle theft. This fact alone suggests that those who engage in robbery differ in some ways from those who commit burglary or theft, along lines we explore in Chapter 3.

Just as robbery differs in an important respect from other crimes of appropriation, homicide differs along a crucial dimension from other crimes of destruction. But the key difference here is not about face-to-face contact between victim and offender. Murder is the only serious crime that can be driven by a preemptive motive: people sometimes kill simply to avoid being killed. Other things equal, those who are fearful are more likely to kill, just as those who are feared are more likely to *be* killed. And since fear is conditioned by stereotypes, patterns of homicide offending and victimization will also be related to the nature of stereotypes. We explore this idea in depth in Chapter 4.

Ebbs and Flows

The FBI's Uniform Crime Reporting (UCR) program aggregates records submitted by several thousand police departments nationwide and can be used to examine trends in the rates of crimes recorded by law enforcement agencies.

These ebbs and flows are shown in Figure 2.1 for crimes of appropriation and Figure 2.2 for crimes of destruction. Since some crimes are much more frequent than others, the units used in constructing the figures were chosen for ease of visual comparison of trends. For instance, among crimes of appropriation, larceny has the highest frequency and robbery the lowest. Accordingly, the larceny rate shown in the figure is per 6,000 persons in the population, while

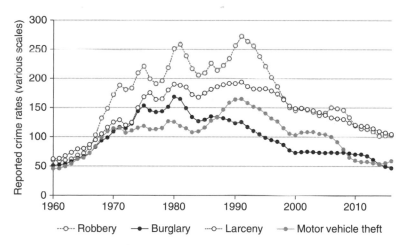

FIGURE 2.1. Crimes of appropriation, 1960–2016. Units have been chosen for ease of visualization. The robbery rate is per 100,000 persons in the U.S. population, motor vehicle theft per 25,000 persons, burglary per 10,000 persons, and larceny per 6,000 persons. Source: FBI Uniform Crime Reports.

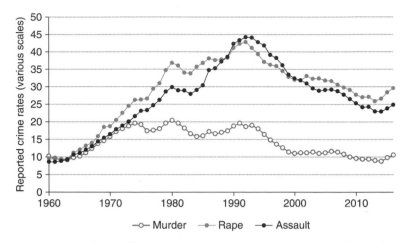

FIGURE 2.2. Crimes of destruction, 1960–2016. Units have been chosen for ease of visualization. The murder rate is per 200,000 persons in the U.S. population, rape per 100,000 persons, and assault per 10,000 persons. Source: FBI Uniform Crime Reports.

the robbery rate is per 100,000. Similarly, homicide is considerably less frequent than rape and assault, and units of measurement have been chosen to ensure that trends over time are clearly visible in the same figure.[2]

According to police reports, the incidence of all index crimes rose sharply during the 1960s and 1970s and fell steadily in the 1990s and 2000s. Peaks were reached in 1991 for robbery, larceny, and motor vehicle theft, and in 1992 for rape and assault. Burglary peaked a decade earlier, in 1980, as did homicide, although homicide was close to peak levels in the early 1990s.

These data are based on police records, so they omit crimes that are not reported to police and those that are reported but not recorded. They may give a misleading picture of overall trends if there have been changes over time in the willingness of victims to report crimes,

44

and in the criteria used by law enforcement agencies in determining how to record them. To check for this, the data can be compared with those obtained using victim surveys, which include unreported and unrecorded crimes.

The National Crime Victimization Survey (NCVS) allows for such comparisons to be made. This data set is constructed from responses to questionnaires by a nationally representative sample of the population. The NCVS samples around 90,000 households composed of about 160,000 persons annually. Respondents provide personal demographic information and various details about each victimization incident that they have experienced over the period in question, regardless of whether the crime was reported to the police. Coverage includes all of the index crimes except murder (for obvious reasons) and arson.

For the six index crimes that are covered by both the NCVS and the UCR, counting methods differ. The NCVS includes crimes that are not reported to the police but does not include crimes against businesses, crimes against children under the age of twelve, and crimes against people who are not in the household population. So the NCVS excludes crimes against residents of nursing homes, homeless people, and inmates of psychiatric hospitals, prisons, and jails. And it includes information about simple assaults (attacks or attempted attacks without either a weapon or serious injury) and unwanted sexual contact, which the UCR does not cover.

A comparison between UCR and NCVS data reveals significant disparities in the incidence of two crimes—rape and aggravated assault—especially in the period before 1990. Specifically, while the UCR shows low and rising levels of these crimes in the 1970s and 1980s, the NCVS shows high and modestly declining levels.[3] Nevertheless, there is agreement across data sources on the sharp decline across all categories of index crime since 1990.

The rate of incarceration, in contrast, continued to rise for two decades after crime rates hit their peaks, reaching levels that were both historically unprecedented and well outside the range observed in other democracies, for reasons that we examine in Chapter 11.[4] This incarcerated population is disproportionately young, male, and poorly educated. It is also disproportionately black and (to a lesser extent) Hispanic. But the rates of arrest and incarceration by race vary quite sharply across different crimes.

Arrests and Offending

Figure 2.3 shows the proportion of African Americans among the pool of arrestees for the four crimes of appropriation over the period 2000–2015. There is a clear outlier here: African Americans are arrested for robbery at far higher rates than they are arrested for burglary, larceny, or motor vehicle theft, and this has remained true even as the overall number of arrests has declined sharply.

Arrest data alone cannot tell us about the racial composition of the offender population, since it is possible that there are significant racial disparities in the likelihood of arrest conditional on the commission of a crime. In the case of nonlethal crimes that typically involve contact between victim and offender—such as robbery, rape, and assault—NCVS data can be used to examine the racial composition of the pool of offenders, as perceived and reported by the surveyed victims. These data fluctuate quite a bit from one year to the next owing to the small sample size, but averaging across multiple years allows for a comparison with the arrest data.

Making this comparison for the 2000–2008 period, we find that in 45 percent of single-offender robberies, the victim identified the offender as black. This statistic rises to 48 percent if one assumes that the racial composition of the pool of offenders who could not be

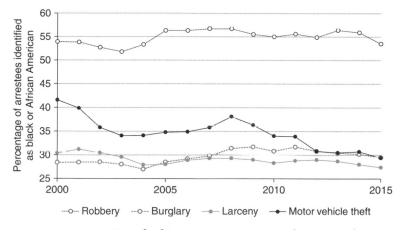

FIGURE 2.3. Proportion of African American arrestees for crimes of appropriation, 2000–2015. Source: Source: FBI Uniform Crime Reports.

classified by victims mirrors the composition of offenders as a whole. Over the same period, about 55 percent of those arrested for robbery were black. While the NCVS data suggest that white robbers are somewhat less likely to be arrested than black robbers, they confirm that among those who commit crimes of acquisition, blacks are more likely to choose robbery while whites are more likely to choose burglary, larceny, and motor vehicle theft. We explore some of the reasons for these patterns in Chapter 3.

Next consider crimes of destruction, for which the proportion of African Americans among the pool of arrestees is shown in Figure 2.4. Again we see an outlier, in this case homicide. While about half of homicide arrestees over this period are black, the corresponding ratios for rape and assault are much lower, and that for arson is lower still. Among those arrested for crimes of destruction, therefore, whites are more likely to be charged with rape, assault, and (especially) arson, while blacks are more likely to be charged with murder and manslaughter. We discuss some possible reasons for this in Chapter 4.

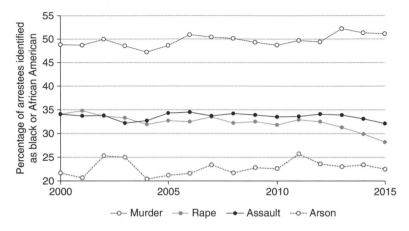

FIGURE 2.4. Proportion of African American arrestees for crimes of destruction, 2000–2015. Source: FBI Uniform Crime Reports.

Victimization

The victims of crime are often people whom offenders actively selected and who did not manage to escape, evade, or avoid the encounter. Crime is a two-way process. If robbery offenders, for instance, could choose between affluent, elderly women and poor young men to be their victims, they would almost certainly choose the former. But, in fact, affluent and elderly women are much less likely to be robbery victims than poor young men, mainly because they stay away from places accessible to offenders.[5]

Crimes of destruction occur mainly within identity groups, and so the victimization patterns are similar to the arrest patterns. For assault and rape we can infer this from the NCVS data. For murder, there are two data sources: the FBI's Supplemental Homicide Reports, which are collected from law enforcement agencies, and the Centers for Disease Control and Prevention's mortality reports, which are

48

collected from medical examiners. The FBI reports contain data on known offenders, showing that murder tends to be an intraracial event—most black victims die at the hands of other blacks, and the killers of whites are typically white themselves.

For crimes of appropriation other than robbery, we can't link victims to offenders because victims rarely see who takes their possessions. In the aggregate, black and white households are about equally likely to be victims of theft, but black households are more than twice as likely to be victims of motor vehicle theft, and almost twice as likely to be victims of burglary.[6] Even though the average black household has fewer automobiles than the average white household, black households are considerably less likely to have access to a garage or carport.[7]

Robbery is different: offenders are typically visible to their victims, which is often not the case with other crimes of appropriation. Furthermore, robbery crosses racial lines in very particular ways: a significant number of whites are robbed by black offenders, but very few blacks are robbed by white offenders. And the manner in which a robbery proceeds—with respect to compliance and the use of force—is contingent on visual attributes of victim and offender in ways that are simply not possible with burglary, theft, or larceny. This has broad implications for offender behavior, arrest rates, and public perceptions of criminality.

Summing Up

All categories of index crimes have become much less frequent since around 1990, but otherwise there are few common elements among them. The crimes differ in their primary motivations, their costs to victims, and the identity groups that are most likely to commit them.

Among the index crimes, two stand out as deserving greater attention in a book about stereotypes—murder and robbery. How these crimes are committed, who commits them, and who is likely to become a victim depend crucially on racial stereotypes. We devote Chapters 3 and 4 to understanding why.

chapter 3

ROBBERY

In Chapter 1 we left Brent Staples whistling Vivaldi to put fellow pedestrians at ease in Chicago. But Staples quickly tired of working so hard to accommodate others and decided instead to act in stereotype-confirming ways:

> One night I stooped beneath the branches and came up on the other side, just as a couple was stepping from their car into their town house. The woman pulled her purse close with one hand and reached for her husband with the other. The two of them stood frozen as I bore down on them. I felt a surge of power. These people were mine; I could do with them as I wished. If I'd been younger, with less to lose, I'd have robbed them and it would have been easy. All I'd have to do was stand silently before them until they surrendered their money.[1]

Staples's recognition that he could turn the negative stereotype to his advantage shows that there are a few circumstances in which such stereotypes can be lucrative. Robbery offenders understand this well.

When confronted, a robbery victim must make a quick and consequential decision about whether to comply with the offender's demands. Compliance involves some loss of property, but a failure to comply may result in injury or even loss of life. Some victims are inclined to comply under all circumstances, while others tend to resist no matter what. Still others comply only if sufficiently fearful that resistance will be met with violence, and these fears depend on observable characteristics of the offender.

Certain characteristics are within an offender's control—for example, whether to use a weapon or to have a menacing facial tattoo. Other attributes, such as height, build, gender, and skin color, are less easily modified. Both types of characteristics can affect the level of victim fear and hence the likelihood of compliance.

In deciding whom to target, offenders also use physical attributes as a guide. They look to avoid victims perceived to be likely to resist, and actively seek out those whom they expect to be compliant.

That is, robbery involves a number of decisions made in rapid sequence, each of which is affected by stereotypes. Offenders choose victims they stereotype as being compliant, and victims comply with offenders they stereotype as being violent. In particular, offenders exhibit a preference for victims whom they expect will hold negative stereotypes about them. Being subject to such stereotypes can be terribly risky and harmful in some contexts, such as interactions with armed and fearful individuals, including some law enforcement officers. But during the commission of a robbery, being stereotyped in this manner can be profitable.

Given these considerations, individuals who are commonly stereotyped as being violent will have more to gain from robbery—relative to burglary, larceny, or any other economic activity for that matter—than those who are not stereotyped in this way. Furthermore, victims who are stereotyped as being resistant will face a very different pool of offenders from those stereotyped as being compliant. Accounting for these factors can help explain certain patterns in the robbery data that are otherwise hard to understand.

Patterns in the Data

The incidence of robbery in the United States quadrupled from 1960 to 1980, remained fairly stable for a decade, peaked around 1990, and then began a steady decline that by 2012 had reversed almost the entire increase of the earlier period.[2]

Victim surveys classify robberies into four types, depending on whether the robbery was completed and whether any victims were injured. This information can be used to compute the likelihood that a victim will resist, as well as the likelihood that one who does so will be injured. As a first approximation, we can interpret robbery attempts that were completed without injury to the victim as those in which the victim did not resist. Over the 2012–2014 period, 43 percent of robberies fell into this category, so 57 percent involved some form of resistance.[3] To compute the likelihood of violence conditional on resistance, we take the ratio of those involving injury (regardless of whether they were completed) to the total involving resistance. Doing this results in an estimate of 56 percent. That is, a majority of attempted robberies involved some resistance, and a majority of those who resisted suffered some injury.[4]

Survey data also tell us about perceived offender race or ethnicity from the victim's perspective. Table 3.1 shows the percentage distribution of single-offender robberies by victim and offender race / ethnicity in recent years.

About 43 percent of robberies involve white offenders, and almost all of their victims are also white. In particular, white offenders almost never target black victims. In sharp contrast, the victims of black offenders are about evenly divided between black and white. As a result, black-on-white robbery is about seventeen times as frequent as white-on-black robbery.[5] It appears that all offenders tend to avoid black victims, but this effect is much stronger among white offenders.

Table 3.1 Single-offender robberies by self-reported victim identity and perceived offender identity, 2012-2014

	Offender Race / Ethnicity as Perceived by Victim				
Victim Race / Ethnicity	White (%)	Black (%)	Hispanic (%)	Other (%)	Unknown (%)
White	39	14	5	3	4
Black	1	14	1	1	1
Hispanic	3	8	4	1	1

Source: Bureau of Justice Statistics.

One might think that offenders selectively target white victims because they are stereotyped as having more cash and valuables in their possession. It turns out, however, that the opposite is true. The monetary value of losses incurred by black victims consistently exceeds those incurred by white victims. In fact, white victims are stereotyped as having less cash on their person, relying more on credit cards and other means of payment. But they are also stereotyped as being more compliant, and this is what makes them attractive to offenders.

Despite these considerations, blacks are about twice as likely as whites to be victims of robbery. In fact, those groups most likely to be targeted under any given circumstances—women, whites, and the elderly—all have lower victimization rates than those least likely to be targeted. This apparent paradox is easily resolved once we consider crime avoidance: those who would be most appealing to offenders are also least willing to expose themselves to risk. This factor helps explain why white households are more likely than black households of comparable means to leave cities for safer suburbs: they would face higher rates of victimization if they were to stay.[6]

As we saw in Chapter 2, robbery arrests show significant black overrepresentation relative to other crimes of appropriation. Over the period 1995–2014, approximately 55 percent of arrestees for robbery were black. The corresponding rate for motor vehicle theft was about 35 percent, and for burglary and larceny was even lower at 30 percent.[7]

Using arrest data to make inferences about rates of offending is fraught with difficulty because arrests can occur only if crimes are reported, and even if crimes are reported, they may be subject to varying levels of enforcement action. However, as we saw in Chapter 2, evidence from victim surveys also suggests that among crimes of appropriation, robbery exhibits by far the greatest levels of black involvement. It is also the only such crime to routinely involve face-to-face interaction.

We argue later in this chapter that these two facts are connected, and that thinking about offending through the lens of stereotypes helps make sense of many patterns in the data. But first, we take a short detour to understand why robberies became more violent even as they became less frequent over the past couple of decades.

Frequency and Violence

As we have seen, crime declined across all major categories since the early 1990s, and robbery was no exception. But even as robbery became considerably less frequent, it became more violent. That is, the likelihood of violence faced by victims offering resistance increased. Between 1993 and 2005, for instance, total robberies declined by 55 percent, but the likelihood of violence conditional on resistance rose from 43 percent to 58 percent. Resistance became more dangerous.[8] What accounts for this?

Robberies became less frequent because more people abandoned the activity than began to engage in it. They did so for a variety of reasons, including better economic opportunities in other occupations and harsher or more certain punishment for offending.[9] The net result has been a reduced pool of robbery offenders.

But the pool did not shrink through random exit and entry. That is, the characteristics of those who left the pool of offenders were systematically different from those who entered or remained. As deterrence became more effective and offending more costly, those exiting the offender pool were, on balance, individuals with the best alternative options for generating an income. Likewise, those remaining were the most desperate to begin with, and the most prone to respond to resistance with violence.

As the incidence of robbery declined, therefore, those victims offering resistance became increasingly likely to get hurt. The offender confronting them was more likely to be desperate enough to try to force compliance, despite the greater risks and penalties involved. The relatively timid offenders who were part of the pool when robbery was frequent had moved on to other lines of work.

Given the greater likelihood of violence, one would expect to see resistance rates decline. And this is indeed what we see, although the effect is not large: rates of resistance fell from about 63 percent in 1993 to 59 percent in 2005.[10] These rates will seem high to many readers, especially to those who have been robbed in the past and chose to comply. But the readers of this book are not typical victims. As we argue below, ethnographic evidence collected by Richard Wright and Scott Decker suggests that victims are often engaged in proscribed activities themselves, such as buying illicit drugs or the services of sex workers.[11] They are also in neighborhoods with high robbery rates and confront such situations often. Most of the offenders in the Wright and Decker sample bore serious scars from resistance, and one of them was killed with his own knife during the data collection period.

Just as any given victim faces different pools of offenders at different points in time, different victims face different pools of offenders at any given point in time. In particular, a black victim will face an offender pool different from the one a white victim will face, even if the two happen to be at roughly the same location at the same time. This is because the latter pool will contain offenders who have chosen to avoid black victims altogether.

Appearance as Deterrence

Robberies became less frequent but more violent over the past couple of decades in part because those offenders most likely to flee in the face of resistance stopped engaging in robbery, leaving behind a more hardened and desperate population of offenders.

This basic mechanism operates not just over time but also at any given point in time. To see the argument, consider the following thought experiment. Suppose that we can divide offenders into two groups, desperate and patient. If whites are stereotyped as being more compliant, then patient offenders will selectively target white victims, while desperate offenders will act on the first opportunity to arise, regardless of victim characteristics. In this case, black victims will face only desperate offenders, while white victims will sometimes face patient ones.

Now suppose that desperate offenders are not just less selective in victim choice but also more likely to try to force compliance with violence if they face resistance. Patient offenders, by contrast, flee when resisted and seek out other opportunities. In this case, black victims will frequently face violence when they resist, while white victims will often resist successfully (whenever they are confronted by a patient offender). Black victims will face a smaller but more violent pool of offenders. If they resist, they will be more likely to get hurt.

This is exactly what we see in the data. Over the 2012–2014 period, the likelihood of violence conditional on resistance was 51 percent for black-on-white robberies and 60 percent for black-on-black robberies. About 30 percent of black-on-white robberies failed without injury, while the corresponding figure for black-on-black robberies was 24 percent.[12] When facing black offenders, white victims on average were more successful than black victims at resisting.[13]

But doesn't this imply that white victims should resist more often? It does not. White victims on average incur smaller losses relative to black victims, both in absolute terms and in relation to their overall wealth. Even though they face a lower risk of violence relative to black victims, this risk is far from negligible and usually not worth taking, given the relatively moderate losses involved. Black victims face larger losses, on average, especially relative to their overall wealth. Their rates of resistance are accordingly higher, which confirms the stereotype held by offenders that whites are more compliant.

Another factor is at play here. The experimental results surveyed in Chapter 1 suggest that whites and blacks differ systematically in the implicit biases they hold. To the extent that whites are more fearful of black offenders, they will tend to resist at lower rates. In fact, there is ethnographic evidence that suggests exactly this.

Conversations with Offenders

Direct evidence on the motives, beliefs, and behavior of active robbery offenders is hard to come by. One notable exception is a study conducted by Richard Wright and Scott Decker, based on detailed interviews with eighty-six active armed robbers in St. Louis over several months in 1994 and 1995. All but three of the offenders were black, so the study tells us very little about the thoughts and actions of white robbers. But the interviews reveal that these offenders select their victims carefully, with the likelihood of resistance being a primary consideration.

At the time of the robberies, many of the victims were themselves engaged in some illegal activity, such as soliciting prostitutes or buying drugs. Such individuals are attractive to offenders because they are unlikely to report the crime or seek help from police. They are especially attractive if they are unlikely to resist, and here stereotypes come into play: "Many of the offenders reported that, other things being equal, they preferred to rob whites because, compared to their black counterparts, such victims were more likely to be cooperative."[14] None of the offenders in the Wright and Decker sample preferred black victims to white victims, although many were willing to target blacks in the absence of an alternative.

One offender states: "Whites accept the fact that they've been robbed. . . . Some blacks would rather die than give you they bucks and you damn near have to be killing [them] to get it." And another: "[Whites] usually don't resist. A black person will try to grab the gun out of your hand. They will make you shoot them if you have to. . . . Black people say 'I don't care if you do have a gun,' and they'll put up a hassle whereas a white person might say, 'Look here, take the watch, take this here, just don't hurt me.' . . . A black person will say, 'No, you gotta kill me, you ain't gonna take my money like that.'"[15]

The preference for white over black victims is not based on the belief that the former possess more cash. Quite the opposite: whites frequently frustrate offenders because they tend to carry little cash. One offender states that "most white people have about two dollars on them, and credit cards, something like that"; another that "whites, they have credit cards and checkbooks on them . . . they get robbed, they cancel it," and yet another that "all they got is plastic and checks."[16]

When asked why whites offer little resistance, offenders offered two kinds of responses. One is based on the (empirically valid) belief that even if whites have less cash on their person, they have more elsewhere on average: "[Whites] can get [the money] back easier [so they seldom resist]. . . . Blacks hard to come by cash so they ain't gonna come up off it too easy." The other, more interestingly, involves a stereotype about a stereotype: "I rob mostly whites. . . . I usually don't have no problem [with resistance], none at all. [Whites] got this stereotype, this myth, that a black person with a gun or knife is like Idi Amin or Hussein. And [a] person [who believes] that will do anything [you say]."[17]

This evidence is anecdotal, of course, and perhaps specific to this particular offender pool. It is also silent on the beliefs and behavior of white offenders, which may be quite different. Nevertheless, it is broadly consistent with the patterns observed in the data from victim surveys and crime reports.

The Public Imagination

Among crimes of appropriation, robbery is unusual in another respect: offenders are more likely than burglars and thieves to be arrested and imprisoned. In 2009, for instance, there were thirty-one arrests per one hundred robberies.[18] The corresponding figures for burglary and motor vehicle theft were fourteen and ten. Furthermore, arrests for robbery were considerably more likely to result in a prison admission than arrests for the other crimes. There were nine prison admissions per one hundred robberies, as compared with three per one hundred burglaries and just one per one hundred motor vehicle thefts. Similar patterns arise in other years.

That is, a robbery is about three times more likely to result in a prison admission than a burglary, and nine times more likely to do so than a motor vehicle theft. In addition, of the four crimes of appropriation, robberies are the least frequent: motor vehicle thefts occur roughly twice as often as robberies, burglaries five times as often, and larcenies fifteen times as often. Most crimes of appropriation are not robberies, and the majority of offenders who are never apprehended are involved with crimes other than robbery.

How does this pool of never-apprehended offenders compare with those who are caught and punished? If the racial composition of the offender pool roughly matches the racial composition of the arrestee pool for crimes of appropriation, then black offenders are caught and punished at significantly higher rates than white offenders. That is, blacks constitute a greater share of arrestees and prisoners than they do of offenders.[19] Note that this argument does not rely on any assumption of bias on the part of law enforcement officials: robberies entail a higher likelihood of arrest for a variety of reasons having little to do with the racial composition of the offender pool. For instance, they are often reported promptly, and robbery victims can describe and identify offenders more easily than victims of burglary, larceny, and motor vehicle theft.

This disparity between the offender pool and the arrestee pool matters, because racial stereotypes about criminal involvement are formed on the basis of arrests, imprisonment, and victim descriptions rather than actual rates of offending. Robbery accordingly plays an outsized role in the public imagination when it comes to beliefs about criminal behavior. In addition, that robbery so often crosses racial boundaries makes it especially salient. As Andrew Hacker has observed, for "white victims caught in interracial robberies, the loss of cash or valuables is seldom their chief concern. Rather, the racial character of the encounter defines the experience."[20]

Richard Wright and Scott Decker note that the offense of robbery "can both provoke and reinforce racial stereotypes in which blacks are perceived to be predatory and violent."[21] As we have argued in this chapter, these very same beliefs make compliance more likely and robbery more lucrative for black offenders. Given the disproportionately high rates of arrest, incarceration, and victim descriptions associated with robbery, these stereotypes are held in place by the very incentives that they help create.

But robbery is not the only offense in which fear-inducing stereotypes play a central role. They are also important in understanding how even minor conflicts can result in homicide, as we argue in Chapter 4.

MURDER

On July 2, 1899, Grace Doyle of Chicago snatched a revolver from the hip pocket of a police officer and shot and killed her husband, Thomas. "If I had not put an end to him this morning he would have killed me tomorrow," she would later claim.[1]

Among serious crimes, homicide is unique in that it has a preemptive motive: people sometimes kill simply to avoid being killed. In some scenarios—such as that of Grace Doyle—the parties involved are well acquainted with each other and able to judge the danger they face with reasonable accuracy. But many homicides result from interactions involving people who scarcely know each other.[2] Under these conditions, how is the level of threat to be assessed?

The Burglar Paradox

In his classic 1960 book *The Strategy of Conflict*, Thomas Schelling examines a scenario that has come to be called the burglar paradox:

> If I go downstairs to investigate a noise at night, with a gun in my hand, and find myself face to face with a burglar who has a gun in his hand, there is a danger of an outcome that neither of us desires. Even if he prefers to just leave quietly, and I wish him to, there is danger that he may think I want to shoot, and shoot first. Worse, there is danger that he may think that I think he wants to shoot. Or he may think that I think he thinks I want to shoot. And so on. "Self-Defense"

is ambiguous, when one is only trying to preclude being shot in self-defense.[3]

If one person has a strong motive to kill another for whatever reason—financial gain, personal hostility, or vengeance—then the potential victim has a motive to kill first, and both parties face danger. But what Schelling's thought experiment makes clear is that a killing can occur even if neither party has any such motive. Fear itself can be a motive, as can fear that one is interacting with a fearful party, and so on, all the way up a hierarchical chain of beliefs. Under these conditions, small changes in underlying conditions can give rise to sharp increases in preemptive killing and investments in lethal weapons that are very difficult to reverse.[4]

One factor that can greatly contribute to one's fear of being killed is the knowledge that one can be killed with impunity. If one's killer faces little prospect of being brought to justice, then one is in greater danger, and the incentive for preemptive action becomes stronger. And if both parties to a dispute are aware that neither is likely to face prosecution for killing the other, these effects are greatly amplified.

Killing with Impunity

For much of the history of the United States, African Americans have been killed with impunity. Before the Civil War, "the law shielded slave-owners from criminal liability for killing a slave if death resulted from violence administered for the purpose of subduing resistance or imposing discipline."[5] Even after the passage of the Fourteenth Amendment in 1868, blatant double standards in the administration of justice persisted. During Reconstruction, whites convicted of murdering blacks could expect sentences less severe than the sentences blacks faced for petty theft, and "many whites still needed to learn that killing a black person amounted to murder."[6]

While this lesson was eventually learned, the severity of punishment continued to depend on victim identity. Consider, for instance, the following account of attitudes in a Mississippi community during the early 1930s, as told by the anthropologist Hortense Powdermaker in her book *After Freedom:*

The attitude of the Whites and of the courts which they control is one of complaisance toward violence among the Negroes, and even toward intra-Negro homicide. There were convictions for only thirty per cent of the killings recorded in 1933. . . . That intra-White killings are not so lightly regarded is a point which does not call for proof. When a white man kills a Negro, it is hardly considered murder. When a Negro kills a white man, conviction is assured, provided the case is not settled immediately by lynch law.

The mildness of the courts where offenses of Negroes against Negroes are concerned . . . may be viewed as one result of the system which treats the Negro as sub-human and therefore places less value on his life than on that of a white person, and exacts less punishment for destroying it. . . . In part also, reluctance to exact a penalty for intra-Negro crime belongs to the policy which by way of "sop" or compensation indulges the Negro whenever license on his part does not infringe on white privileges. Such a policy finds support in the paternalistic white attitude, which views Negroes as children— irresponsible, volatile, unaccountable.

Whatever its causes, its results are not in the direction of diminishing violence among the Negroes. While the high percentage of assaults may not be attributable solely to white policy and attitudes, some connection can hardly be denied. The courts punish with drastic severity Negro violence against Whites. But they function in a way that serves as inducement to the Negro to take the law into his own hands when his difficulties involve other Negroes. Since he can hope for no justice and no defense from our legal institutions, he must settle his own difficulties, and often he knows only one way. He is the more ready to use it, since the same court which would crush him if he accused a white man of cheating him will probably let him off if he is accused of killing a black man.[7]

The community Powdermaker describes was not unusual, and many similar accounts exist.[8] In *Locking Up Our Own,* James Forman describes a report from the Commission on Interracial Cooperation based on gatherings involving concerned members of Atlanta's black community in 1936. The report complains of extremely light sentences for identified killers whose victims were black, observing that "murderers have been known to get off with two and three years, and in some cases with six months."[9] As David Hardy of the *New York Daily News* communicated to the Kerner Commission three decades later: "If a black man kills another black man, the law is generally enforced at its minimum."[10]

Some of the most striking evidence for the relevance of victim race in determining the severity of punishment comes from studies of the death penalty. In 1972, the Supreme Court ruled in *Furman v. Georgia* that the death penalty could not be applied in a capricious or discriminatory manner, and effectively imposed a moratorium on executions in the United States.[11] Several states responded by amending their laws and procedures to comply with the decision, and capital punishment was allowed to resume in 1976. In 1990, the United States Government Accountability Office published a report on racial disparities in the imposition of the death penalty during the post-*Furman* period, based on a survey and evaluation of twenty-eight separate studies (using twenty-three data sets). The report found that in more than four-fifths of the studies, "race of victim was found to influence the likelihood of being charged with capital murder or receiving the death penalty, i.e., those who murdered whites were found to be more likely to be sentenced to death than those who murdered blacks. This finding was remarkably consistent across data sets, states, data collection methods, and analytic techniques."[12]

Subsequent work has confirmed these findings: among those convicted of capital murder, the killers of whites are significantly more likely to end up on death row than the killers of blacks.[13]

Clearance

Before an offender can be sentenced, a murder needs to be solved, and here again victim race appears to matter. A study conducted for the *Los Angeles Times* examined all 9,442 "willful homicides" reported in Los Angeles County over the 1990–1994 period, tracking their clearance status until mid-1996. After accounting for general characteristics of the crime related to the ease of identifying the perpetrator, the study found that the odds that the murders of whites would be solved were more than 1.4 times greater than the odds that murders of blacks and Hispanics would be solved.[14]

This study did not simply find that homicides with white victims were more likely to be solved than those with black and Hispanic victims in the raw data; it also accounted for a variety of other aspects of the crime that could conceivably have affected clearance rates— including whether the killing occurred during a robbery or was gang related, the relationship between the victim and the offender, and the age and gender of the victim.[15] The findings indicate that these other factors, taken together, are insufficient to account for the differences across victim groups in clearance rates.

Law enforcement sources quoted in the report denied that the disparity was due to the explicit neglect of cases with black and Hispanic victims, arguing instead that "whites tend to be killed in middle- and higher-income neighborhoods where witnesses are more inclined to cooperate with police."[16] As it happens, this explanation cannot be ruled out: the study did not account for the neighborhood in which the crimes occurred or the cooperativeness of potential witnesses.

The *Washington Post* recently conducted a comprehensive study of clearance rates nationwide that is based on a mapping of more than fifty thousand murders over the past decade.[17] The authors found large variations in homicide clearance rates both within and between cities. While about half the cases were solved (in the sense of being cleared by arrest), many neighborhoods had clearance rates of less than one-third. Some cities, such as Baltimore and Chicago, had much lower clearance rates than others.

The study found that neighborhoods with especially low arrest rates were primarily home to low-income black residents. Partly for this reason, clearance rates showed significant variation across victim groups: an arrest was made "in 63 percent of the killings of white victims, compared with 48 percent of killings of Latino victims and 46 percent of the killings of black victims."

As in the Los Angeles study, police officials blamed the low clearance rates on "frayed relationships with residents and on witnesses who are unwilling to cooperate." This "makes it almost impossible to close cases in areas where residents already distrust police. As a result, distrust deepens and killers remain on the street with no deterrent." The very real threat of retaliation also keeps witnesses from

coming forward. According to residents of low-clearance neighborhoods and even a few officers, responsibility also lies with "apathetic
police departments."

Support for the view that neighborhood attributes matter more
than victim characteristics in accounting for disparities in clearance
rates may be found in an analysis of 802 homicides in Columbus,
Ohio, over the period 1984–1992.[18] The authors of this study found
that neighborhood racial composition has a significant effect on clearance rates, with homicides in predominantly black neighborhoods
being solved at lower rates than those in predominantly white neighborhoods. In fact, once neighborhood demographics are taken into
account, the race and gender of victims cease to have independent explanatory importance. The authors interpret this finding as arising
from a lack of trust in police in black neighborhoods, which lowers
rates of witness cooperation.[19]

The link between witness cooperation and clearance rates, and the
mediating role of police tactics and trust, is extremely important and
so we return to it in subsequent chapters. Here we focus on the incentive effects of low clearance rates: knowing that one can be killed
with impunity makes preemptive killing more likely, which in turn
amplifies fear in a cascading psychological sequence with a predictably violent end.

A minor dispute between two parties who are confident that the
police will apprehend and the courts severely punish either one of
them for committing murder will evolve in very different ways from
a dispute on which no such expectation exists. If one party fears that
he can be killed with impunity, he will become more dangerous as a
result, and more likely to kill and be killed preemptively. And this
effect is substantially amplified if both parties to the dispute expect that
either one of them could be killed with impunity.[20] Low clearance
rates and high homicide rates are two sides of the same coin.

This very same logic extends to the effects of "stand-your-ground" laws, which have been shown to result in an increase in rates of criminal homicide.[21] Such laws allow civilians to legally kill others if they reasonably consider themselves to be under threat in public places, even if safe retreat is an option. Since the laws, by definition, restrict the set of homicides that are subject to criminal penalties, the finding that they cause increases in murder and manslaughter might appear puzzling at first glance. But the logic of preemption suggests that this is precisely what one should expect: if one party to a dispute can kill with impunity, the other is more likely to kill first.

The following account from the early 1930s, related by Hortense Powdermaker, illustrates both the salience of the preemptive motive and the impunity with which killing could occur at the time:

> One shooting concerns two men, both with wives and children, who were courting a widow. One man came in and found the other there; and said to him: "Didn't I tell you what I'd do if I ever found you here?" The other man got up to go out and the first followed him. Suddenly the one who was leaving turned and shot the one who had threatened him. The shot was fatal, but the killer was considered a good plantation hand and was not taken into custody.[22]

In an environment where killing with impunity is frequent, individuals will be both fearful and dangerous. In his book *Between the World and Me*, written as a letter to his young son, Ta-Nehisi Coates describes the Baltimore of his youth:

> When I was your age the only people I knew were black, and all of them were powerfully, adamantly, dangerously afraid. . . . The fear was there in the extravagant boys of my neighborhood, in their large rings and medallions, their big puffy coats and full-length fur-collared leathers, which was their armor against their world. . . .

The fear lived on in their practiced bop, their slouching denim, their big T-shirts, the calculated angle of their baseball caps, a catalog of behaviors and garments enlisted to inspire the belief that these boys were in firm possession of everything they desired. . . . I heard the fear in the first music I ever knew, the music that pumped from boom boxes full of grand boast and bluster.

They were "dangerously afraid" because one response to fear is preemptive violence, which has the effect of making others more fearful and hence more violent. As Coates puts it, "Violence rose from the fear like smoke from a fire," including the violence inflicted by loving parents on their children in trying to drill into them habits that would keep them safe in the outside world.[23]

Guns and Lawyers

The preemptive motive can result in increased likelihood that a dispute will end in a killing, and thus amplify homicide rates. This is especially the case when alternative means of dispute resolution are unavailable. Parties to a legally binding contract have recourse to the courts when a dispute arises, but no such option exists when the contract involves prohibited activities such as gambling, prostitution, or the sale of illicit drugs. As noted by Jeffrey Miron, "Under prohibition, market participants substitute guns for lawyers in the resolution of disputes."[24]

In principle, therefore, prohibition of the so-called vices can raise homicide rates, which the preemptive motive can then push even higher. There is some evidence that this effect can be large. Daniel Okrent, for instance, traces scores of mob killings in Chicago during Prohibition to "broken contracts that did not lend themselves to polite resolution."[25]

But to argue that legalization or decriminalization of currently proscribed activities would lower homicide rates, one needs to take account of a countervailing effect: indulgence in the activities may rise, and this itself may affect the incidence of homicide. Intoxication with some substances can lead to more disputes and more violence, as can the desperation induced by withdrawal.

These mutually offsetting effects make it difficult to separately isolate and quantify the increase in transaction-related violence and the decrease in intoxication-induced violence. However, as Emily Owens argues, the strength of these effects varies at different points of the age distribution, with victims of transaction-related violence concentrated among young adults in their twenties, and victims of intoxication-related violence more evenly distributed by age. Using data on the timing and repeal of dry laws across states in the first half of the twentieth century, she confirms that the net effect of temperance laws was compression in the age distribution of homicide victims. As a result, "banning the commercial sale of alcohol appears to have protected children and teens from homicide, but at the cost of exposing young adults to more violence."[26]

Howard Bodenhorn has recently uncovered much stronger overall effects of Prohibition on homicide at a different time and place. He examines the passage of an 1893 South Carolina law that prohibited the private manufacture and sale of alcohol, causing several hundred saloons, taverns, and liquor stores to shut down or go underground.[27] Citing reports by the attorney general, he documents a sharp increase in homicide and assault prosecutions in the wake of the law's passage. But what makes the analysis especially compelling is that there were substantial variations in enforcement of the law across counties. Enforcement in Spartanburg, for example, was strict, while the authorities in Charleston essentially ignored the law. Bodenhorn finds systematic differences across counties in the rate of increase in homicide prosecutions, with stricter enforcement going hand in hand with greater numbers of homicides.

Melissa Dell discovered a similar phenomenon in twenty-first-century Mexico. After his election in 2006, President Felipe Calderón began aggressive enforcement actions against drug trafficking. Towns where mayors from his Partido Acción Nacional (PAN) won electoral victories cracked down much more severely than towns where his party's candidates suffered defeats, in part because stricter enforcement was an integral element of the PAN platform, and also because PAN-controlled towns were more likely to get help from the federal government. To uncover a causal effect of the change in policy, Dell focused only on those towns in which the election was close; with the exception of the electoral outcome, these towns had similar characteristics on average. She found that the towns in which PAN won close electoral victories experienced large increases in homicides relative to those in which the party suffered narrow defeats. Because the former set of towns was on average similar to the latter, she inferred that it was the policy itself, and not some extraneous factor that just happened to be correlated with the crackdowns, that caused the bloodbath.[28]

Jason Lindo and María Padilla-Romo also looked at the war on drugs in Mexico and found similar effects. Capturing a drug kingpin caused large and sustained increases in the number of murders in the area in which he operated, presumably as people lower down in the organization clashed in an attempt to move upward.[29]

While laws restricting the sale of drugs and alcohol have countervailing effects on violence, this is not the case for the prohibition of trade in goods such as ivory or timber, since their consumption has no intoxicating effects. In these latter cases, prohibition might be expected to result clearly and unambiguously in increased violence, and this is precisely what we see in the data. The restriction and eventual prohibition of extraction of and trade in Brazilian big-leaf mahogany has resulted in both continued illegal export and a greater incidence of homicide in precisely those regions where production was concentrated before the ban.[30]

The Geography of Murder

The 1968 Kerner Commission report determined that "the police maintain a much less rigorous standard of law enforcement in the ghetto, tolerating there illegal activities like drug addiction, prostitution and street violence that they would not tolerate elsewhere."[31] This geographic concentration of street vice had been documented thirty years earlier by Gunnar Myrdal, who observed that prostitution, gambling, and the selling of narcotics were far more common in black neighborhoods, where "police do not stand on the law so much."[32] Even earlier, in 1915, Booker T. Washington made the point that segregated black neighborhoods provide "hiding-places from the law," with the consequence that all manner of street vice is openly paraded.[33]

The lack of adequate police protection is one factor for the concentration of street vice but not the only one. Given that violence is the default contract enforcement mechanism in markets for illicit goods, individuals who are stereotyped as threatening will more effectively deter contract noncompliance. This is especially the case for small-scale transactions among strangers, where other means of building a reputation for toughness may not be available. Just as stereotypes of violence are useful to robbery offenders, they can be useful to those who have no recourse to the courts to ensure contract fulfillment.

Furthermore, stereotypes about locations can be particularly explosive in the chains of inference that lead to murders. If the two of us meet in a place stereotyped as particularly dangerous, I know that you are the type of person who goes to a place like that, and you know that I am that type of person too. Moreover, I know that you know, and you know that I know. So just being in this kind of place makes both of us more dangerous to each other. A dispute that starts at Moby Dick's Bar in Minneapolis is more likely to escalate than one that starts at a garden show on the East Side of Manhattan.

It should not be surprising that the location of murders is very concentrated—more concentrated than the location of any other index crime, and more concentrated than poverty or race. In the Newark metropolitan area in 2011, six municipalities with reputations as high-crime areas accounted for 2.6 percent of the land and 24.9 percent of the population, but were the location of 86 percent of murders, 80 percent of robberies, 77 percent of motor vehicle thefts, 73 percent of aggravated assaults, 52 percent of burglaries, and 35 percent of larcenies.[34]

Murder is concentrated in social as well as physical space: an individual whose social network includes someone who has previously suffered a gunshot injury is significantly more likely to be shot than someone whose network does not include any such person.[35] That one's likelihood of being shot is predictably greater if an associate (or even an associate of an associate) is shot means that any given shooting creates a heightened sense of risk among a clearly identifiable group of individuals. The preemptive motive for killing can then take hold, prompting other shootings, and so on in an escalating cycle of violence. As Andrew Papachristos puts it, "Murders spread through an epidemic-like process of social contagion" within networks.[36]

The combination of concentrated street vice, with its concomitant violent contract enforcement mechanisms, and the lower likelihood of homicide clearance in these very same communities makes life dangerous, and these effects are amplified by the preemptive motive. Holding this structure in place is a lack of trust in the law enforcement community and the absence of witness cooperation that this entails. As Janice Puckett and Richard Lundman note:

When citizens do not trust police enough to tell them what they saw, what they know, and what they suspect, the odds of a clearance decrease. . . . Scholars have regularly noted that citizens in African American neighborhoods do not trust police because police have long brought a far more heavy handed and intrusive style of policing to Black as compared to White communities. . . . It thus is possible that citizens in African American neighborhoods provide detectives with less information, which necessarily translates into lower clearance rates.[37]

We consider these "heavy handed and intrusive" tactics in some detail in chapters to follow.

Summing Up

In Chapters 2 and 3 we saw how racial stereotypes combine to result in racially specific and elevated rates of robbery and murder. These empirical realities can be accounted for by considering beliefs and incentives, without any need for essentialist arguments. But one needs to consider the beliefs and incentives of victims and offenders alike, and their manner of interaction, since these are crimes that cannot occur without at least two people involved.

Just looking at victims and offenders, however, is not enough to understand how and why crimes occur. Many other actors are involved: potential witnesses, police, prosecutors, judges, juries, parole boards, legislators, and voters, to name just some of the main players. We have already seen how legal prohibitions of alcohol and drugs, and the reluctance of witnesses to testify or provide tips affect murder rates.

Therefore, starting with Chapter 5, we look beyond victims and offenders to consider the workings of the criminal justice system.

chapter 5

PUBLIC ACTION

You can't think about crime without thinking about what police, corrections officers, prosecutors, judges, legislators, and other public employees do. In Chapter 2 we defined crime (somewhat reluctantly) as something that could not exist as a concept without governments to threaten to punish it. In the next few chapters we discuss what governments do about crime, including stops and searches, the use of force, criminal proceedings, and incarceration.

These topics are all controversial, for many reasons. First, public officials are rightly held to higher standards than private citizens. For instance, a real estate developer who hints that people who come to visit him will be treated better if they stay at a very expensive hotel he owns has done nothing inappropriate, but a public official who does the same thing has done something wrong and possibly illegal. Many public agents also have significant powers: most people are not permitted to lay a hand on a stranger, but police officers can punch or jail or shoot people in the normal course of their day if they think their duties require it.

Second, in a democracy, public officials represent citizens, and these citizens can end up paying for mistakes those public officials make. We can deplore sexual assault by Roger Ailes or Harvey Weinstein, but we do not consider ourselves responsible for it, either morally or financially. But after the United States government interned Japanese Americans during World War II, all taxpayers had to contribute to reparations. And when New York police officers beat and sodomized Abner Louima at the Seventieth Precinct station house in Brooklyn in 1997, all New Yorkers contributed to the resulting $8.75 million settlement—even those who marched in the streets to protest the abuse.

Finally, sometimes public decisions are more complex than private decisions and the motives are less obvious, if motives for these decisions can be said to exist at all. For instance, no single individual or organization decided to implement a fourfold increase in the rate at which Americans were incarcerated, but somehow this increase occurred over a span of thirty years, through a decentralized and often uncoordinated web of policies and actions. Most prisoners in the United States are held in state and local facilities, for violations of state and local laws. They have been arrested by local police, tried in local courts, and judged by local peers. Local prosecutors, wielding considerable discretionary power, have made decisions regarding charges, sentencing recommendations, and plea bargains based on preferences and principles that can vary sharply from one county to the next.[1]

When we think about complex public actions, then, the simplest schema of racial discrimination—person A did something to person B because of B's perceived race—no longer seems sufficient. As the philosopher Michele Moody-Adams notes, "Sometimes people don't tell us that they are in fact attempting to put racism into practice, and sometimes institutions can embody racist assumptions about the nature of human populations in the absence of any kind of overt justification or explanation in terms of racist convictions."[2] So before we consider complex public actions, we need to discuss discrimination at some length.

Two Kinds of Discrimination

Discrimination in employment has probably seen more thought and litigation than any other kind of discrimination, and we can learn something from it. Employment law distinguishes between two kinds of discrimination.

In *disparate treatment* discrimination, an individual treats or plans to treat one person differently from another because of race or gender (or age or sexual orientation). Disparate treatment is about motives. In the context of police use of force, disparate treatment would correspond to a situation in which an officer shoots a black civilian even though she would not have shot a white civilian under the same circumstances. This can happen even in the absence of malice or racial animus—for instance, if the officer is more likely to mistake a harmless object as a weapon when it is held by a black civilian.

Since disparate treatment speaks to motives and psychological states, it is extremely difficult to identify beyond a reasonable doubt in specific cases. In February 1999, Amadou Diallo was shot and killed in a hail of bullets from four plainclothes New York Police Department (NYPD) officers while standing in a poorly lit vestibule outside his apartment.[3] He held a black wallet in his hand that the officers mistook for a gun. The officers were acquitted of all charges, including second-degree murder, and Diallo's family accepted a $3 million wrongful death settlement from the city. But neither the verdict nor the settlement can tell us conclusively whether this was a case of disparate treatment, since we cannot be certain that a white suspect would have been spared in similar circumstances.

In *disparate impact* discrimination, an organization maintains a practice or policy that adversely affects members of a protected class, without any "business necessity" for the policy. Disparate impact grew out of employment litigation in the late 1960s, most importantly the unanimous Supreme Court decision in *Griggs v. Duke Power Co.* in 1971. Chief Justice Warren Burger wrote in that opinion: "The [Civil Rights] Act proscribes not only overt discrimination, but also practices that are fair in form but discriminatory in operation. The touchstone is business necessity. If an employment practice which operates to exclude Negroes cannot be shown to be related to job performance, the practice is prohibited." Thus disparate impact is about policies and their consequences.

While the idea of disparate impact discrimination was enunciated explicitly in a case involving a private employer, the logic can be extended to public entities. For instance, consider the "grandfather clauses" that several southern states enacted in the late nineteenth and early twentieth centuries.

These states required potential voters to pay onerous poll taxes and pass demanding literacy and constitutional knowledge tests, but exempted men who were eligible to vote in 1866 or 1867, or whose ancestors ("grandfathers") were eligible to vote at that time. On their face, these laws were racially neutral, but in practice they were discriminatory since blacks were not permitted to vote in these states in those years. They were "fair in form but discriminatory in operation." The laws were in fact ways to permit voting by poor, uneducated whites while excluding virtually all black citizens.

For instance, of the 58,000 blacks who lived in Oklahoma in 1900, only 57 came from states where their ancestors could vote in 1867. In 1915, the Supreme Court ruled that grandfather clauses like that in Oklahoma were unconstitutional, but Oklahoma responded by "grandfathering the grandfather clause" and switching the magic date from 1867 to 1914—a law that stayed in place for a quarter of a century.[4] What Oklahoma did was clearly discrimination, but it was not disparate treatment discrimination. It's appropriate to label it disparate impact discrimination.

How should we look for disparate impact discrimination in public policies? The first step is the same as that for private employers: are racial minorities (or other protected classes) disproportionately harmed by the policy? With the Oklahoma grandfather clauses, a few whites lost the right to vote, but blacks disproportionately lost that right—in fact, almost all African Americans in Oklahoma did so.

The second step is harder to translate, because governments are not enterprises that can have "business necessities." The equivalent test is a sort of cost-benefit calculation—is there some legitimate nonracial goal that the policy achieves that cannot be achieved as well as or better by some other policy that is less harmful to minorities? With the Oklahoma grandfather clauses, it is hard to think of a legitimate nonracial goal that they served uniquely well. Even if the goal were to reduce the number of people who had to take literacy tests, a criterion like elementary school education would have worked as well. So, as expected, the Oklahoma grandfather clauses fail both tests—they were disparate impact discrimination.

Note that while business necessity can excuse behavior that involves disparate impact, it cannot do so in the case of disparate treatment: employers that fire a black worker when doing so increases their profit—for instance, because it ends a boycott by customers—are still guilty of disparate treatment discrimination.

Public decisions also often differ from simple private decisions in the extent of the consequences for decision makers and hence the care that those decision makers exercise. A judge who decides a hundred cases a year is not as affected by any one of them as much as a consumer is in deciding which make of car to purchase, or a student in deciding which college to attend. The thinking that goes into the public decisions may therefore be more susceptible to shortcuts. This is especially true for routine decisions that occur frequently, such as police stops, rather than rare occurrences that could have significant consequences, such as the discharge of a firearm.

Furthermore, even in the case of frequent and routine decisions, some kinds of errors are much costlier than others. Denying bail to someone who is highly unlikely to miss a court appointment or commit a crime while free is relatively costless for a judge; granting bail to someone who later commits rape or murder is much costlier. To ensure against the latter outcome a judge may be willing to tolerate many errors of the former kind.

Another way of looking at disparate impact studies of public policies is that they cast aside the question of motive: a government is a disparate impact discriminator if it acts the way a racist government would act and an unbiased government would not. The difficulty of proving motives was in fact what led judges to turn to disparate impact arguments in employment cases.

Even with the simplest private decisions, uncovering the motives behind an action is extremely challenging, especially when the actor has no incentive to reveal these. Moreover, even the ability to read minds may not be enough: we often do things without understanding why we do them and how we would have acted under slightly different circumstances. In the case of public policies such as mass incarceration, which is the consequence of a very large number of localized decisions, ascribing motives is probably conceptually impossible. Even if each prosecutor had a clear and articulable motive, no common motive could be ascribed to all.

Stigma, too, may be especially important in public as opposed to private decisions. As Glenn Loury has observed, some "social disparities are salient while other are not. The salience of social facts is not determined in an entirely rational, deductively confirmed manner."[5] He points out that after welfare reform legislation in 1996, states with a higher proportion of black recipients tended to be more punitive in implementing laws they enacted.[6]

To carry this example forward in time, the crack epidemic among African Americans in the 1980s engendered an almost entirely punitive response, while the opioid epidemic in the 2010s, which has afflicted significant numbers of whites, has engendered a response with a large treatment component and considerable investment in harm-reduction technologies. The psychologist Carl Hart has written about this continuing pattern of using cops and correction officers to treat drug use among blacks, and doctors and social workers to treat it among whites: "The characteristically American pattern of cognitive flexibility on drug policy, with harsh penalties for some and sympathetic treatment for others . . . continues to this day."[7]

As we shall see, there is considerable evidence to support the claim of a yawning gap between offending and incarceration when it comes to the possession of illicit drugs. The evidence for index crimes, however, is much less clear.[8]

While disparate impact is a valuable conceptual tool, we will continue to look at disparate treatment too. Whether individuals do things for racist reasons says something about society and may also affect the victims of racism directly. The attack on Abner Louima was brutal and wrong, even if it was not part of a broader NYPD policy.

With large organizations, moreover, combining disparate treatment and disparate impact has the advantage of spreading responsibility throughout all levels of the organization, not just the bottom. In a police department, for instance, disparate treatment concentrates by necessity on police officers on the street, because they have the most contact with the public. Disparate impact looks at what mayors and commissioners do, too, and the voters who elect them.

So when we look at public responses to crime, we have to look at both disparate treatment and disparate impact.

What's Next?

Now that we've covered the preliminaries, we can begin our examination of the criminal justice system—how it affects crime, and how stereotypes affect its actions. We begin with three chapters about

police, since police interact with civilians more than any other officials in the justice system. Chapters 6–8 are about the different kinds
of interactions police can have with civilians, and are arranged in
increasing order of invasiveness or harm: police can stop civilians
and question them, police can use nonlethal force against civilians,
and police can kill civilians. For each type of interaction, we try to
assess why police act the way they do and what the consequences are.
Chapters 9 and 10 look at what happens when people are accused of
crimes: what sort of testimony (if any) witnesses give and why they
give it, and what sorts of decisions judges and juries make. Chapter 11
is about incarceration.

chapter 6

POLICE STOPS

The Fourth Amendment of the United States Constitution protects citizens from "unreasonable searches and seizures" of their person or property by law enforcement officers and requires a high legal standard of "probable cause" to be met before such actions are considered permissible. However, for some less invasive searches, including certain traffic and pedestrian stops, a lower standard of "reasonable suspicion" is enough.[1] This lower standard is still high: police must be able to point to "specific and articulable facts" that indicate that the person is—or is about to be—engaged in criminal activity.

The total number of involuntary, police-initiated stops in the United States is substantial. In 2011, for instance, about twenty-five million people were subjected to a traffic stop, and a further million and a half to a street stop.[2] About 3.5 percent of all stopped drivers had their person or vehicle searched, although this proportion varied substantially across groups: among stopped white drivers 2.3 percent were searched, while the corresponding rates for black and Hispanic drivers were 6.3 and 6.6 percent, respectively.

Race is not one of the "specific and articulable facts" on which a police officer's reasonable suspicion can be based, even if using race for that purpose could improve policing, reduce crime, make an officer's job easier, or serve some other law enforcement objective. According to United States law, one group of people (the police) cannot do something to another group of people (motorists or pedestrians) even if doing so is beneficial for the former, or beneficial for some third parties.

Preventing somebody from doing something to someone else is what most laws are about, after all. For an analogy, consider the case of New York City taxi drivers, who are not permitted to refuse service to a rider on account of the latter's race, or indeed their membership in any protected class under the city's Human Rights Law.[3] Drivers may have a preference for some passengers over others for a variety of reasons, including choice of destination, anticipated size of a tip, likelihood of robbery victimization, or simply a distaste for sharing space with members of some groups. Were they free to do so, they might use outward appearance to make judgments about these things, and bypass passengers whom they would prefer not to serve. But the law prevents them from doing so, and significant fines have been assessed against drivers who fail to comply.[4]

Similarly, according to the same law, a store "may reserve the right to inspect your bags, check your bags at the door, or closely observe your conduct in the store in an effort to prevent shoplifting; however, such actions may not be based on a protected class, e.g. race."[5] Regardless of whether a security guard at a store finds race to be informative about the likelihood of larceny, he is not legally permitted to condition his behavior on such information.

Such laws are in place so that people can go about their lives and pursue their goals without worrying about suffering costs on account of what the philosopher Sophia Moreau calls "extraneous traits":

> In a liberal society, each person is entitled to decide for herself what she values and how she is going to live in light of these values. This means that, in addition to certain freedoms of action, we are each entitled to a set of "deliberative freedoms," freedoms to deliberate about and decide how to live in a way that is insulated from pressures stem-

ming from extraneous traits of ours. Many of us already have these deliberative freedoms. . . . Anti-discrimination law attempts to give them to all of us, because each of us has an independent entitlement to them. It attempts to give them to us by preventing our employers, service providers, landlords, and others from acting in ways that deny us opportunities because of these traits, so that when we deliberate about such things as where to work and where to live, we do not have to think about these traits as costs.[6]

The rationale for restrictions on the behavior of law enforcement officers is similar—even if their ability to fight crime is compromised by the requirement that they inform suspects of their Miranda rights, secure a warrant before entering a home, shovel the sidewalks outside police stations after a snowstorm, or refrain from using race as a proxy for suspicion in the absence of specific evidence.

But how can we know whether officers are complying with the last of these imperatives? We noted above that among drivers who are stopped, blacks and Hispanics are more than twice as likely to be searched than whites. But this fact alone cannot be used to deduce the presence of disparate treatment. It remains possible that the same standards of suspicion were applied to all motorists, but that members of different groups exhibited suspicious behavior to different degrees. To test for disparate treatment, we need information not only on the likelihood with which a search was conducted, but also on the frequency with which it was productive. By comparing contraband recovery rates across groups it may be possible to infer whether different standards of suspicion were indeed applied. This approach to diagnosing discrimination is called the hit-rate test.

The Hit-Rate Test

In his 1957 book *The Economics of Discrimination,* Gary Becker introduced the idea that discriminatory treatment may be revealed by the outcomes of decisions; he argued that anyone engaged in discrimination must "either pay or forfeit income for this privilege."[7] Becker expanded on this idea in his Nobel lecture, asserting that in the context of loan origination, "the correct procedure for assessing whether banks discriminate . . . is to determine whether loans are more profitable to blacks (and other minorities) than to whites. . . . If banks discriminate against minority applicants, they should earn greater profits on the loans actually made to them than on those to whites. The reason is that discriminating banks would be willing to accept marginally profitable white applicants who would be turned down if they were black."[8]

In the case of police stops, the cost of discrimination takes the form of a reduced rate of contraband recovery, called the *hit rate.* Ian Ayres describes the logic as follows: "The ex post probability that a police search will uncover contraband or evidence of illegality is strong evidence of the average level of probable cause that police require before undertaking a search. . . . Any finding that the police searches of individuals with a particular characteristic (such as minority status) induce a systematically lower probability of uncovering illegality suggests that police search criteria unjustifiably subject that class of individuals to the disability of being searched."[9]

Becker and Ayres are using the word "discrimination" here in a very specific sense. They are referring to actions that are not motivated by pecuniary gain or any work-based motive—discrimination out of sheer malice. Economists refer to this as taste-based discrimination and contrast it with statistical discrimination, which is motivated by pecuniary gain or workplace incentives. Legal scholars have also been attentive to the distinction and refer to *prejudiced* versus *strategic* discrimination.[10] On a conventional metric that ignores psychic costs and benefits, prejudiced discrimination is costly to the discriminator, while strategic discrimination is profitable.

Civil rights laws and constitutional protections in the United States make no such distinction between motives for discrimination, nor should they. To see why, consider again the case of a taxi driver who is reluctant to pick up a black passenger. If the driver's behavior is based on his beliefs about anticipated earnings, he is engaged in strategic discrimination; if his behavior is motivated by a distaste for sharing space with a black passenger, he is engaged in prejudiced discrimination. Even though these motives are quite different, in both cases the actions of the driver take away a right from the would-be rider. Those who have to wait longer for a cab or find alternative transportation do not generally know or care whether the discrimination is prejudiced or strategic.[11] And neither does the law.

The tests that Becker and Ayres propose are ones that tell us *why* someone is breaking the law, not *whether* someone is breaking the law. But even for that limited purpose, the tests may not work as advertised.

The Problem with Averages

The word "average" in the reasoning by Becker and Ayres about police stops is critical: even if contraband is found at the same rate in searches of two groups, it is entirely possible that the groups have been subject to different thresholds of suspicion. By the same token, the application of a uniform standard across groups can give rise to very different hit rates. This is because the distribution of characteristics among those who meet the common threshold may differ substantially across groups. Thus the Becker-Ayres criterion may sometimes miss discrimination when it is occurring, and indicate discrimination when none is occurring.

The problem may be illustrated as follows.[12] Consider two groups, each of which has an average likelihood of contraband possession (as perceived by an officer at a stop) of 40 percent. But individuals are heterogeneous within groups, with some being perceived as much less likely to carry contraband than others. In one group this variation is wide, with some appearing highly suspicious and others much less so. In the other group there is less variation: individuals are harder to distinguish, and most fall into an intermediate range of suspicion as perceived by the officer. We refer to the first group as relatively heterogeneous and the second group as relatively homogeneous (see Figure 6.1).

Now suppose that all officers apply the same standard to both groups and conduct a search if their perceived likelihood of finding contraband is above 10 percent. This is shown by the dashed vertical line in the figure; all those who lie to the right of this line are searched. Two things are then apparent: a greater proportion of those in the relatively homogeneous group will be searched, and this group will also have a smaller hit rate. This is because both groups have the same average likelihood of carrying contraband, and many more of those unlikely to do so in the relatively heterogeneous group are not searched at all. So in this case, when officers don't discriminate, the Becker-Ayres test makes it look like they are discriminating. The opposite could also be the case—we could draw the lines differently for the groups and show that even though the officers were discriminating, the hit rates were the same.

The point is this: a proper application of the hit-rate test requires that we calculate and compare hit rates for those individuals who barely meet the threshold for a search in each group (called marginal hit rates), rather than the hit rates for all those who are searched (called

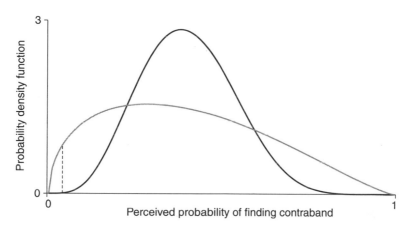

FIGURE 6.1. The two groups shown have the same average likelihood of carrying contraband, but the one shown in light gray is relatively heterogeneous, while the one in dark gray is relatively homogeneous (as perceived by officers). Facing a common threshold of suspicion for stops, the relatively homogeneous group will be stopped more often and will have a smaller hit rate than the relatively heterogeneous group.

average hit rates). But the former individuals cannot easily be identified in the data, so the average hit rate is typically used as a proxy.

Setting aside for the moment the shortcomings of the average hit-rate test as a method of detecting bias in police searches, what do the data on search outcomes tell us?

In a recent analysis of about a half million traffic stops across nine states, a team of researchers at Stanford University found that the hit rates for black and white drivers are about the same, although searches of Hispanic drivers are consistently less productive.[13] These results are roughly consistent with earlier findings based on more limited data.[14]

But given the size and richness of the data available to them, the researchers were also able to jointly estimate the entire distribution of the perceived likelihood of contraband possession, together with the thresholds used for searches, allowing for variation by driver identity and the county in which the stop occurred.[15] They find that at almost all locations, black and Hispanic drivers face a lower bar for searches relative to white drivers. This analysis provides evidence of bias in police searches and also demonstrates the value of going beyond the simple hit-rate test.

Notice that even if the Stanford group had found that police used the same threshold of suspicion for both groups, they might still be engaged in strategic discrimination, motivated by maximizing the expected amount of contraband recovered. They might assign a higher perceived probability of finding contraband to black civilians than to white civilians with the same observed nonracial characteristics. That is, they might think, possibly correctly, that young black men driving five miles per hour above the speed limit in green Chevrolet Camaros are more likely to be carrying drugs than white men driving at the same speed in the same make, model, and color of car. The requirement for nondiscrimination under the law is that for any set of nonracial characteristics, the probability of being stopped is the same for all groups. In the absence of "specific and articulable facts," a law-abiding police department can't stop black motorists in circumstances where it would not stop otherwise similar whites.[16]

Pedestrian Stops

Although traffic stops are by far the most frequent form of involuntary contact between the police and citizens nationwide, pedestrian stops are routine occurrences in certain neighborhoods. The widespread use of such stops has sometimes been deployed by police departments as a crime reduction strategy, most famously in the case of New York City's Stop, Question, and Frisk program.[17] At its peak this program involved well over a half million stops annually, most of which were concentrated in a few precincts. Legal challenges and a change of administration in the city have since led to a substantial decline in its use.

Officers making stops under this program must fill out form UF-250, which requires them to describe the rationale for the stop and report any instances of contraband recovery. This is in keeping with the legal requirement that suspicion be reasonable, based on facts that are specific to individuals and clearly articulable. In cases where there is suspicion of illegal drug or gun possession, hit rates can be computed from these data and compared across groups.

Sharad Goel, Justin Rao, and Ravi Shroff conducted one of the largest studies to date of the New York policy, examining about three million stops over the period 2008–2012.[18] Four-fifths of stops involved black or Hispanic civilians, who together constitute about half of the city's population. About a quarter of all stops were motivated by suspicion of criminal possession of a weapon, as recorded on the form. More than half of these involved a frisk, and about one in ten involved a more invasive search. The overall hit rate for weapon recovery was about 3 percent, but this varied widely across groups: 2.5 percent for blacks, 3.6 percent for Hispanics, and 11 percent for whites. Most of the recovered weapons were knives.

The data reveal that whites were infrequently stopped, but searches of whites conditional on being stopped were substantially more productive. At first glance this might suggest discrimination against blacks and Hispanics relative to whites, but for reasons that we have discussed, the simple hit-rate test cannot convincingly support such an inference. As it happens, most stops occurred in high-crime areas with low stop thresholds and predominantly black or Hispanic populations. If whites, on average, were stopped in low-crime areas with high stop thresholds (or if the whites stopped in high-crime areas were extremely likely to possess illegal weapons), the hit-rate disparities could arise even if a single threshold was applied to all groups at any given location. As the authors note, "Without understanding the location-specific nature of stop-and-frisk, it is easy to conflate racial discrimination with generally low—but not necessarily discriminatory—stop thresholds in predominately [sic] minority neighborhoods."[19]

But this does not mean that the data are silent on the issue of discrimination. Given the large number of detailed observations at their disposal, the authors are able to estimate with a high degree of precision the likelihood that any given stop will be productive. They do this using information that is readily available or that could be provided to officers, such as nonracial characteristics of the suspect, the characteristics of the stop location (including a measure of the local hit rate), and the time and day of the week when the stop was made.[20]

This empirical approach allows for the computation of stop-level hit rates, and the authors find that for most stops the likelihood of weapon recovery is predictably low, based on such nonracial factors as location and the stated reason for the stop. By focusing only on those stops with the highest likelihood of weapon recovery, the total number of stops could be dramatically reduced without substantially reducing overall productivity. Half the weapons could have been recovered with just 6 percent of stops, and 90 percent of weapons with 58 percent of stops.

Furthermore, a curtailment of stops along these lines would have dramatic consequences for the racial composition of the population searched. A disproportionate share of the (predictably) least productive stops involves searches of African Americans, so a more restrained and tightly focused policy would lead to a reduction in racial disparities within the population searched. Fewer innocents would be stopped, but the benefits would accrue disproportionately to black civilians, and "optimizing for weapons recovery would simultaneously bring more racial balance to stop-and-frisk."[21]

Racial Profiling

The hit rate test is designed to detect discriminatory treatment based on prejudice, which results in lower overall rates of police performance. But such tests cannot detect statistical or strategic discrimination, in which the selective targeting of particular groups is motivated purely by the maximization of contraband recovery. While it is true that the NYPD could have recovered most of its seized weapons with substantially fewer stops by ignoring race and concentrating on the appropriate nonracial characteristics, it is also true that even fewer stops would have been needed if both race and the appropriate nonracial characteristics had been used.

That is, a police force that was unconstrained in its use of diagnostic or preventive stops would have an incentive to engage in widespread racial profiling. As long as this is motivated by performance goals rather than racial animus or inaccurate stereotypes, it will not be detected by hit-rate tests. In fact, some economists have argued that discriminatory treatment based on strategic considerations alone can account for racial disparities in some search rates.

John Knowles, Nicola Persico, and Petra Todd have made an argument along these lines, using a theoretical model in which optimizing behavior by police and citizens gives rise to equality between average and marginal hit rates under the hypothesis that only performance goals motivate police behavior (and that police ignore constitutional constraints on their activity).[22] The equality of marginal and average hit rates in this model arises because the authors assume that within groups, those who are carrying contraband are behaviorally indistinguishable from those who are not; an officer making a stop will not observe any outward signs of guilt.[23] Under this assumption, the average hit-rate test can indeed be used to make inferences about discrimination. Using data on Maryland State Police stops on the I-95

95

Highway, they find support for the hypothesis of performance-based stops in the case of black and white drivers. Hispanic drivers, however, are stopped more often than a pure performance motive would imply.

If police officers consider only the likelihood of contraband recovery when deciding whether to conduct a search, then the probability of a search conditional on a stop ought not to depend on the racial identity of the officer making the decision. In a study of stops by the Boston Police Department over a two-year period starting in 2001, however, Kate Antonovics and Brian Knight found that a mismatch between officer and motorist race increased the likelihood that a search would be conducted. That is, although all groups of officers were more likely to search the vehicles of black motorists relative to those of whites, this difference was significantly more pronounced in the case of white officers.[24] It appears that black and white officers profile motorists to different degrees and in different ways.

Along similar lines, Shamena Anwar and Hanming Fang examined data from the Florida Highway Patrol that allowed them to test for differences across troopers in their propensities to conduct searches. They too found that vehicles were searched more often when the stopped motorist was black, but this disparity in the likelihood of search was greatest when the officer was white.[25]

Of course, the real job of police is to fight crime, not to maximize contraband recovery. These two goals can be in conflict, since racial profiling gives rise to incentive effects, leading civilians (including those who are not negatively stereotyped) to act differently.[26] If officers set different thresholds of suspicion for searching members of different groups, individuals contemplating carrying contraband will alter their behavior. For instance, if police target black drivers in luxury vehicles for searches, drivers carrying contraband will shift to more modest cars, in which case African Americans continuing to drive luxury vehicles will typically be innocent.

This is not just a hypothetical scenario. In the early 1990s, officers with the Washington, DC, Metropolitan Police's Rapid Deployment Unit (RDU) selectively targeted black drivers in luxury cars, believing such vehicles to be favored by drug dealers. They eventually came to the realization that "drug dealers were leaving their fancy cars at home to avoid vehicular stops" and began to target black drivers in all manner of vehicles.[27]

Once adjustments by citizens in response to police practices are taken into account, maximizing the rate of contraband recovery need not minimize the aggregate level of crime. The crime rate will decline in the most heavily targeted groups but rise in groups that face neglect from police under the policy. The net result of these changes will depend on the relative strengths of these two effects: if the response of the targeted groups is small relative to the response of those not targeted, overall crime can rise.[28] This is because a targeted group may be less responsive to the police strategy than a group that is neglected under the policy. In this case the discriminatory stop policy may create the appearance of effective policing while having counterproductive effects on the level of crime.

Furthermore, as Bernard Harcourt argues in *Against Prediction*, racial profiling in police stops creates a divergence between the population of offenders and the population of arrestees.[29] We saw in Chapter 3 that this divergence can arise even in the absence of statistical discrimination by law enforcement, but targeting individuals for stops and searches on the basis of racial or ethnic markers further amplifies the effect. It can lead naive (or prejudiced) observers to think that whites are relatively more law abiding than they actually are.

So the theoretical effects of statistical discrimination on the volume of crime are indeterminate. What do the data say?

Business Necessity

Does a program of police-initiated stops in which officers engage in racial profiling actually reduce crime? This is not a precisely worded question; to answer it, we have to know, "relative to what?"

A more relevant question is this: Does racial profiling reduce crime relative to the best other program that uses the same resources? But even this phrasing is ambiguous: we don't know what the best other program is, and it's not clear what resources go into a program like this. In particular, are the losses of dignity and time suffered by innocents who are stopped and searched counted as resources used by the program?

This question of effectiveness is important in its own right, but it's also important if we are to assess whether these programs are instances of disparate impact discrimination. So far in this chapter we have looked at disparate treatment (whether individual police officers treat motorists or pedestrians differently on account of their race) but not disparate impact (whether the programs that these police stops are part of disproportionately burden minorities without any "business necessity"). We know that most of these programs disproportionately affect black and Hispanic civilians, and the harm they do to innocents is significant.[30] The issue of business necessity then boils down to this: Does racial profiling reduce crime, and is there no better alternative?

We attempt to answer this question for two programs that have attracted national attention: drug interdiction traffic stops on Interstate 95, and the stop-and-frisk program of pedestrian stops in New York City. As a practical matter, we'll take as the alternative business-as-usual policing. Scholars have made a number of observations about what happens to crime on average when police departments expand or when police officers start patrolling an area, doing nothing out of the ordinary. The best program, whatever it is, is surely no worse than this. The "resources" that innocent victims provide to the program are difficult to measure, but they involve significant costs; we ignore them for now but will bring them back into the picture in due course.

First consider traffic stops on I-95, the heavily traveled highway that runs from Miami to the Canadian border in Maine. After two decades of controversy and scores of research papers, it seems that somebody would have asked whether stopping racial profiling on a highway raises violence or illicit drug overdoses in nearby cities, but we haven't found any work that tries to answer this simple question. The only relevant piece of evidence comes from Mexico and so is very indirect. Melissa Dell looked at crackdowns on drug trafficking in various Mexican cities between 2007 and 2010 and examined how they affected the movement of drugs northward to the U.S. border.[31] She found that when one town became tougher on drugs, traffic was rerouted through other towns in a fairly predictable manner. In the end, the price and quantity of illicit drugs at the U.S. border changed very little, despite a massive, expensive, and bloody crackdown in Mexico, costing about $9 billion and the loss of more than 60,000 lives.

The eastern region of the United States has a much denser network of high-quality roads over which drug shipments could be rerouted, and so it is dubious that a policy of occasional traffic stops by a few dozen or even a few hundred state troopers, even if they were untrammeled by the constraints of constitutionality, could have a significant effect on drug supply. The policy of using traffic stops to interdict shipments of illicit drugs sounds so misguided that, whether or not state troopers engaged in racial profiling, it could have little impact on crime.[32]

For pedestrian stops, especially the stop-and-frisk program in New York City, there is both more evidence and more potential justification. But in looking at the evidence and thinking about alternatives, we have to be clear about what various interventions actually look like when police officers implement them on the street.

One way to look at pedestrian stops is as a variety of "hot spots" policing. The idea of hot spots policing is to concentrate police resources on a small space—often a particular block or even a particular intersection—where crime is heaviest. As Lawrence Sherman and coauthors showed in their paper about Minneapolis, an enormous proportion of crime occurs in only a few places, and so targeting those places could reduce crime substantially, especially if good substitute locations are hard to find.[33]

Substantial evidence—over a half dozen well-administered randomized control trials—supports hot spots policing as an effective strategy. The National Research Council Committee to Review Research on Police Policy and Practices found that "studies that focused police resources on crime hot spots provide the strongest collective evidence of police effectiveness that is now available. On the basis of a series of randomized experimental studies, we conclude that the practice . . . is effective in reducing crime and disorder and can achieve these reductions without significant displacement of crime control benefits. Indeed, the research evidence suggests that the diffusion of crime control benefits to the areas surrounding the treated hot spots is stronger than any displacement outcome."[34]

But the studies give no clear picture of what police should do when they get to a hot spot. According to the National Research Council Committee: "There is strong evidence that focusing on hot spots reduces crime and disorder, [but] research has not yet distinguished the types of strategies that lead to the strongest prevention benefits."[35] Stop-and-frisk involves the interrogation of civilians who exhibit "reasonable suspicion," but the studies have found promising crime-reduction effects with a wide variety of police activities, from merely walking around, to meeting with nearby property owners and solving their problems, to stopping vehicles in the street.

In recent years, some high-quality studies have been performed that try to tease out the best strategies for officers to use while patrolling hot spots. No consistent picture emerges: targeting known high-volume violent offenders and frequently reminding them about police presence works better than less aggressive strategies, but just directing rookies to patrol as they see fit also works.[36] Telling police to engage in "self-initiated activities" at their discretion—which might include stopping and questioning civilians but might not—reduces crime more than discouraging them from taking initiatives.[37]

Crime is concentrated in hot spots in New York: just 5 percent of street segments are responsible for half of the crime on street segments, and 5 percent of intersections are responsible for half of the crime at intersections.[38] Stop-and-frisk activity was concentrated on hot spots: 5 percent of street segments accounted for 77 percent of stops on street segments, and 5 percent of intersections accounted for over half of stops at intersections. And the top 5 percent of locations in each domain overlapped heavily. So we should not be surprised to find that stop-and-frisk polices reduced crime—many other police activities probably would have done the same if they had occurred in the same places. And that is what two recent studies found.

David Weisburd and coauthors looked at how stop-and-frisk affected crime rates at the level of street segments.[39] To avoid problems with reverse causality (more stops on street segments with more crime), they isolated changes in the rate of stops that were due to borough-wide policy changes. One additional stop on a street segment decreased crime on that segment in the week by about 20–25 percent in the Bronx and Brooklyn, less in Manhattan, and much less in Queens (but more on Staten Island). There was little, if any, displacement of crime. This effect was quite modest: it implied that the large investment made in the policy in the 2000s reduced overall crime by only about 2 percent.

These findings raise the question, What else were police doing on the street segments on which the stops were recorded? The authors of the study don't have information on this. Police had to be present and on foot on the street segment at some point in order to conduct the stop, and they had to take some time to do it, but how many were there, how long did they stay, and what other activities did they engage in? The stops could have been a proxy for other kinds of crime-fighting activity that happened but that the study authors could not observe.

To see how this might work statistically, think about the activity of drinking water. If a researcher had data only on when and where police officers drank water, and she used the methods of this study but substituted drinking water for making stops, she would probably conclude that drinking water reduced crime, because officers tended to drink water at times and places where they were engaged in more directly productive activities. And they never drank water where they were not engaged in such activities.

The other study—by John MacDonald, Jeffrey Fagan, and Amanda Geller—confirms this basic result and adds a little information about what police were doing. These authors study Operation Impact, a program under which precinct commanders identified small areas of high crime—called impact zones—and saturated them with police. This was a classic hot spots policing operation. Police conducted large numbers of stops between 2003 and 2012 as part of the operation; in most years the majority of stops were tied to this initiative, and in some years this share was over two-thirds. The authors found that Operation Impact reduced crime in targeted zones by around 10 percent. This is the result of all the crime-fighting activities that went on in the average zone.[40]

The authors then turn to their data on stop-and-frisk. They divide stops into two classes: those with reasons that meet the standards of probable cause (for instance, "casing a location" or engaging in an apparent drug transaction) and those that don't (for instance, furtive movements or a suspicious bulge). They use this division to try to find out how well the numbers of each type of stop explain the crime reductions that Operation Impact caused. If the pattern of crime reductions by place and time follows the pattern of stops of one type or both (if, for instance, crime reductions are large whenever probable cause stops are many, and small when they are few), then stops might play an important role in bringing about crime reductions (although they might still just be correlated, like drinking water, with some other activity that is really doing the work). On the other hand, if the crime reductions don't follow the stops, then we can be fairly sure that the stops were not a major factor.

MacDonald, Fagan, and Geller found that non-probable-cause stops seem to have no effect on crime reduction. Probable-cause stops are correlated with crime reductions, but the effect is quite small, in part because probable-cause stops are fairly rare—on average only about four per month in an impact zone. The average estimated effect of such stops was a drop of about 0.2 crimes per month—a notable part of the overall zone effect, but not large in absolute terms.

To put these results in perspective, we can look at a number of good estimates that scholars have made of what happens to crime when police presence increases, even if officers are not doing anything special. For instance, in 2002 and 2003, the Washington, DC, police department beefed up its forces whenever the federal Department of Homeland Security ordered high-alert days because of the possibility of terror attacks (these were not publicized); crime on the National Mall fell by 15 percent on these days, although public activity was little affected. This effect is greater than the estimated overall effect of impact zones.

Researchers have also looked at crime in Buenos Aires after a bomb struck the major Jewish center in that city, and the police stepped up their presence around all the Jewish and Muslim institutions; crime in central London after the terrorist attacks in 2005; and hockey and football hooliganism in Stockholm after 9 / 11 and the South Asian tsunami caused the government to redeploy officers away from these events. There are also studies of the average effect on crime of adding more officers to a police department, doing whatever they do on average. Generally, these papers find that for every 10 percent increase in this kind of mundane police presence, crime falls by about 3–5 percent.[41]

If we knew how much Operation Impact increased police presence in the affected zones, or how much greater police presence was on an average street segment on which a stop occurred, we could compare the effect of stops and the other activities that the operation involved, to the effect of just average policing behavior. Although we don't know the size of the increase in police presence, we can make some speculative remarks. Operation Impact was supposed to be a surge in police presence. If this surge increased police presence by only 25–35 percent, then police presence alone could explain the crime decrease that MacDonald, Fagan, and Geller found. That seems like a modest increase to be called a surge. Similarly, if segments on which stops occurred had on average 50–75 percent more police presence, then the effect that Weisburd and coauthors found is like the effects of the mundane expansions of police presence.

What sort of numbers would these surges involve? Most street segments have no police presence most of the time. There are 82,000 street segments in New York City and at most around 3,600 officers on patrol duty at an average moment in the early 2000s.[42] If officers patrolled in pairs, then the average street segment had about half an hour of police presence a day. A 75 percent increase would require the pair to spend an extra twenty-four minutes a day.

Thus the program of widespread, low-threshold stops produced no miracle of crime reduction. There's no reason to think that the program reduced crime any more than it would have if the same officers in the same locations had acted in the way that officers routinely act. That would have included some field interrogation, but mainly for probable cause. And if those officers had engaged in some of the newer initiatives that are showing some favorable results in rigorous tests, like problem-oriented policing, crime might have been lower than it actually was.

Many people like to believe that there is an inherent trade-off between fairness and safety: that fairness can come only at some cost to safety. There are probably cases where that is true. But in the two cases considered in this chapter, drug interdiction traffic stops on I-95 and the stop-and-frisk program in New York City, there appears to have been no trade-off, in the sense that the concomitant crime reductions could have been achieved by relying on probable cause searches that were considerably less frequent and did not involve the use of profiling.

There could very well be other programs that are much more effective than these—and also some that are considerably less effective. However, even if it were true that profiling was effective in reducing crime in the short run, one would still have to consider the costs imposed on innocents, the erosion of trust, and the consequences for witness cooperation.

Expressive Harm

The set of innocents affected by police stops is substantial. The New York City Police Department engaged in over five million stops and interrogations over the period 2002–2016, with a peak above 685,000 in 2012.[43] Firearms were recovered in less than 0.2 percent of cases, and nine out of every ten people stopped were determined to be completely innocent. Only a tenth of those stopped in any given year were white; the rest were predominantly black and Hispanic. Many in the latter group doubtless believed that they had been targeted simply because they fit a particular demographic profile, and the logic of performance-based statistical discrimination suggests that they might well have been.

How great is the harm to those who are stopped on the basis of racial profiling? Being singled out for a stop or search for no reason other than one's physical features is galling in a way that a random stop or one triggered by genuinely reasonable suspicion is not. As Claude Steele observes in his memoir *Whistling Vivaldi,* the reason for the inconvenience often matters more than the inconvenience itself. As a black child growing up in Chicago, Steele was prohibited from using the local swimming pool except on Wednesday after-noons, to which he reacted as follows:

> To my seven- or eight-year old self this was a bad condition of life. But the condition itself wasn't the worst of it. For example, had my parents imposed it on me for not taking out the garbage, I wouldn't have been so upset. What got me was that it was imposed on me because I was black. There was nothing I could do about that, and if being black was enough to restrict my swimming then what else would happen because of it?[44]

Along similar lines, in an article on the killing of Trayvon Martin, Charles Blow argues that the "idea of universal suspicion without indi-vidual evidence is what Americans find abhorrent and what black men in America must constantly fight. It is pervasive in policing policies—like stop-and-frisk, and in this case neighborhood watch—regardless of the collateral damage done to the majority of innocents."[45]

Stops are more than just simple inconveniences. According to Matthias Risse and Richard Zeckhauser: "Acts of profiling are harmful because they make concrete and real the fact of some people's inferior social standing; they express the underlying injustice of racism."[46] Thus they call this harm "expressive" and compare it to "the harm done to Holocaust survivors when Neo-Nazis march through the neighborhood. . . . Such harm is expressive even if the Nazis do nothing beyond march in uniform. There would be little harm caused by their marching in uniform had the Nazi movement been condemned to insignificance in the 1920s."[47]

Risse and Zeckhauser point out that targeting a group of people that is not defined by some history of subordination usually does not arouse anger. In the Vietnam-era draft lottery, for instance, men born on May 24, 1951, had a very low draft number and were therefore singled out for involuntary military service. They may have considered themselves very unlucky, especially if they were opposed to the war, but since there was no history of men born in May being a demeaned and subordinated class, they did not think that they were unfairly treated relative to men with higher draft numbers.

Risse and Zeckhauser then argue that much of the outrage that black and Hispanic civilians feel about profiling would still be present if profiling were to cease, because the underlying racism that triggers the outrage would still be present. The sting of being racially profiled, in their view, is tied to the many other insults and dangers that one anticipates. As long as these insults and dangers remain, the cessation of profiling would not substantially improve well-being.

Steven Durlauf answers this objection as follows: "By analogy, the pain of slapping my back is far greater when I am sunburned than when I am not. So while the effect of the slap is almost entirely contingent on the sunburn, it is because of the sunburn that my pain is severe."[48] That profiling is painful for black and Hispanic civilians because of underlying racism does not make the pain any less real or any easier to tolerate.

Durlauf argues that a policy of stops should adhere, under most circumstances, to the following fairness principle: among innocent people, the probability of being stopped should not depend on race. For an innocent person, being stopped is a burden that the government imposes in order to achieve some other objective, and so it should not be imposed in a discriminatory fashion. He recognizes that this principle may have to yield to other objectives at times, but only when those objectives are very serious and fairly certain. So if police stops were effective at reducing crime and there were no good alternatives, the fairness principle might countenance them even if they were unfair. However, as we have seen, the simple aggregated data show that Durlauf's fairness principle is violated for traffic stops on I-95 and pedestrian stops in New York—in both cases, innocent black and Hispanic civilians were far more likely to be stopped than innocent whites.[49]

Expressive harm—in conjunction with more tangible costs such as inconvenience and loss of time—inevitably affects the willingness of citizens to serve as witnesses or informants in precisely those neighborhoods where cooperation with law enforcement is most desperately needed. So while performance-based profiling might result in somewhat greater recovery of contraband than would otherwise be the case, it can also make homicides harder to solve, and preemptive killing more common. These effects are amplified if stops are accompanied by the excessive and indiscriminate use of force.

chapter 7

USE OF FORCE

Using force is part of a police officer's job. In his influential book *The Functions of the Police in Modern Society*, the sociologist Egon Bittner calls the capacity to use force the core of the police role. After describing in detail a normal working day for a pair of modern urban officers, Bittner concludes:

> Whatever the substance of the task at hand, whether it involves protection against an undesired imposition, caring for those who cannot care for themselves, attempting to solve a crime, helping to save a life, abating a nuisance, or settling an explosive dispute, police intervention means above all else making use of the capacity and authority to overpower resistance to an attempted solution in the native habitat of the problem. There can be no doubt that this feature of police work is uppermost in the minds of people who solicit police aid or direct attention of the police to problems, that persons against whom the police proceed have this feature in mind and conduct themselves accordingly, and that every conceivable police intervention projects the message that force may be, and may have to be, used to achieve a desired objective.[1]

Bittner argues that "the role of the police is best understood as a mechanism for the distribution of non-negotiably coercive force employed in accordance with the dictates of an intuitive grasp of situational exigencies," and that "police authorization to use force is essentially unrestricted." There are restrictions on the use of lethal force, against the use of force "to advance . . . own personal interest or the private interests of other persons," and against frivolous or malicious use of force. But in 1970 Bittner found that these restrictions carried little weight because police had few guidelines on how to act and after-the-fact reviews of police actions were "exceedingly rare."[2]

Word and Manner

Most police officers today, in most encounters, probably use this discretion responsibly. But in American history there have been some conspicuous exceptions to the responsible use of police force.

Extreme brutality by police against black civilians was once commonplace and routinized. In the South, the police used discretionary force to maintain a caste hierarchy as well as to enforce the law. Often, when the law would have protected black citizens, enforcing the law was a secondary goal.[3] But whatever the police did, they did brutally. Gunnar Myrdal, in his 1944 study *An American Dilemma,* reported on the use of bodily punishment at the slightest sign of insubordination, as well as routine assaults on black arrestees and prisoners: "When once the beating habit is developed in a police department, it is, according to all experience, difficult to stop. It appeals to primitive sadistic impulses ordinarily held down by education and other social controls."[4]

This violence was motivated, in part, by the "common belief" that blacks "respond only to violent methods."[5] This belief was reinforced by the fact that the only black civilians that a southern police officer encountered in the course of his working life were thought to be "criminals, prostitutes, and loiterers" or "stool pigeons" seeking immunity for petty crimes in order to provide information on more significant targets. These interactions with the public are "strongly selective and only magnify his prejudices," with the result that "probably no group of whites in America have a lower opinion of the

Negro people and are more fixed in their view than Southern policemen."[6]

In his 1963 *Letter from Birmingham Jail*, Martin Luther King Jr. explains that his campaign of direct action was motivated, in part, by the city's "ugly record of brutality" against its black residents, including "grossly unjust treatment in the courts" and numerous "unsolved bombings" of homes and churches.[7] The letter was addressed to a group of local clergymen who had urged restraint and praised the local police force for maintaining order without resorting to violence. On the latter point, King responded as follows:

> I doubt that you would have so warmly commended the police force if you had seen its dogs sinking their teeth into unarmed, nonviolent Negroes. I doubt that you would so quickly commend the policemen if you were to observe their ugly and inhumane treatment of Negroes here in the city jail; if you were to watch them push and curse old Negro women and young Negro girls; if you were to see them slap and kick old Negro men and young boys; if you were to observe them, as they did on two occasions, refuse to give us food because we wanted to sing our grace together. I cannot join you in your praise of the Birmingham police department.[8]

The "unspeakable horrors of police brutality" is also among the long list of injustices cataloged in King's "I Have a Dream" speech.[9]

Moving forward in time, James Forman describes his experience working with court-involved teens at the Maya Angelou Public Charter School in Washington, DC, in the spring of 2000 as follows:

> About once a week that entire spring, a team of officers would descend on our block, throw students against the wall, and search them for weapons or drugs. I had learned the concepts of "stop-and-frisk" and "search and seizure" in law school, and as a lawyer, I had filed

hundreds of motions alleging that the police lacked "reasonable articulable suspicion" or "probable cause," the legal standards for conducting searches of this kind. But the searches on our corner defied those standards: if the police had a rationale for choosing their targets among the assembled teenagers, I couldn't see it. Nor was I prepared for the force and violence that can accompany these police actions. . . . When the police rushed onto our corner, our students were forced to "assume the position," with their legs spread, faces against the wall or squad car, and hands behind their heads. Then they were searched, with the officers feeling every inch of their bodies, turning backpacks and pockets inside out, leaving the sidewalks strewn with notebooks, broken pencils, lipstick, and combs. Not once, over the course of about ten searches, did the police recover anything illegal. . . . Unable to distinguish between a student on break and a drug dealer working the corner, the police treat them both as menaces to public safety. . . . In the ghetto, you are not presumed innocent until proven otherwise. Rather, you are presumed guilty, or at least suspicious, and you must spend an extraordinary amount of energy—through careful attention to dress, behavior, and speech—to mark yourself as innocent.[10]

Anecdotal evidence of this kind is consistent with statistical analyses of large-scale data sets. For example, in the case of New York's stop-and-frisk program, the same forms used to compute rates of contraband recovery can be used to examine whether the use of nonlethal force varies systematically by the race and ethnicity of the suspect. In a study based on these data, Roland Fryer has argued that, relative to whites, blacks and Hispanics are more likely to be held, pushed, struck, sprayed, cuffed, or threatened with a weapon during a police stop. These differences cannot be accounted for by variation across stops in nonracial demographic, behavioral, or environmental characteristics. And even greater differences in treatment are observed in the Police-Public Contact Survey, which relies on a nationwide sample of citizen reports.[11]

Such indiscriminate and excessive use of force against innocents has implications for attitudes toward the police and the willingness of witnesses to cooperate with law enforcement officials investigating serious crimes. In *Locking Up Our Own,* James Forman references a 1936 report by the Commission on Interracial Cooperation that laments the light sentences of black homicide offenders whose victims were also black. The very same report also mentions the rough treatment that innocent blacks routinely experienced at the hands of law enforcement officials:

> White police were not only indifferent to black suffering; they were also "abusive in word and manner" toward black citizens. This caused a vicious cycle: black citizens often refused to cooperate with police, which stymied police investigations, halfhearted to begin with, leaving blacks yet more vulnerable. This description of the problem—dispiritingly similar, in many respects, to accounts of the dysfunctional relationship between police departments and black communities today—led the group to call for hiring black police.[12]

The irony is that most of the officers involved in the raids at the Maya Angelou School were themselves black, and "shared racial identity did little to make the encounters less humiliating."[13] Breaking the vicious cycle of excessive force, witness recalcitrance, and unpunished crime will require more than a change in the racial composition of the law enforcement community.

The Talk

On July 16, 2013, three days after a Florida jury found George Zimmerman not guilty of second-degree murder in the shooting death of

Trayvon Martin, then attorney general Eric Holder addressed the NAACP (National Association for the Advancement of Colored People) Annual Convention. He spoke about the "complicated and emotionally-charged issues" that the case has raised in the following terms:

> Years ago, some of these same issues drove my father to sit down with me to have a conversation—which is no doubt familiar to many of you—about how as a young black man I should interact with the police, what to say, and how to conduct myself if I was ever stopped or confronted in a way I thought was unwarranted. . . . Trayvon's death last spring caused me to sit down to have a conversation with my own 15 year old son, like my dad did with me. This was a father-son tradition I hoped would not need to be handed down. But as a father who loves his son and who is more knowing in the ways of the world, I had to do this to protect my boy. I am his father and it is my responsibility, not to burden him with the baggage of eras long gone, but to make him aware of the world he must still confront. This is a sad reality in a nation that is changing for the better in so many ways.[14]

Holder was describing here a conversation that was instantly familiar to many in his audience as "the talk." It takes different forms in different households but generally is as follows:

> If you are pulled over in your car, keep your hands on the steering wheel. Give the officer your license. If your registration is in your glove box, tell the officer that you're going to retrieve it from there, and move slowly.
>
> If you are stopped by an officer while you are on the street, keep your hands visible. Don't say anything besides "yes" and "no." Be compliant. Be polite.[15]

The purpose of this ritual, as Holder made clear, is to protect one's children. In cases where the script is followed, the interaction between officer and suspect takes a different path, as indeed it is designed to do. But this makes any statistical inferences of police use of force (lethal and nonlethal) very difficult to make based simply on recorded data. The interaction contains race-contingent textures that simply cannot be captured quantitatively. For instance, suppose that one found that the rate at which police use force in encounters with black citizens is roughly comparable to the rate experienced by white citizens. Can one treat this as evidence of the absence of bias? Not if these encounters were qualitatively different in a manner contingent on race. Those encounters in which the citizen is mindful of the importance of being compliant and polite ought to result in fewer incidents of the use of force.[16]

Further complicating matters is that people who believe that they have been singled out because of their race may be angered by this and induced to act in ways that are far from compliant or polite. Just as Brent Staples grew tired of whistling Vivaldi to put others at ease on the streets of Chicago, even those who have been exposed to the talk may be unable to restrain feelings of frustration of anger. This can change the dynamic of the interaction between officer and citizen in entirely different ways.

In *Race, Crime, and the Law,* Randall Kennedy makes this point using a hypothetical interaction between a "nonracist, courteous officer" and a black civilian:

[The] quality of the interaction between officials and at least some of those stopped for questioning is likely to be degraded by everyone's knowledge that race played a role in the decision to question. Officers who begin by seeking to discharge their duties with courteousness will confront people who will resent being stopped in part because of their racial heritage. The people stopped will vent their resentment. The officer . . . will respond in some defensive manner, which will in turn provoke further negative responses from those who feel aggrieved. That, in turn, will further aggravate the officer, leading to a deteriorating relationship that will often create bruised feelings, sometimes generate needless arrests, and occasionally spark violence.[17]

These words were written more than two decades ago, long before the arrests of Sandra Bland and Henry Louis Gates Jr., whom they seem to describe almost perfectly.

Two Arrests

On July 10, 2015, Sandra Bland was driving in Prairie View, Texas, when she saw a police vehicle closing in behind her. She moved over to let it through but did so without signaling, and so the trooper stopped her. After completing the necessary paperwork, the officer returned to Bland's vehicle, observed that she seemed irate, and asked her to put out her cigarette. She refused to do so, asserting a right to smoke in her car, at which point the trooper ordered her out of the vehicle. When she again refused to comply, he attempted to drag her out by force. Unable to do so, he drew his Taser and threatened to "light her up." She then exited her vehicle, was physically restrained, and was arrested for assaulting a public servant. These events were recorded on the officer's dashboard camera.[18]

Three days later Bland was found hanging lifeless in her jail cell, and the death was ruled a suicide. The arresting officer, Brian Encina, was charged with perjury in connection with the incident and fired from his job. The charges were subsequently dropped on the condition that he "never seek, accept or engage in employment in any capacity with law enforcement."[19] A number of policy violations were uncovered at the facility where Bland had been held, and her family settled a wrongful death lawsuit against the county for $1.9 million and a commitment to change several procedures at the jail.[20]

Sandra Bland's arrest and her terrible and lonely death were entirely avoidable events. The officer had no need to mention that she seemed irritated, to ask her to put out her cigarette when no further interaction between the two was necessary, to attempt to drag her out of her vehicle, to threaten her with a weapon, to pin her forcefully to the ground, or to respond with callous indifference when she disclosed that she had epilepsy. That all this occurred in the knowledge that it was being recorded makes it all the more disturbing, and it is hard to imagine what would have transpired had no dashboard camera been present.

When two strangers interact they each bring to the encounter a personal history, and in America these histories are deeply contingent on racial identity. Sandra Bland had accumulated numerous traffic tickets, fines, and court costs in this area and elsewhere over several years.[21] Inspired by the movie *Selma*, she had been posting video commentary on civil rights and racial justice on her Facebook page for several months before her death. She suffered from occasional bouts of untreated depression and frequent financial difficulties. We cannot know precisely what role her race played in affecting the behavior of the officer, or his race in her interpretation of his actions. But these factors were surely not without significance.

Another interaction in which beliefs about bias appear to have played a role involved Harvard professor Henry Louis Gates Jr., who was arrested on his front porch in July 2009. The incident drew national attention, eventually culminating in a "beer summit" at the White House involving Gates, the arresting officer James Crowley, and both the president and the vice president of the United States.

What appears to have happened is this.[22] Upon returning home from the airport after a trip to China, Gates found his front door damaged and jammed. He entered through the rear of the house with a key and then, with the help of his limousine driver, forced open the front door to get his luggage through. A neighbor who witnessed this activity called the police to report a possible burglary in progress. Crowley was the first officer at the scene.

At this point the accounts of the two parties diverge, but they agree on the following points: Gates refused to step outside when asked to do so, was followed into the home by the officer, provided identification establishing that he was the rightful occupant, followed the officer out onto the porch, accused him of being racially motivated, and was arrested for disorderly conduct. The charges were dropped five days later.

A grainy, widely circulated photograph of Gates in handcuffs shows him straddled by two white officers, with a black officer, Leon Lashley, in the foreground.[23] Lashley was subsequently interviewed by Anderson Cooper on CNN, where he defended the conduct of his colleague and insisted that racism was not involved.[24] But he also added the following cryptic comment: "Would it have been different if I had shown up first? I think it probably would have been different." When asked what he meant by this, he said simply: "Black man to black man, it probably would have been different."

Although we can never know for sure, there are many reasons to think that the encounter would have followed a different trajectory had Lashley been first officer on the scene. Perhaps he would have been quicker to recognize that the "slight, elderly man" at the door was unlikely to be a burglar, and would have been less fearful and more courteous. But even if Lashley had behaved in every respect as Crowley did, the encounter would probably have evolved differently because Gates would have been less inclined to believe that the officer's actions were motivated by racial animus.

Interactions between strangers take paths that depend not only on words and actions but also on imputed motives and character. And these inferences are shaped by the racial identities of all parties involved. We have seen how this phenomenon affects offender-victim interactions in the case of robbery, and the likelihood that escalating disputes can turn violent and possibly homicidal. Police-citizen interactions are no different. Even if a white police officer behaves in exactly the same way toward all suspects, regardless of race, he will be viewed and treated in a manner that is not similarly neutral. Black men who suspect the officer's motives may react with an abundance of caution, taking elaborate steps to avoid being seen as provocative. Or they may react, as Gates did, with indignation and outrage. In either case, the reaction will be contingent on race, even if the officer's behavior is not.

In fact, the problem is far more general. If a doctor appears inattentive to a patient, and both are white, the latter may attribute this to poor training or a momentary lapse. If the patient is black, there is the additional suspicion that the behavior is racially motivated. The same words and actions are assigned different meanings in the two cases and lead to different reactions and responses. This raises a serious problem when one is called on to make statistical inferences from aggregate data. Quantitative measures of conduct are harder to interpret when the qualitative nature of police-citizen interactions is shaped by the racial identities of the interacting parties. This is especially important when considering police homicides, as we will see in Chapter 8.

Trust

Terrence Cunningham, president of the International Association of Chiefs of Police, gave a speech at the association's 2016 annual conference that was remarkable for its candor. He acknowledged and apologized for the police profession's role in "society's historical mistreatment of communities of color" and recognized that this had led to a "historic cycle of mistrust" between law enforcement officers and some of the communities they serve:

> There have been times when law enforcement officers, because of the laws enacted by federal, state, and local governments, have been the face of oppression for far too many of our fellow citizens. In the past, the laws adopted by our society have required police officers to perform many unpalatable tasks, such as ensuring legalized discrimination or even denying the basic rights of citizenship to many of our fellow Americans.
>
> While this is no longer the case, this dark side of our shared history has created a multigenerational—almost inherited—mistrust between many communities of color and their law enforcement agencies.[25]

Officers are no longer called on to enforce segregation laws.[26] Nevertheless, the dark side of this shared history is not entirely in the past. The Department of Justice opened an investigation of the Ferguson Police Department in September 2014 in the wake of sustained and significant public protests after the shooting of Michael Brown by Officer Darren Wilson. The resulting report described a department whose enforcement practices were driven by a "focus on revenue rather than by public safety needs," pressured by a city that "budgets for sizeable increases in municipal fines and fees each year, exhorts police and court staff to deliver those revenue increases, and closely monitors whether those increases are achieved." The result was a pattern of "unnecessarily aggressive and at times unlawful policing" involving "stops without reasonable suspicion and arrests without probable cause . . . retaliation for protected expression . . . and excessive force."[27]

The weight of these practices falls disproportionately on the city's black community, which is subjected to "routinely disrespectful treatment." The department "appears to bring certain offenses almost exclusively against African Americans," and "police and municipal court practices both reflect and exacerbate existing racial bias, including racial stereotypes." Not surprisingly, there is "deep mistrust between parts of the community and the police department, undermining law enforcement legitimacy." As a result, "the partnerships necessary for public safety are, in some areas, entirely absent."[28]

While this report on the Ferguson Police Department was scathing, a separate and concurrent report by the Justice Department found that the decision not to prosecute Wilson for the shooting of Brown was justified, and that the officer's actions were not "objectively unreasonable" under the circumstances.[29] Furthermore, the very same study by Roland Fryer that documented significant disparities in the use of nonlethal force claimed an absence of bias in police use of lethal force.[30] Is it possible that there are biases in stops and searches and the use of nonlethal force but not in the application of lethal force? We turn to this question next.

chapter 8

LETHAL FORCE

Chapter 4 began with Grace Doyle's quote about how she killed her husband before he could kill her. Police officers, too, sometimes shoot to save their lives—at least in the way that they perceive the situation. These perceptions may well be shaped by stereotypes based on statistical generalizations or implicit and explicit bias. But given a perceived threat, the preemptive motive for killing is operative for police officers, just as it is for civilians.

Indeed, in the United States, preemption is the only reason why police may lawfully try to kill someone, even though they are allowed to use nonlethal force for a wide variety of reasons. According to the 1985 Supreme Court ruling in the case of *Tennessee v. Garner,* police officers may not use deadly force against a suspect trying to escape "unless it is necessary to prevent the escape and the officer has probable cause to believe that the suspect poses a significant threat of death or serious physical injury to the officer or others."[1]

Police officers in the United States have good reason to fear being killed while they are working, probably more than members of any other lawful occupation. In 2010, police were 11 percent of the victims of workplace homicide, even though they were less than two-thirds of 1 percent of total workers.[2] Over the decade 2007–2016, 485 officers across forty-six states were feloniously killed in the line of duty.[3] Thus it should not be surprising that sometimes police kill civilians.

But how many civilians do police kill? To this day there is no reliable official data source that can answer this question, a situation that then FBI director James Comey described in 2015 as "embarrassing and ridiculous."[4] As Paul Butler observes, the "information about itself that a society collects—and does not collect—is always revealing about the values of that society. We know, as we should, exactly how many police officers are killed in the line of duty. But we do not know, as we should, exactly how many civilians are killed by the police."[5]

Newspapers have stepped into the breach, with the *Washington Post* and the *Guardian* each collecting and posting data on such incidents, based largely on local media reports.[6] According to the latter source, police killed 1,146 civilians in 2015 and 1,093 in 2016. By way of comparison, the average annual loss of life from terrorism in the United States between 1995 and 2014 was about 163, about one-seventh the average annual loss of life from police use of lethal force in recent years.[7]

Police-related killings—both civilians killed by police and officers killed in the line of duty—are far more prevalent in the United States than in other countries at comparable levels of economic development. While approximately fifty police officers are killed annually in the United States, just three on-duty officers were killed in the United Kingdom over the entire five-year period between 2010 and 2014, for an average of 0.6 per year. Between 2008 and 2012, two on-duty officers were killed in Germany, or 0.4 per year.

In contrast to the approximately 1,100 civilians killed by police annually in the United States, German police kill about 6–9 civilians a year. In England and Wales the corresponding rate is about 2 per year on average, and none were killed between 2012 and 2014.[8] The mechanisms explored in Chapter 4 suggest that killings of police by civilians should correlate with killings of civilians by police, and at least in international comparisons they appear to do so. The United Kingdom and Germany seem to be in a different world from the United States.

Guns and Kevlar

The most obvious explanation for why police-related killings are so rare in the United Kingdom and Germany relative to the United States is the prevalence of firearms. With few exceptions, civilians in the United Kingdom and Germany don't have guns, but large numbers of civilians in the United States have access to weapons. In all three countries, firearms are responsible for almost all police deaths by assault.[9] Police have much less reason to fear civilians in Europe, and civilians there don't have to worry about how they can demonstrate that they are not carrying a gun.

The inference is that tougher gun control laws in the United States would make both police and civilians safer—police would be safer because civilians would not be able to kill them so easily, and civilians would be safer because police would feel less urgency to preemptively kill.

The Law Center to Prevent Gun Violence grades each state's laws on how well, in its opinion, they avert gun violence (it does not grade the District of Columbia). The grade can be interpreted as a measure of how strict gun control law is in that state. Most states get Fs, and no state gets straight As.[10] We can use this rating to take a rough and preliminary look at how gun control laws correlate with police-related killings, by combining it with the LEOKA (Law Enforcement Officers Killed and Assaulted) database compiled by the FBI and the *Guardian* data on civilians killed by police.

Comparing states receiving an A or B grade with states receiving an F, the raw correlations indicate that police are a lot safer in states with strict gun control. The rate of police deaths from assault by civilians, averaged over the period 2006–2015, are 0.97 and 1.91 per million residents in the strict and lax gun control states, respectively. Civilians overall seem safer from police in these states also, but the effect is not large; the rates of civilian deaths from assault by police over the period 2015–2016 are 2.48 and 3.01 per million residents in the strict and lax gun control states, respectively. Black civilians are less safe—the victimization rates being 7.37 and 6.61, respectively. The general murder rate is also somewhat lower in states with strict gun control (4.32 versus 5.56).[11]

No causal inference can be drawn from these correlations, of course, but it does not appear that in states where police are a lot safer they are much more relaxed around civilians, especially black civilians.

Another way to examine the link between greater police safety and the incidence of police homicide is to trace the effects of a major innovation in protective gear: Kevlar.[12]

Kevlar is a fabric used to make soft and lightweight body armor that can stop a .38 caliber lead bullet. It was invented by Stephanie Kwolek in 1965, and by 2008 over 70 percent of law enforcement agencies had issued it to all officers, and 53 percent required officers to wear the vest while on duty.[13] During the decades when Kevlar was being adopted (1976–2012), the rate at which police were killed per year of service fell by three-quarters.[14] Kevlar was not responsible for the entire decline, although it probably played a major role.

As far as we can tell, police killings of civilians did not fall when civilian killings of police fell.[15] Two sources of data are available on civilians killed by police before 2015, one from the FBI and one from the Centers for Disease Control and Prevention, both of which are known to be seriously incomplete. Over the 1976–2012 period, both series were mostly flat, with a gentle upward trend. Again, this evidence is very weak, but it suggests that improvements in police safety do not easily or automatically translate into declines in the use of lethal force.

The Fear Hypothesis

Police killings in the United States have an unmistakable racial dimension. In his 1944 book *An American Dilemma,* Gunnar Myrdal notes that a majority of the whites who killed blacks in the 1930s were police officers. In fact, during the 1930s, African Americans were killed by police at more than four times the rate at which they were lynched.[16] It remains true today that close to a majority of the whites who kill blacks are police officers.[17]

This phenomenon has achieved great visibility in recent years, with the increasing emergence of video evidence from witnesses as well as police body cameras and dashboard cameras. But the phenomenon is not new. In 1933, for instance, 5,000 people attended the protest funeral of Grover Davis, a blind black man shot by Atlanta police, and in 1938 about 2,000 marched in Washington, DC, with several thousand more lining the streets, to protest the shooting of Wallace McKnight in the back by an officer "over a bag of food."[18]

Many of today's videos depict white officers shooting black civilians under conditions where there was no objective threat to the officer or anyone else. In some cases, there was not even a credible perception of a threat—for instance, in the shooting of Laquan McDonald by Jason Van Dyke in Chicago, or that of Walter Scott by Michael Slager in North Charleston. The officers in these cases were indicted on murder charges after video evidence emerged, with Slager eventually pleading guilty to a civil rights violation under federal law and Van Dyke convicted of second-degree murder.

In most instances, however, officers have successfully argued that they were reasonable in perceiving a threat even when none was subsequently found to exist. This was the case, for instance, in the shooting of twelve-year-old Tamir Rice by Timothy Loehmann in Cleveland. Rice possessed a replica pistol that Loehmann claims he mistook as a functioning firearm.[19] Although the victim's family received a substantial settlement from the city, no charges were filed against the officer.

Similarly, no charges were filed against Darren Wilson for the fatal shooting of Michael Brown in Ferguson, Missouri, in August 2014. Wilson convinced a grand jury that Brown was a genuine threat, using language that was quite extraordinary. He felt like "a five-year old holding on to Hulk Hogan," while Brown looked "like a demon," made a "grunting, aggravated sound," and was "almost bulking up to run through the shots, like it was making him mad that I was shooting at him."[20] Wilson was six feet four inches tall, and weighed about 210 pounds, while Brown was an inch taller and weighed 289 pounds. Perhaps the officer's statements were embellishments meant to convince grand jurors that he was in genuine fear, but as Jamelle Bouie has observed, his language "sits flush with a century of stereotypes and a bundle of recent research on implicit bias and racial perceptions of pain."[21] Even if Wilson embellished his testimony to convince others that he had acted in fear, it is telling that he believed these remarks to be persuasive.

A number of witnesses offered conflicting sworn testimony in this case, but—as we discuss in Chapter 9—a federal investigation concluded that some of the most credible of these corroborated the officer's account. While Wilson may well have faced a real threat from Brown, this was clearly not the case when South Carolina trooper Sean Groubert shot Levar Jones in September 2014. On leaving work,

Jones entered his pickup truck, drove around the corner into a gas station, and exited his vehicle, not realizing that a police car was following him on account of a seat belt violation. Officer Groubert pulled up behind the truck, exited his own vehicle, and asked Jones for his license and registration. Jones reached back into his vehicle to grab his wallet, at which point he was shot at several times and suffered a nonfatal bullet wound. The entire incident was captured on the officer's dashboard camera, and Groubert was dismissed from his position with the South Carolina Highway Patrol on the grounds that he "reacted to a perceived threat when there was none."[22] He later pleaded guilty to charges of assault and battery.

In July 2016, during a traffic stop in Falcon Heights, Minnesota, Philando Castile was shot and killed in the presence of his girlfriend, Diamond Reynolds, and her four-year-old daughter by Officer Jeronimo Yanez. Castile had provided the officer with his proof of insurance, informed him calmly and respectfully that he was in possession of a licensed firearm, and was reaching for his wallet to produce his driver's license when Yanez appeared to panic, thinking Castile was reaching for a gun. In announcing charges of second-degree manslaughter against the officer, the county attorney John Choi offered the following reasoning:

> When evaluating the reasonableness of a police officer's use of deadly force, we must take into account that police officers are often required to react quickly—in tense, uncertain and rapidly evolving situations. To justify the use of deadly force, it is not enough, however, for the police officer to merely express a subjective fear of death or great bodily harm. Unreasonable fear cannot justify the use of deadly force. The use of deadly force must be objectively reasonable and necessary, given the totality of the circumstances. Based upon our thorough and exhaustive review of the facts of this case, it is my conclusion that

the use of deadly force by Officer Yanez was not justified and that sufficient facts exist to prove this to be true.[23]

In an emotional statement to investigators on the day after the shooting, Yanez repeatedly confessed to being scared and fearing for his life. He believed that Castile fit the description of a robbery suspect, on account of his dreadlocks, glasses, and "a wide set nose," and this presumably contributed to his level of fear.[24] A jury later found this fear to be warranted, and he was acquitted at trial.

But the question remains: Would Castile have been shot under the same circumstances had he been a white driver with a young woman in the seat beside him and a four-year-old child in the back? Mark Dayton, the governor of Minnesota, did not think so.[25] Neither did Peter Moskos, a professor at the John Jay College of Criminal Justice and a former Baltimore police officer, who wrote on his blog: "Honestly, in this shooting, with this cop, in this locale, I don't think there's a chance in hell Castile would have been shot had he been white."[26]

The Jones and Castile cases, among many others, suggest that the fear experienced by officers is often amplified when they face a citizen who is young, black, and male. That is, the level of threat perceived is out of proportion with the threat actually present. From this perspective, which we call the *fear hypothesis*, black civilians face a heightened likelihood of being subject to police use of lethal force because they are more commonly stereotyped as dangerous.

While the 250–300 deaths that African Americans suffer at the hands of police every year are not a large source of mortality for African Americans overall (around 300 times as many die every year from heart disease), these deaths result from deliberate government actions—actions by people who are sworn to protect the safety of all citizens. As Paul Butler has observed, there is "a categorical moral difference between antisocial conduct that is harshly punished . . . and authorized violence by the state committed with impunity."[27] To many, the unpunished killings reveal a widespread attitude that black lives don't matter.

Some historical evidence in support of the fear hypothesis may be found in a report issued by the Kerner Commission, which was established in order to better understand the violence that engulfed many American cities during the summer of 1967.

The Summer of 1967

The summer of 1967 was a tumultuous one, with prolonged and violent civil disturbances breaking out in scores of American cities.[28] The resulting deployment of police and military resources led to the greatest concentration of civilian deaths at the hands of law enforcement officers in recent history. In Newark and Detroit alone, more than fifty civilians were killed in less than a week; the current rate of civilian deaths at the hands of police officers is about three a day in the nation as a whole.

Even as riots were still raging in Detroit, President Johnson established the National Advisory Commission on Civil Disorders under the leadership of Illinois governor Otto Kerner. Seven months later, the Kerner Commission released a report with the following ominous warning: "Our nation is moving toward two societies, one black, one white—separate and unequal."

As part of its mandate, the commission was tasked with uncovering what had happened and why. To address the latter question, the commissioners tabulated grievances voiced by members of the affected communities. At the top of this list—ahead of unemployment, inadequate housing and education, white attitudes, and the administration of justice—was a category called "police practices."

In fact, the triggering incident in many of the riots examined in the report was some form of police action. In the case of Newark it was the arrest of taxi driver and army veteran John Smith, who was falsely rumored to have been killed in custody. And in Detroit it was the raid on a blind pig (an unlicensed drinking and gambling establishment) during a large party for servicemen.[29]

In Chapter 4, we observed that a climate of fear amplifies violence by increasing the incentive to kill preemptively. This effect is documented very clearly in the Kerner report. The police and National Guard members tasked with quelling the riots were largely young, inexperienced, and unfamiliar with the local conditions and communities. They were especially fearful of sniper attacks, and this led to indiscriminate firing and multiple fatalities. At around 6 p.m. on July 15, for instance, the following sequence of events occurred in Newark:

> National Guardsmen and state troopers were directing mass fire at the Hayes Housing project in response to what they believed were snipers.
>
> On the 10th floor, Eloise Spellman, the mother of several children, fell, a bullet through her neck.
>
> Across the street, a number of persons, standing in an apartment window, were watching the firing directed at the housing project. Suddenly, several troopers whirled and began firing in the general direction of the spectators. Mrs. Hattie Gainer, a grandmother, sank to the floor.
>
> A block away Rebecca Brown's 2-year-old daughter was standing at the window. Mrs. Brown rushed to drag her to safety. As Mrs. Brown was, momentarily, framed in the window, a bullet spun into her back.
>
> All three women died.[30]

According to the report, "the amount of sniping attributed to rioters—by law enforcement officials as well as the press—was highly exaggerated." In particular, "most reported sniping incidents were demonstrated to be gunfire by either police or National Guardsmen. . . . The climate of fear and expectation of violence created by such exaggerated, sometimes totally erroneous, reports demonstrates the serious risks of overreaction and excessive use of force." According to one police source: "Guardsmen were firing upon police and police were firing back at them."[31]

The report offers several reasons for the exaggerated fear of sniper attack:

> Several problems contributed to the misconceptions regarding snipers: the lack of communications; the fact that one shot might be reported half a dozen times by half a dozen different persons as it caromed and reverberated a mile or more through the city; the fact that the National Guard troops lacked riot training. They were, said a police official, "young and very scared."

In contrast with the jumpiness exhibited by the police and National Guard members, one section of Detroit was policed by a group of professional soldiers, one-fifth of them black, under the command of Lieutenant General Throckmorton. The behavior and experience of this group is instructive.

> According to Lieutenant General Throckmorton and Colonel Bolling, the city, at this time, was saturated with fear. The National Guardsmen were afraid, the residents were afraid, and the police were afraid. . . . The general and his staff felt that the major task of the troops was to reduce the fear and restore an air of normalcy.
>
> In order to accomplish this, every effort was made to establish contact and rapport between the troops and the residents. Troopers . . .

began helping to clean up the streets, collect garbage, and trace persons who had disappeared in the confusion. Residents in the neighborhoods responded with soup and sandwiches for the troops. . . .

Within hours after the arrival of the paratroops, the area occupied by them was the quietest in the city, bearing out General Throckmorton's view that the key to quelling a disorder is to saturate an area with "calm, determined, and hardened professional soldiers." . . . Troopers had strict orders not to fire unless they could see the specific person at whom they were aiming. Mass fire was forbidden.

During five days in the city, 2,700 Army troops expended only 201 rounds of ammunition, almost all during the first few hours, after which even stricter fire discipline was enforced. (In contrast, New Jersey National Guardsmen and state police expended 3,326 rounds of ammunition in three days in Newark.) Hundreds of reports of sniper fire—most of them false—continued to pour into police headquarters; the Army logged only 10. No paratrooper was injured by a gunshot.[32]

Not only did Throckmorton's troops inflict less violence on innocent civilians, but they were also more effective in executing their mission. This phenomenon is familiar to military units involved in occupations of civilian areas. A U.S. Army counterinsurgency manual, for instance, states that "many of the . . . best weapons for countering an insurgency do not shoot."[33]

What happened in Newark and Detroit in the summer of 1967 happens routinely on a much smaller scale across the country. Officers armed with lethal weapons confront civilians whom they may have reason to fear. The fears are not without basis, but exaggerated perceptions of danger can result in the unwarranted killing of innocents.

The fear hypothesis is about disparate treatment: Are officers more likely to shoot a black civilian than a white civilian who is otherwise identical in appearance, indicia, location, and behavior? We next consider an alternative hypothesis, focused on the rate at which police make contact with people belonging to different groups. As we have seen, there are large differences across groups in rates of offending, victimization, stops, and arrests, which means that the population as a whole is not the right benchmark to assess disparities in the use of lethal force. To determine the extent to which racial bias is implicated in police killings, we need to examine deaths in relation to some measure of police-citizen contact.

The Contact Hypothesis

In October 2015, the Harvard economist Sendhil Mullainathan published an article in the *New York Times* in which he made the following claims:

> According to the F.B.I.'s Supplementary Homicide Report, 31.8 percent of people shot by the police were African-American, a proportion more than two and a half times the 13.2 percent of African-Americans in the general population. . . . But this data does not prove that biased police officers are more likely to shoot blacks in any given encounter. . . . Having more encounters with police officers, even with officers entirely free of racial bias, can create a greater risk of a fatal shooting.
>
> This claim is based on nationwide data. Since rates of killing vary tremendously across the country, this is almost certainly the wrong level at which to begin analysis. But we can see where it leads us.
>
> Arrest data let us measure this possibility. For the entire country, 28.9 percent of arrestees were African American. This number is not very different from the 31.8 percent of police-shooting victims who

were African Americans. If police discrimination were a big factor in the actual killings (and every place were roughly the same), we would have expected a larger gap between the arrest rate and the police-killing rate.

This, in turn, suggests that removing police racial bias will have little effect on the killing rate.

Mullainathan was correct in pointing out that there is rough parity between the arrest rate and the rate at which black civilians face lethal force. But in inferring that removing bias will have a negligible impact, he was making several implicit assumptions. One of these is that encounters between black civilians and police are as likely to be objectively threatening to officers as encounters between other civilians and police.

But is the assumption reasonable? As we saw in Chapter 3, racial stereotypes can provide incentives for black offenders to specialize in robbery as opposed to other crimes of appropriation such as burglary and motor vehicle theft, while the opposite is true for white offenders. And within this set of crimes, robbery is the one that triggers the most immediate and widespread police action. Victims are able to provide descriptions to police officers within minutes of the crime, and officers accordingly take actions to apprehend offenders. But this means that innocent individuals who are most likely to fit the description of a robbery offender will also be most likely to be stopped and to have contact with police—as in the case of Philando Castile. A large number of contacts with innocents also arise through certain policing strategies, such as New York City's stop-and-frisk policy.

And whenever a contact occurs, there is always the possibility of an arrest on some charge. In fact, officers are obliged to take punitive action if they uncover a small amount of marijuana possession, even if the stop was motivated by more serious considerations such as robbery or gun law violations.[34] Furthermore, even without any prior violation, arrests can result from contacts that escalate in unpredictable ways when citizens suspect that they are being racially profiled. We saw this in Chapter 7, for the cases of Sandra Bland and Henry Louis Gates.

As a result, the arrest pool for black civilians looks quite different from that of white civilians. It is inflated by the arrest of individuals on minor infractions that would not have arisen, or would have remained undetected, if the civilian in question had not been black. The arrests of Rashon Nelson and Donte Robinson at a Philadelphia Starbucks in April 2018 illustrate this point.[35] These two men were seated in the coffee shop, waiting for an associate, but had not made a purchase. A manager called the police, and the two were arrested when they refused demands to leave. A video of the incident attracted national media attention, and the men eventually reached settlements with both the city and the company. Starbucks also closed down several thousand stores for a day of "racial bias training" for its employees.

The ubiquity of mobile devices capable of recording video and audio has brought many such incidents to light. And since the individuals who are caught up in this way are not generally objectively threatening to officers, we ought not to expect parity between arrest rates and the rate of lethal force experienced by black civilians even in the absence of bias.[36] Put differently, the respective rates of arrest and lethal force that we see in the data are entirely consistent with the presence of racial bias.

This does not mean, of course, that the evidence is conclusive. To make a more confident claim one would need to consider a pool of police-civilian contacts that are roughly comparable across groups, at least in the level of threat faced by officers. One could then examine whether contacts with members of one group were systematically more likely to result in a shooting. And for this we need data not only on those who were shot and killed but also on those who could have been shot but were not, including some who were peacefully disarmed.

Another Harvard economist, Roland Fryer, has attempted to do precisely this.[37] Fryer looks at shootings, not killings—incidents in which an officer discharges his or her weapon, whether or not anyone is actually hit.[38] He uses detailed incident reports obtained from the Houston Police Department, and so does not face the problem of aggregating across vastly differing environments. He wants to find out how likely an officer is to shoot in an encounter with a white civilian as compared with an encounter with a black civilian, holding all other relevant factors constant. But he can't observe every encounter that police have with civilians while on duty—buying coffee, directing traffic, sharing jokes with friends, giving directions, and so on. Instead, he has to settle for observing arrests for just a few crimes, for which he codes large amounts of data from Houston Police Department reports.

These are arrests for which it seems most likely that lethal force might be justified: attempted capital murder of a police officer, aggravated assault on a public safety officer, resisting arrest, evading arrest, and interfering in an arrest. He has an arrest pool (reports of arrests that seem especially likely to lead to shootings) and a shooting pool (reports of shootings). The shooting pool is not a subset of the arrest pool: the two pools are from different sources, and either pool can contain interactions that are not in the other.

What does he find? In the raw data, blacks were just as likely to be in the shooting pool (to be shot at) as they were to be in the arrest pool (to be arrested for the sort of activity that might endanger an officer's life). When Fryer adds a large number of controls based on incident reports, the result persists. Holding constant all the information in the incident reports, he finds no evidence that black civilians are subjected to biased treatment by the Houston Police Department, and describes this as "the most surprising finding of my career."[39]

The Fryer study raises many questions, some of which future researchers may be able to address. To begin with, there is direct evidence that black arrestees are systematically different on average than white arrestees in his arrest pool. According to the incident reports from which these pools are constructed, two-thirds of white arrestees and one-half of black arrestees "attacked or drew weapon," a difference that is statistically significant. On this measure at least, the black arrestees were less threatening on average and ought to have faced a lower rate of lethal force than the white arrestees. Fryer's statistical methods are designed to adjust for this possibility so that a net measure of bias can be inferred. That he finds no evidence of bias after this adjustment is therefore noteworthy and suggests that officers in Houston tend to treat genuinely threatening individuals in a manner that is not contingent on race. But what about nonthreatening individuals?

Many of the civilians whose injuries or deaths have attracted national attention—Philando Castile and Levar Jones among them—were not engaged in acts that would have led to inclusion in the kind of arrest pool constructed by Fryer. In fact there was no basis for them to end up in any pool of arrestees at all. Fryer's results are therefore consistent with the possibility that Houston police officers are relatively color-blind when dealing with genuinely threatening situations, but mistakenly perceive interactions with harmless black civilians as threatening from time to time. And even these findings may not generalize to other jurisdictions, given the enormous regional variability in police use of lethal force. They may not even generalize to all of Houston, since around a third of the civilians killed by police in

Houston according to the *Guardian* data set were killed by law enforcement agencies other than the Houston Police Department.[40]

Weapon Recovery

A different approach to testing for disparate treatment in the use of lethal force is to consider whether black victims are less likely to be armed than victims belonging to other groups, under the assumption that armed victims are more likely to be objectively threatening to officers. Possession of a weapon does not imply the existence of a threat—as the Philando Castile case illustrates—and threats can certainly arise from unarmed civilians. Of the 491 officers feloniously killed over the 2006–2015 period, for instance, 24 were killed with their own weapon.[41] Nevertheless, most officers are killed with weapons other than their own, primarily firearms.

The data on victims of fatal police shootings reveal disparities in the frequency with which victims from different groups were unarmed. For the period 2015–2016, about 21 percent of black victims in the *Guardian* database were classified as unarmed, while the corresponding proportions for whites and Hispanics were 17 percent and 18 percent, respectively. The *Washington Post* database treats all manner of objects—from toy weapons and flashlights to crowbars and chainsaws—as arms, so the proportion of unarmed victims is much lower.[42] Still, the basic pattern remains: over the same period, 11 percent of black victims were classified as unarmed, while the corresponding proportions for whites and Hispanics were 6 percent and 8 percent, respectively.

The *Post* data also record whether an attack was in progress at the time of the police shooting, and this makes clear that most of the victims of lethal force were plausibly dangerous to officers and fellow citizens. Over the two-year period, about two-thirds of incidents involved an attack in progress, with virtually identical rates for cases with black and white victims. In the 2015 data a greater proportion of whites were engaged in an attack relative to blacks, but this pattern was reversed in 2016, with no net difference overall. In both years, Hispanics were less likely than whites and blacks to be engaged in an attack when killed.[43]

Some attacks on police or other civilians are designed to provoke a lethal response, a phenomenon known as suicide-by-cop. Such incidents are not rare—one study of officer-involved shootings in Los Angeles County estimated that 13 percent of the resulting fatalities were of this nature, and a more recent study with a large sample including cases throughout North America found that over a third of shootings were precipitated by suicidal individuals. In most cases the victims possessed loaded and operational firearms, though some instances involved unloaded, inoperable, or replica weapons.[44] It is possible that the incidence of suicide-by-cop varies systematically by victim identity, which makes detecting bias in the data even more challenging. For instance, in the *Post* data, about 6 percent of white victims and 3–4 percent of black and Hispanic victims possessed toy weapons.

As Sendhil Mullainathan observed when evaluating the data, the rate at which civilians are exposed to lethal force varies dramatically across locations.[45] A detailed examination of these variations can tell us something about where exactly the fear hypothesis may be most relevant, and why the aggregate data appear to support the contact hypothesis.

Geography

The variation across regions in the rate at which civilians are subject to lethal force in the United States is staggering. Figure 8.1 shows the number of people killed annually by police per million residents for

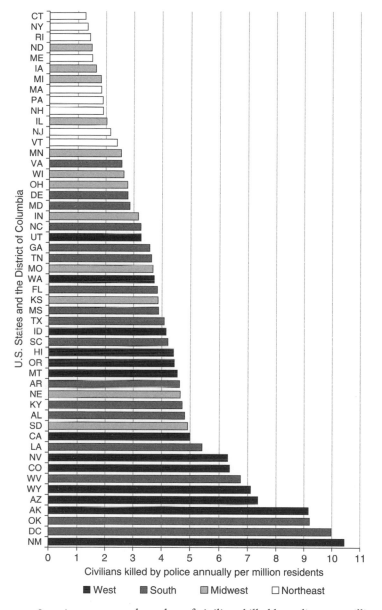

FIGURE 8.1. Average annual number of civilians killed by police, per million residents, for 2015–2016, based on the *Guardian* database.

all fifty states and the District of Columbia, with different shades identifying the four census regions of the country—Northeast, Midwest, South, and West. The figure is based on the *Guardian* data for the period 2015–2016.[46] The deadliest state, New Mexico, has more than eight times the rate of lethal force than the least deadly, which is Connecticut.

Although some of the variation across states is due to random factors that may not persist, we still see a great deal of clustering by region. The nine states in the Northeast—composed of New England and the Middle Atlantic States (New York, New Jersey, and Pennsylvania)—are among the safest as far as police use of lethal force is concerned. The Midwest is next, followed by the South and West. In the South the safest states are those adjacent to the Northeast—Delaware, Maryland, and Virginia.

Eight states—Colorado, Nevada, Arizona, West Virginia, Wyoming, Alaska, Oklahoma, and New Mexico—together with the District of Columbia, all have more than six civilians killed annually per million residents. Six of these eight states are in the West, with the remaining two in the South. Each of them has a black population well below the national average, ranging from less than 1 percent in Wyoming to 8 percent in Nevada. The District of Columbia is clearly an outlier here: it is a majority black urban center while the other regions are relatively rural and predominantly white.

What accounts for such large geographic variations? One possibility is preemption—perhaps police kill more frequently at locations where they are in more danger. We have already seen—based on variations across states in gun laws, and the effects of the introduction of Kevlar—that support for this hypothesis is relatively weak. However, the correlation between police victimization and police homicide is still positive, as can be seen in Figure 8.2. States where civilians were more likely to be killed by police (in 2015–2016) also

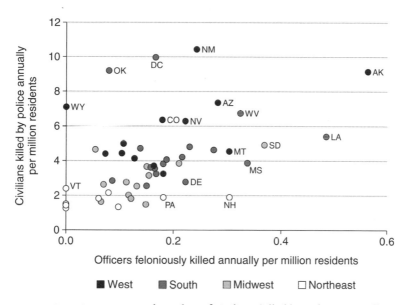

FIGURE 8.2. Average annual number of civilians killed by police, per million residents, for 2015–2016, based on the *Guardian* database, and average annual number of police officers killed, per million residents, for 2006–2015, based on the LEOKA database.

tended to be states where police were more likely to be killed by civilians (in the 2006–2015 decade). Preemption tells us something about police-involved killings: the correlation between the two rates was 0.44.

Yet there are some extreme deviations from this regularity. California and New York are large, affluent, liberal, and coastal states with strict gun control laws, but California civilians were almost four times as likely to be killed by police as New York civilians. This cannot be accounted for by dangers that officers face: the per capita rate of killings of police was less than 10 percent higher in California than it was in New York.

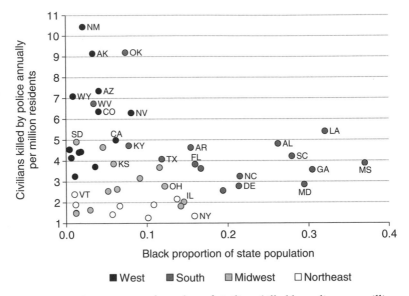

FIGURE 8.3. Average annual number of civilians killed by police, per million residents, for 2015–2016, based on the *Guardian* database, and the black proportion of the state population based on the 2010 Census.

The nine areas (eight states and the District of Columbia) where civilians were killed at the highest rates vary widely with respect to the rates at which officers were killed, ranging from none in Wyoming to 0.56 annually per million residents in Alaska. Again, some of this variation is random: we are looking at a ten-year period in which four officers in Alaska were feloniously killed, so the high rate is a consequence of the small size of the resident population.

Over the decade 2006–2015, thirty-three police officers were killed in Louisiana, Alaska, and South Dakota combined, but in Connecticut, Maine, Rhode Island, and Vermont, which have a greater combined population, none were killed.[47] And there are some states in which the mismatch between officers killed and civilians killed by officers is considerable: Oklahoma is among the safer states for officers while it has among the highest rates of civilian deaths.

Next consider the racial composition of states in relation to the rates of use of lethal force, as shown in Figure 8.3. We have omitted from the figure the District of Columbia, which is majority black and unusual in other respects. The eight states with the greatest incidence of lethal police force all have small black populations. The states with the largest black populations all lie in the South, and lie in an intermediate range as far as lethal force is concerned—above the rate of the Northeast but below the cluster of eight states with the highest rates. All the states of the original confederacy—South Carolina, Mississippi, Florida, Alabama, Georgia, Louisiana, and Texas—lie within this intermediate range, with civilians killed at rates ranging from 3.6 in Georgia to 5.4 in Louisiana.

Finally, consider the variation across states in the rates at which black citizens were subject to lethal force, relative to their presence in the residential population (Figure 8.4). Again we see enormous geographic variation. In eleven states, police officers did not kill any black civilians in 2015–2016, and these span the entire range of overall use of lethal force, from Connecticut to New Mexico. These states belong to a group of fifteen in which black civilians faced lethal force at lower rates than white civilians (these states are shown to the left of the steeper dotted line). Some other states, such as Arizona and Alabama, lie close to the line, indicating rough parity in black and white rates of victimization. Arizona and New Mexico together accounted for 137 deaths, with half the victims being white, 37 percent Hispanic, 10 percent Native American, and 2 percent black.[48]

One might expect that the eleven secessionist states of the former Confederacy would exhibit high rates of lethal force against black civilians relative to whites, but this is not the case.[49] Many of these states are arrayed close to the steeper dotted line in Figure 8.4, which

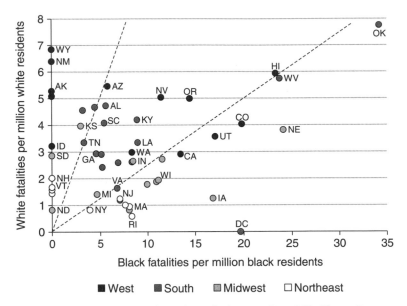

FIGURE 8.4. Average annual number of white civilians killed by police, per million white residents, and the average annual number of black civilians killed by police, per million black residents, for 2015–2016, based on the *Guardian* database and the state populations in the 2010 Census.

indicates parity between rates of lethal force faced by black civilians and white civilians. In fact, in Mississippi, Arkansas, and Tennessee, black civilians faced a lower likelihood of being killed by police than whites. This is despite the fact that white racial attitudes remain less favorable to blacks in the South than in most of the rest of the country.[50]

These eleven states are not generally peaceful—they have high rates of police victimization and high overall murder rates—so the finding that black citizens face relatively low rates of lethal force and rough parity with whites in this region is puzzling. This is especially the case since the rate at which black civilians were killed by police in these states was many times greater than the rate at which whites were killed in the 1930s.[51]

It is possible, of course, that killings are systematically underreported or mischaracterized, in ways that prevent them from making it into the databases compiled by media outlets.[52] It is also possible that citizens are more cautious and compliant in their interactions with officers, or that lower levels of residential segregation in the South, relative to the Northeast and Midwest, make misinterpretation of words and actions less likely when communication crosses racial boundaries.[53] The bottom line is that we don't know why black civilians appear to be relatively safe from police use of lethal force in this set of states today. The data revealing this regularity were not available until very recently, and remain too limited to select among competing explanations.

At the other extreme are several states in which black civilians are killed at rates that are significantly higher than those of white civilians. To the right of the flatter dotted line in Figure 8.4 are states where the victimization rate for black civilians is more than four times that for whites. For the most part, these are states in the Northeast and Midwest, where the overall use of lethal force is relatively low.

Oklahoma is in a category of its own, with very high use of lethal force, which black civilians face to an extreme degree, even as its police officers are much less exposed to felonious killing than officers in the country at large. The District of Columbia is also unique, being a city rather than a state, with a majority black population. Use of lethal force is high and all twelve victims here were black, even as the threat faced by officers in the District is well below the national average.

To summarize, there is enormous geographic variation in the rates at which civilians are killed by police officers, as well as the degree to which African Americans face greater force relative to the general population. States with the greatest use of lethal force have relatively small black populations and, with the notable exception of Oklahoma, are responsible for a relatively small proportion of black lives taken.

Cities

We can get a slightly more fine-grained picture of civilian deaths by looking at big cities (because of the paucity of data, we can look only at the largest cities). Table 8.1 compares police killing rates for blacks, whites, and Hispanics in five major cities.

In the two largest cities, New York and Los Angeles, two patterns stand out. The first is how different these two affluent, large, and diverse cities are: every group is much safer in New York than in the nation at large, and every group is less safe in Los Angeles than in the nation at large. Blacks in New York are almost as safe as the average white in the rest of the nation, and not much more likely to be killed by police than the average white in Los Angeles. Whites in Los Angeles are almost four times as likely to be killed by police as those in New York, though still less likely to be killed by police than blacks in the nation at large. Hispanics in Los Angeles are more than eight times as likely to be killed as Hispanics in New York.

The other pattern is the huge disparity in New York City between blacks and other groups, especially whites. There are 2.7 million whites in New York City, and slightly more than the 2.6 million in Oklahoma, but in 2015–2016 police killed 3 white civilians in New York City, while killing 42 in Oklahoma. Blacks in New York are six times as likely to be killed by police as whites, which is more than twice the national ratio. Even though black civilians in New York are almost as safe from lethal force as whites in Los Angeles, this ratio suggests that police use of force in New York has a racial dimension that is less salient in Los Angeles.

Table 8.1 Annual rate of civilian deaths from police action, five largest American cities, 2015-2016, per million population

	Los Angeles	New York City	Chicago	Houston	Philadelphia
Black	15.1	3.4	10.7	15.1	6.0
Hispanic	7.6	0.9	1.3	4.3	2.7
White	2.3	0.6	0.6	3.7	0.9

Source: *Guardian*, "The Counted." *Note:* Civilian deaths are attributed to a city if they occur within the city's boundaries, no matter which law enforcement agency is responsible, or if a member of the city police department is responsible, no matter where the death occurred.

How do other large cities look? Chicago, Houston, and Philadelphia—the only other cities with populations over two million—are not as safe as New York, and Houston is even deadlier for whites than Los Angeles. In fact, Houston is deadlier for white civilians than New York is for black civilians. Still, as in New York, police killings are heavily concentrated on African Americans in these cities too: the ratio of black to white victimization ranges from four in Houston to eighteen in Chicago. In Chicago, blacks are killed at a rate much higher than the national average, and whites are killed at a rate much lower than the national average. Many other large cities exhibit a similar pattern, with the rate at which police kill black civilians being much higher than the rate at which they kill whites.

Putting together the information about cities and states, we can paint a general but tentative picture of police killings in the United States. The highest rates are in two kinds of areas: the rural and semirural areas of the West and Midwest, and the African American neighborhoods of large cities (other than New York). The former areas are mainly white and the latter, by definition, mainly black.

There are two salient differences between the two types of dangerous areas. The first is that the fraction of the white population nationally that lives in the rural West is much smaller than the proportion of the black population that lives in big cities. That alone would make the national black rate higher than the national white rate. The second difference is that in the rural West there is no contrasting group. In large cities, the police agencies that kill a lot of blacks also patrol areas with a lot of whites, whom they hardly ever kill. But in the rural West there is no one whom the police agencies treat much better than whites—either because the area is almost entirely white or because the local Hispanics or Native Americans are also killed at a high rate.

Nevertheless, variation is still wide within these general categories (as we saw in the New York–Los Angeles comparison). It's hard to believe that all of the differences between New York and Los Angeles are due to how civilians behave, and nothing is due to how police behave.

American Dilemma

The Carnegie Corporation funded a project in the 1930s that can give us some insight into how rates of police-related violence have changed over time. The project examined the so-called Negro question, and it eventually led to the publication of Gunnar Myrdal's *American Dilemma*. As part of this project, Arthur Raper, a sociologist who had written an influential book about lynching, undertook a study of criminal justice, especially in the South, and surveyed a large number of police departments by mail about police-related homicides in the five years ending in 1940. A total of 228 departments responded. The responding departments represented about 13 percent of the national population in 1930, and about 20 percent of the national black population.

We don't know how representative Raper's respondents were of the nation at that time, but if they were reasonably representative, then the rate at which police are killed has fallen substantially.[54] Among Raper's respondents, 1.3 police officers were killed per year per million population, and current figures are between 0.1 and 0.2 per year per million. The rate at which black civilians are killed by police has also fallen, but not quite so substantially: from more than 20 per year per million to less than 10 in the *Guardian*'s data set for 2015–2016. The rate for whites seems to have risen since the 1930s: 2.5 per year per million in the Raper data set, as opposed to more than 5 in the *Guardian* data set, although Raper has little data from the western states, where the rate of whites being killed is currently highest. Because Raper's data set was not designed to be representative, we cannot be sure about any trend for white civilians, but the differences for police and black civilians are so large that the direction of change seems unmistakable.

Raper's data for 1935–1940 include only deaths caused by the main police department in each city, while the *Guardian* data include deaths that occurred within the city but were caused by other law enforcement agencies, like sheriff's officers and transit police. So the reduction in killings of black civilians may be even larger than it appears, and the increase in killings of white civilians may be smaller. These other law enforcement agencies cause a significant number of deaths in the *Guardian* data, around a quarter.

Mutual fear, amplified by the logic of preemption, appears to have been at work in interactions involving white officers and black civilians at the time. Drawing on prior work by H. C. Brearley, Raper observed that between 1920 and 1932, more than half of interracial homicides in which the killer's identity was known were either slayings of black civilians by white police officers or slayings of white officers by black civilians.[55]

As Raper puts it, "Sensing the danger of scared policemen, Negroes in turn frequently depend on the first shot."[56] Other sources from the time confirm the prevalence of this effect; according to "dozens of letters written by black suspects and convicts to the NAACP in the 1920s, self-defense was one of the most frequently cited causes of interracial homicide of white male citizens and police officers by black men."[57]

For black civilians, some confirmation for this conclusion comes from looking at relatively large cities. Many cities had much higher rates of killing in the 1930s than they do today. Denver, Jacksonville, and Covington, Kentucky had rates over fifty per million in the Raper data, and Atlanta, Nashville, Kansas City, and Chattanooga had rates above forty per million. A separate study found a very high rate for Washington, DC, from roughly the same period.[58] In 2015–2016, only Miami and Stockton, California had rates above forty, and only Miami a rate above fifty.[59]

Restricting attention to the fifty-two cities in Raper's data that had over 50,000 people in 1940, the picture is similar. In this group of cities as a whole, the rate at which blacks were killed by police fell from about twenty per million in 1935–1940 to about ten in 2015–2016. But the average rate at which whites were killed in these cities rose from about two to above four. (The average rate at which Hispanics were killed was about five.)[60]

For African Americans especially, the level of danger in 1935–1940 does not predict the level of danger eight decades later: the correlation in per capita victimization rates was slightly negative. That is, cities that were more dangerous for blacks in 1935–1940 were a little safer on average in 2015–2016. But the correlation for whites indicates some very weak predictive ability: the correlation was low but positive.[61] These low correlations are encouraging: proclivity to kill does not seem to be some deeply entrenched part of the culture of cities.

In the American South, at least, and the non-southern cities for which Raper had data, the use of lethal force by police against black civilians has declined appreciably since that time (though starting from an extremely high level). So has the rate at which police officers are killed while on duty. In these cities, there is no evidence for a decrease in the rate at which white civilians are killed. For other regions of the country we have no basis for comparison.

Simpson's Paradox

While Roland Fryer characterized his findings on the use of lethal force as the "most surprising" of his career, not everyone was surprised. Writing on his blog, Peter Moskos responded as follows:

> Jonathan Ayers, Andrew Thomas, Diaz Zerifino, James Boyd, Bobby Canipe, Dylan Noble, Dillon Taylor, Michael Parker, Loren Simpson, Dion Damen, James Scott, Brandon Stanley, Daniel Shaver, and Gil Collar were all killed by police in questionable to bad circumstances. . . . What they have in common is none were black and very few people seemed to know or care when they were killed.[62]

Recall that Moskos did not think there was "a chance in hell" that Philando Castile would have been shot had he been white. But how can these two views—bias in individual cases but not in the aggregate—be reconciled?

We have already seen that there are enormous differences across states in the use of lethal force, as well as in the demographic structure of the population. Under these conditions a surprising possibility emerges: black citizens can face higher rates of lethal force relative to arrest rates at a set of locations, viewed separately, but not in the aggregate when these locations are viewed as a whole. The following simple example illustrates this logical point.

Consider a country composed of two regions, A and B, where A has a small black population and a high rate of lethal force, and B has a large black population but a lower incidence of lethal force. Suppose that both regions have a million arrests annually, in which black citizens are 20 percent of arrests in A and 40 percent of those in B. Suppose further that there are 200 victims of lethal force in A, of whom one-fourth are black, and 50 victims in B, of whom one-half are black. Then, clearly, the rate at which black civilians face lethal force exceeds the rate at which they face arrest in both regions. By the contact hypothesis proposed by Sendhil Mullainathan, there is evidence of bias at every location.

But what about the nation as a whole? Looking at the two regions as a single entity, we have two million arrests, with 30 percent of them involving black citizens. And there are 250 victims of lethal force altogether, of whom 75 are black—a ratio of precisely 30 percent. Thus, we find no evidence of bias in a country in which each region exhibits clear evidence of bias. Of course, it is also possible to construct hypothetical examples to generate the opposite result, showing no bias in each region but bias in the aggregate.

This fallacy of composition is known as Simpson's paradox.[63] Recognition of this possibility cautions us against relying too much on aggregate data, especially when geographic variations are substantial. While the example above is hypothetical, one can find groupings of areas that generate the same phenomenon—for instance, with Region A representing rural and semirural areas and Region B corresponding to the large cities.

Treatment and Impact

The usual way that scholars study disparate treatment is to send "auditors"—pairs of job applicants, for instance, who are trained to give employers almost identical information—and see whether the manner in which auditors are treated varies with such attributes as race, ethnicity, or gender. While this may be a feasible approach to test for bias in certain kinds of traffic stops, it is clearly impossible in the case of lethal force and would be highly unethical even in the case of nonlethal force.

Furthermore, it is not clear that the disparate treatment question is even meaningful in this context, since interactions that result in police killings typically involve a sequence of actions performed by multiple parties. Black and white civilians are likely to react differently to the same objective circumstances, as we have seen. Greater fear could result in more compliant behavior, while greater suspicion and hostility could have the opposite effect. Reactions to encounters with law enforcement are likely to differ widely both within and across groups, which makes it challenging to answer the equal treatment question even in principle.

The disparate treatment question also does not deal well with differences within the ranks of officers or the level of decision making at which bias arises. For instance, suppose that some officers are hot-headed and quick to shoot, while others are calm and try to defuse situations, but neither group acts in a manner that is contingent on the racial identity of suspects. Then disparities in police killings could be substantial but due largely to where hot-headed officers tended to be assigned, rather than the racial attitudes of particular individuals.[64]

While the disparate treatment question seems like the obvious one to ask, on closer examination it turns out to be poorly posed. Even if it were well posed (and could be answered with data we could gather ethically), it may not be the most important question to ask. Whether or not police officers are guilty of disparate treatment on average, they are still responsible for taking more than a thousand lives a year, about a third of which are black lives. To understand why, we need to attend to policies and practices and not just the hearts and minds of individual officers.

Recall that the issue of disparate impact involves two questions: do the policies and practices disproportionately harm members of protected classes, and are they a "business" necessity? Clearly, facing an elevated risk of death is a harm, and there is no doubt that this risk is greater for African Americans: about a quarter of the people whom police officers killed in 2015–2016 were black, which is twice as great as the black share of the general population. The disproportion is much larger in most big cities. Native Americans were also disproportionately likely to be killed in the *Guardian* data.

The business necessity or public benefit question is harder to answer, but many relationships that we have seen so far suggest that the number of police killings (of people of all identity groups) could be reduced substantially without serious offsetting problems. The comparisons with the United Kingdom and Germany, for instance, and between different states (for instance, California and New York) and different cities that we have already presented suggest that some police departments could do a much better job of keeping civilians safe.

But showing that Germany or New York City has lower rates of civilians being killed by police (and in many cases, lower rates of police being killed) does not really tell us that they are doing something right. To answer the business necessity question, we should be able to show specific policies and practices that make these places safer and that could work in the places where civilians are not safe now. That's impossible with current knowledge, but in Chapter 12 we point to some policies that appear promising.

The policies are likely to be most effective—in terms of lives saved—in the places where rates of killing are currently the highest and the most out of line with the rest of the nation. For instance, lowering the overall rate of police killing in the ten largest or most dangerous states to that of Ohio would reduce the number of police homicides nationally by about one-fifth.[65]

While all groups face extremely high rates of lethal force in the United States, the available evidence suggests that they do so for different reasons. African Americans are killed out of fear, anger, and loathing, while whites are killed because they tend to live in parts of the country where overall rates of lethal force are especially high. Since there seems to be two kinds of places where the rate of police killings is very high—the rural West and the black neighborhoods of large cities—this reasoning would imply that efforts should be concentrated there. It is entirely possible, and indeed likely, that the reasons for the high rate of police killings and the best policies to deal with them are different in these two kinds of places. If serious action is taken to reduce police killings, either kind of place could see the greater decrease.

This reasoning has some ironic implications, among which is the following: if the Black Lives Matter movement is successful in drawing attention to the excessive use of lethal force in the United States, leading states with the highest rates to bring these down to the current national average, some of the greatest beneficiaries could be the white residents of the rural and semirural West.

Summing Up

Chapters 5–7 showed that police are more likely to take aggressive actions of all kinds against black civilians than against white civilians: they are more likely to stop African Americans, to use force against them, and to kill them. Especially when it comes to shooting, American police are also more aggressive with just about everybody than police in other prosperous countries (although comparative international data on stops and nonlethal force are hard to come by).

Part of this greater aggressiveness is justified by circumstances and probably not discriminatory. But it is very hard to point to any rigorous evidence that the greater aggressiveness, either in general or in that directed toward African Americans, results in reduced crime or greater overall civilian safety. The important stereotypes here are probably not those held by individual officers but those held by policy-makers, both police and civilian, who have been willing to countenance aggressive tactics for many years without evidence that they work, and who have not even bothered to count how many people police kill. Disparate treatment matters too, but it is hard to measure or even define when people belonging to different identity groups differ in how they interpret and react to the words and deeds of police officers.

Courts are one place where the consequences of harsh policing tactics are revealed, especially in the willingness of witnesses to testify. The ability of police to convince potential witnesses that they will be safe is also a factor. Chapters 9 and 10 look at how these factors, and stereotypes more generally, affect the courts.

chapter 9

TESTIMONY

The effectiveness of a criminal justice system depends crucially on the level of cooperation that law enforcement officers get from witnesses to crimes, especially when it comes to the most serious offenses. As David Simon says in his book *Homicide:* "In truth, when all is said and done, the surest way for a cop to solve a murder is to get his ass out on the street and find a witness."[1]

This is easier said than done. Witnesses provide an enormously valuable but largely uncompensated benefit to society. Aside from the satisfaction of seeing justice done, citizens often have little incentive to devote time, effort, and expense to assisting police and prosecutors.[2] The system must therefore rely either on goodwill and public spiritedness or on witnesses who are themselves in trouble with the law and are therefore willing to trade testimony for leniency.

Furthermore, some potential witnesses face huge costs of cooperation. Witnesses risk life and limb if they testify against defendants with ties to gangs or organized crime. More generally, they face social ostracism, especially in communities that have experienced heavy-handed police tactics. And if they themselves lack trust in the law enforcement community, they may fear mistreatment or prosecution on trumped-up charges. All these considerations make it harder to clear homicides and other violent crimes in precisely those communities where the need for protection is greatest.

Why, indeed, are any civilians willing to face the risks and incur the costs of witness cooperation? For much the same reason that they abide by the law when it is not in their interest to do so: because they believe in the legitimacy of the rules and the process through which they are enforced. In the absence of such legitimacy, we see an unwillingness to assist police and prosecutors, and in some cases deliberate distortions of the truth, even under penalty of perjury.

As Tom Tyler and Jeffrey Fagan observe, "Strategies appealing to self-interest are often an inadequate basis for managing crime and security."[3] Using interviews with a large and diverse group of New York City residents at two points in time, and collecting information about their interactions with law enforcement officials in the intervening period, these authors found that "people who received a negative outcome via a just procedure increased their views about the legitimacy of the police and the law." That is, procedural fairness rather than positive outcomes were the key determinant of perceived legitimacy. Furthermore, they found evidence to support the view that "legitimacy shapes willingness to cooperate with the police in fighting crime."[4]

Legitimacy eroded through improper behavior or shortsighted tactics can be hard to restore. In Chapter 7 we discussed a Department of Justice probe of the Ferguson Police Department that uncovered evidence of highly aggressive and sometimes unlawful policing practices largely targeting black residents of the city. This investigation was prompted by days of unrest after a Ferguson police officer, Darren Wilson, fatally shot Michael Brown. It was rumored that Brown had been killed with his hands in the air in an act of surrender, and the slogan "hands up—don't shoot" quickly became a rallying cry for the protests.[5]

A concurrent investigation by the Department of Justice examined the shooting itself, to determine whether the officer had acted lawfully. A large number of witnesses were interviewed, many of whom had previously offered statements to police and testified under oath before a grand jury. The resulting report concluded that the physical and forensic evidence, as well as the most credible witness accounts, was generally consistent with the officer's version of events.[6] But this report also revealed just how varied and complicated the incentives faced by witnesses can be, and the salience of community pressure.

The Ferguson Witnesses

The Department of Justice investigators partitioned the Ferguson witnesses into three groups on the basis of their credibility and material relevance. The most crucial group comprised eight witnesses whose accounts of the incident were "materially consistent with prior statements, physical evidence, and other witnesses" and therefore credible. None of the accounts of these witnesses inculpated Wilson, and this was the basis of the conclusion in the report that no prosecution of the officer was warranted.

But most of these witnesses were extremely reluctant to come forward, and some refused to make formal statements or testify. Witness 103 was a fifty-eight-year-old man whose son had been shot and injured by police during the commission of a crime, and who exhibited "apparent antipathy toward law enforcement." Fearful of being targeted as a snitch, he insisted on confidentiality, but offered a version of events consistent with Wilson's account in its essentials. Witness 113 was a thirty-one-year-old woman who initially claimed that Brown had been shot in the back while he lay on the ground, then admitted to having lied when confronted with autopsy evidence. Her initial testimony was motivated by a fear of community backlash, but she eventually provided an account consistent with the officer's own.

Witness 108 was a seventy-four-year-old man who stated that the shooting was justified but refused to provide a formal statement and refused to appear before the grand jury, claiming that "he would rather go to jail than testify," and expressing a "fear of reprisal should the . . . neighborhood find out that his account corroborated Wilson." Witness 109, a fifty-three-year-old man, also refused to testify for much the same reason but provided an account in a phone call that also corroborated Wilson.

Even among the more willing witnesses in this group, neighborhood sentiment was salient. Witness 102, a twenty-seven-year-old male, came forward because he thought that community pressure would prevent others from doing so. And Witness 105, a fifty-year-old woman, came forward after realizing that her neighbors held beliefs about the incident that she knew to be false.

Where did these beliefs come from? They appear to have originated with statements made by Dorian Johnson (Witness 101), who was walking with Brown at the start of the encounter with Wilson, and who claimed in initial statements to the media that Brown had been shot execution-style while attempting to surrender. That so many people in the neighborhood found this to be a credible claim is surely connected to the abuses uncovered by the other Ferguson report.

Furthermore, as Jonathan Capehart observes, "the false Ferguson narrative stuck because of concern over a distressing pattern of other police killings of unarmed African American men and boys around the time of Brown's death . . . Eric Garner was killed on a Staten Island street on July 17. John Crawford III was killed in a Wal-Mart in Beavercreek, Ohio, on Aug. 5, four days before Brown. Levar Jones survived being shot by a South Carolina state trooper on Sept. 4. Tamir Rice, 12 years old, was killed in a Cleveland park on Nov. 23, the day before the Ferguson grand jury opted not to indict Wilson. Sadly, the list has grown longer."[7] Less than three weeks after Capehart wrote those words, Walter Scott was shot in the back while unarmed and running away from a police officer after a traffic stop in South Carolina.[8]

Capehart faced some pressure from his community of readers but stood his ground, observing that the report came from a justice department "helmed by Eric Holder, the nation's first African American attorney general appointed by the nation's first African American president."[9] He also emphasized the distinction between moral and legal culpability, stating that Wilson was legally judged and that, according to the available evidence, the homicide was legally if not morally justified.

The case of the Ferguson witnesses is unusual in that the defendant was a police officer and the pressure was on witnesses who considered him to have acted lawfully. More typically, defendants are members of the community and the pressure is on those whose testimony would inculpate rather than exonerate them.

Collective Silence

In his book *First in Violence, Deepest in Dirt,* Jeffrey Adler describes a series of homicides in early twentieth-century Chicago that were attributed to a secret society of extortionists and assassins known as the Black Hand. The killings were "brazenly public" and followed a scripted ritual, with multiple offenders, sawed-off shotguns fired at close range, and weapons left at the scene.[10] They were also geographically concentrated within the Little Sicily neighborhood, with victims, offenders, and witnesses all drawn from the surrounding Italian immigrant community. Testimony from terrified witnesses was almost impossible to obtain: they would "first instinctively turn toward the sound of the shotgun blasts and then, recognizing what had just transpired, immediately look away, close their windows, shut their doors, and go about their business, purposefully oblivious to the shooting of their neighbor."

Not surprisingly, this made the arrest and prosecution of the offenders extremely unlikely:

> Between 1910 and 1920 Chicago policemen and prosecutors secured convictions for 21 percent of the city's homicides. Among homicides labeled Black Hand killings, only 4 percent of killers were convicted. . . . Similarly, police made arrests in only 21 percent of Black Hand killings, compared with 71 percent for all of the city's homicides. During the trial in one of the few cases in which law enforcers made an arrest and secured an indictment, a stranger walked into the courtroom and waved a red handkerchief. Seeing this, the Italian immigrant on the witness stand instantly fell silent and "refused to answer any questions by the prosecutor."[11]

Under such circumstances it made sense for all manner of offenders to feign a Black Hand affiliation, by imitating the brazen style and accompanying rituals, with the consequence that neither "law enforcers nor newspaper reporters were able to distinguish Black Hand murders from murders merely committed in the Black Hand style."

What was true of Chicago's Little Sicily a century ago is true of many neighborhoods across the country today. Even when the victims are innocent bystanders, the reluctance of witnesses to testify can be unshakable. The following incident from Trenton, New Jersey, in 2007 provides a vivid example:

> A woman who was standing 10 feet away when a stray bullet from a gang fight struck 7-year-old Tajahnique Lee in the face told the police she had been too distracted by her young son to see who fired the shots.

A man who was also in the courtyard when that .45-caliber round blew Tajahnique off her bicycle told detectives he had been engrossed in conversation with neighbors and ducked too quickly to notice what had happened.

Indeed, at least 20 people were within sight of the gunfight among well-known members of the Sex Money Murder subset of the Bloods gang 15 months ago, but the case remains unsolved because not a single one will testify or even describe what they saw to investigators. The witnesses include Vera Lee, Tajahnique's grandmother, who declined to be interviewed for this article. People who have spoken to her about the shooting said she would not talk to the police for fear she would "have to move out of the country."[12]

A witness has a great deal to fear from a violent offender, especially one affiliated with a gang or organized crime syndicate. But this fear depends, in part, on beliefs about the willingness of other witnesses to come forward. Testimony is more convincing when it is corroborated, and conviction accordingly becomes much more likely when multiple witnesses provide mutually consistent accounts. Since offenders are less able to retaliate against witnesses if convicted, a generalized belief in collective silence can become self-fulfilling. Just as homicide itself can spiral upward through chains of preemption and retaliation, witness recalcitrance can become entrenched as the silence of some pushes others toward silence.[13]

Public messages predicting violence against witnesses further contribute to holding collective silence in place. Witness 103 in the Ferguson case explained his reluctance to testify by referencing signs in the neighborhood warning that "snitches get stitches." But even in the absence of any threat of violence or fear of abuse at the hands of law enforcement officials, a culture of noncooperation can emerge, in which witnesses are perceived as traitors to the community.

The killings of several high-profile hip-hop artists—including Tupac Shakur, Biggie Smalls, and Jam Master Jay—remain unsolved in part because no witnesses were willing to come forward. The same applies to their associates: Israel Ramirez, a security guard for Busta Rhymes, was shot dead in front of several dozen witnesses, none of whom were willing to identify the offender.[14] Lil' Kim was a witness to a shootout involving rival groups but chose to commit perjury before a grand jury rather than implicate her manager Damion Butler and bodyguard Suif Jackson.[15] For this she was sentenced to a year in prison.

While anti-snitching norms may well be understandable responses to aggressive policing in some communities, they have the inevitable effect of lowering clearance rates for serious crimes. This results in lower expected costs of offending and, in extreme cases, killing with impunity. As we saw in Chapter 4, such conditions can result in highly elevated murder rates, as people involved in escalating disputes have stronger incentives to kill preemptively.

Floodgates

There are some crimes involving serial offenders—domestic violence, sexual assault, and rape, for instance—where the victim is often the only witness. Victims of domestic violence have good reason to fear escalation in response to a report to police and may therefore endure years of abuse. And well-intentioned laws can give rise to lower rates of reporting and ultimately greater danger to victims. Radha Iyengar has shown that laws requiring police to arrest domestic violence offenders, no matter whether the victim pressed charges or not, increased the rate at which women were killed by their partners, largely because the law dissuaded them from reporting earlier incidents.[16]

Victims of sexual assault may fear retaliation in the form of negative publicity or damage to their careers, especially if the offenders are affluent and powerful. And they may also be only dimly aware of the extent to which others have also been victimized. Doubts about the existence of other victims, or their willingness to come forward, are what hold collective silence in place. In such cases a single precipitating event can result in a flood of allegations as a state of collective silence rapidly unravels. The knowledge that others are likely to come forward can ease fears of retaliation and lend credibility to each individual account.

Consider, for instance, the case of Larry Nassar, who was sentenced to 40–175 years in prison in January 2018 for multiple sex crimes dating back to 1995. Nassar was described by prosecutors as "possibly the most prolific serial child sex abuser in history" and was confronted by 156 of his victims during sentencing. The youngest of these was six years old at the time of abuse, and the earliest-known victim was ten. Among the victims were four Olympic gold medalists.[17]

Over the two-decade period during which the abuses occurred, at least thirteen complaints were filed with various organizations— including USA Gymnastics, Michigan State University, and multiple law enforcement agencies—but none that led to serious protective or punitive action. The floodgates eventually opened when Rachael Denhollander came forward without cover of anonymity in August 2016, and the *Indianapolis Star* corroborated and published her account.[18] Nassar was fired by Michigan State within days and charged with possession of child pornography and multiple counts of sexual assault within months.

This was a story of organizational failure at multiple levels, of "ineptitude, inaction and willful neglect," according to a lawyer defending many of the victims.[19] But it was also a story of isolated and vulnerable victims, largely unaware of the presence of others, and an offender protected by the status accorded to the medical profession.

The dangers of speaking out alone are illustrated by the fate of Anita Hill, who was called to testify at the 1991 Senate hearings on the nomination of Clarence Thomas to the Supreme Court. Under oath, Hill disclosed repeated instances of sexual harassment by Thomas, but faced a powerful backlash that Jane Mayer described in a recent interview as follows:

> She was just dragged through the dirt. They accused; they questioned her motives; they suggested that she was something they called an "erotomaniac"; they questioned whether she was a woman scorned, whether she had personal motives, whether she had professional motives, political motives. . . . They basically questioned her sanity and made her out to be a liar and potentially a lunatic. . . . She served as kind of a canary in the coal mine for women about what happens when you do speak up against a powerful man, even though she hadn't even asked to speak up.[20]

A generation later, another nominee for the Supreme Court was accused under oath of sexual assault. This time the nominee was Brett Kavanaugh, and the accuser was Dr. Christine Blasey Ford. Like Hill, Ford was a reluctant witness. According to her prepared remarks before the United States Senate, she had struggled with "fears of the consequences of speaking out" and believed that were she to come forward, her "voice would be drowned out by a chorus of powerful supporters."[21] She agreed to testify only after it became clear that her allegations and her name had been released to the media.

Ford's fears were not groundless: within days of the hearing she was taunted and mocked by the president himself at a rally.[22] A survey released shortly thereafter asked voters which claim they tended to believe most, "the accusation of sexual assault made by Dr. Christine Blasey Ford or the denial made by Judge Brett Kavanaugh." Among self-identified Democrats, 86 percent said they believed Ford's accusations while just 5 percent believed Kavanaugh's denial. Among Republicans this was almost exactly reversed: just 10 percent believed Ford and 84% believed the denial.[23]

In a similar case about a year earlier, Leigh Corfman was slandered and had her credibility questioned by Roy Moore and his surrogates after she accused the Senate candidate of having engaged in unwanted sexual touching at his home in 1979, when she was fourteen years old. Initially silent in response to the attacks on her character, Corfman eventually repeated her claims on national television and demanded in an open letter that he cease his "smears and false denials."[24]

The risk of defamation creates strong incentives to refrain from coming forward in the first place, and it is such risks that Judge Rosemarie Aquilina presumably had in mind when she described Rachael Denhollander as "the bravest person I've ever had in my courtroom."[25] The fact that a single credible accusation can give rise to an avalanche of similar claims that have remained hidden for years creates incentives for accused parties and their supporters to aggressively challenge the character and credibility of a first accuser. By imposing sufficiently high (and highly visible) costs on the first to speak out, this strategy is designed to dissuade other victims or corroborating witnesses from coming forward. Out-of-court settlements with nondisclosure agreements involving large sums of money but no admission of wrongdoing have a similar purpose and effect.

But the strategy doesn't always work. Nassar's abuse eventually came to light, and many other instances of serial abuse have followed a similar trajectory. In the case of Harvey Weinstein, the floodgates opened after a story in the *New York Times* on October 5, 2017, and one in the *New Yorker* five days later.[26] In Bill Cosby's case it was a video clip featuring comedian Hannibal Buress that referenced rape allegations against Cosby; the clip went viral after being posted on the website of *Philadelphia Magazine* in October 2014.[27] The precipitating event for Roger Ailes was a lawsuit alleging sexual harassment, filed by former Fox News anchor Gretchen Carlson in July 2016; this prompted six other women to come forward within three days. And at the same channel, Bill O'Reilly experienced a "swift and steep" downfall in April 2017 after the *New York Times* reported on out-of-court settlements with several women.[28]

In many of these cases there had been prior reports alleging misconduct or criminal behavior, but the scale of the abuse remained largely concealed and was able to continue for decades. It was the coordinating force of a public event that prompted victims to speak out, in the expectation that they would not be alone in doing so and would accordingly be safer from ridicule, neglect, or retaliation.

In an opinion piece in the *New York Times*, Lupita Nyong'o described her own sordid interactions with Harvey Weinstein and also explained why she had not previously brought these to light:

> I had shelved my experience with Harvey far in the recesses of my mind, joining in the conspiracy of silence that has allowed this predator to prowl for so many years. I had felt very much alone when these things happened, and I had blamed myself for a lot of it, quite like many of the other women who have shared their stories.
>
> But now that this is being discussed openly, I have not been able to avoid the memories resurfacing. I have felt sick in the pit of my stomach. I have felt such a flare of rage that the experience I recount below was not a unique incident with me, but rather part of a sinister pattern of behavior. . . .

Now that we are speaking, let us never shut up about this kind of thing. I speak up to make certain that this is not the kind of misconduct that deserves a second chance. I speak up to contribute to the end of the conspiracy of silence.[29]

Many of Weinstein's victims were affluent and famous in their own right—Angelina Jolie, Gwyneth Paltrow, and Ashley Judd among them. Nyong'o offers an explanation for why even these women, who had little to fear from him, nevertheless failed for so long to sound the alarm.

Errors and Hoaxes

People often have trouble recognizing faces of people from groups with which they have infrequent contact. In the United States, this means that many whites do poorly in recognizing blacks. Because whites are more numerous, African Americans generally do quite well in recognizing white faces.[30] This need not reflect animosity or a lack of concern on the part of whites; scarce cognitive resources tend to be utilized in ways that are most useful, and distinctions that need to be made with high frequency, or that result in high reward, will be made with greater accuracy.[31] One consequence of this is that white eyewitnesses are especially prone to mistakes when they try to identify African Americans.

Rape convictions usually rely on eyewitness testimony, with the victim often being the most important (if not the only) witness. Fewer than a tenth of rape convictions are for rapes where the offender is black and the victim is white, but this category of rape accounts for half of all DNA rape exonerations.[32] This suggests that the inability of some whites to identify blacks correctly routinely results in serious miscarriages of justice.

The problem stems, in part, from residential and social segregation, a point made by Elizabeth Anderson: "If whites led more racially integrated lives, they would be more competent witnesses for crimes involving black offenders and would cause fewer grave miscarriages of justice against blacks."[33]

Innocent mistakes by witnesses are only part of the problem—deliberate falsifications can also exploit stereotypes. A century ago, homicide offenders in Chicago imitated the Black Hand–style of killing to suppress witness cooperation. By adopting the signature of a ruthless organization of Italian immigrants, these killers were attempting to turn a stereotype to their advantage. Along similar lines, some offenders have attempted to escape detection by inventing narratives that appear plausible because they seem to fit a profile.

On October 23, 1989, Charles Stuart shot his pregnant wife in Boston's Mission Hill neighborhood after the couple returned home from a childbearing class. Carol DiMaiti Stuart died within hours, and her child, delivered by caesarean section two months premature, succumbed a few days later. Stuart had a severe and self-inflicted wound to the stomach. He claimed that a black male with a raspy voice, about six feet tall and thirty years old, had forced his way into the car and shot them both. He later picked out William Bennett from a police lineup and identified him as the killer.

The truth eventually came to light when Stuart's brother Matthew, who had disposed of the gun and some allegedly stolen jewelry, confessed to his role in the plot. He was apparently unwilling to let another man be charged with the crime. Charles Stuart committed suicide by jumping off the Tobin Bridge before he could be arrested.[34]

On October 25, 1994, Susan Smith allowed her car to roll into a lake in Union County, South Carolina, with her two toddlers strapped to their car seats inside. She then reported that an armed black male had forced her out of the car and disappeared with her vehicle and children. Her tearful, televised pleas for their return attracted national media attention and led to an intensive search for the suspect and the children. Smith confessed to the killings after nine days of sustained deception.[35] Had she taken her own life before confessing, as investigators feared she would do, her story may never have been proven false.

Perhaps the most famous instance of a racial hoax in American history involved nine black youths accused of raping two white women aboard a freight train in Scottsboro, Alabama, in 1931. The youngest of the "Scottsboro Boys" was thirteen at the time. The prosecution's case was fully dependent on the testimony of the women, one of whom later recanted and testified on behalf of the accused. The boys were convicted and sentenced to death, in trials that Randall Kennedy has described as "parodies of due process." The Supreme Court eventually reversed the convictions, but the defendants collectively served over a hundred years in prison before their eventual release.[36]

Accusations of rape once led to instant vigilante justice in the form of lynching, as Ida B. Wells painstakingly documented in her pioneering studies of this savage practice. To avoid even the perception of bias, Wells used only mainstream publications—owned and staffed at the time by whites—as her sources. She identified several consensual relationships involving black men and white women that, when discovered, led to accusations of rape. Given the essentialist notions of black criminality so prevalent at the time, and the impunity with which blacks could be killed, the accusation alone was often enough to result in a lynching.[37]

Here, from *A Red Record*, is an account of a racial hoax that was used to cover up a petty theft, and openly confessed:

The excuse has come to be so safe, it is not surprising that a Philadelphia girl, beautiful and well educated, and of good family, should make a confession published in all the daily papers of that city October, 1894, that she had been stealing for some time, and that to cover one of her thefts, she had said she had been bound and gagged in her father's house by a colored man, and money stolen therefrom by him. Had this been done in many localities, it would only have been necessary for her to "identify" the first Negro in that vicinity, to have brought about another lynching.[38]

Racial hoaxes are false narratives that rely on stereotypes to appear more credible. Miscarriages of justice can also arise from false confessions offered under pressure, threat, or the power of suggestion, and these too can be shaped by stereotypes.

False Confessions

On the night of April 19, 1989, a young woman jogging through New York City's Central Park was brutally raped, beaten, and left for dead.[39] Five teenagers—four black and one Latino—had been picked up in the vicinity of the park for unrelated offenses and became prime suspects after her body was discovered clinging to life. After more than a day in custody, all five confessed to involvement in the crime, and all were convicted at trial, largely on the basis of these confessions. But DNA evidence recovered from the victim was later found to match Matias Reyes—a convicted rapist and killer—who confessed to the crime and claimed to have acted alone. All judgments against the original defendants were vacated, but by that time all had completed their prison terms for this crime.

At the time of this writing, the Innocence Project lists 351 cases of individuals who have been exonerated by DNA evidence after serving time in prison.[40] Ninety-eight of these involved convictions based on false confessions or admissions, thirty-five involved guilty pleas, and twenty were death penalty cases. Sixty-two percent of the exonerated defendants were black, 30 percent white, and 7 percent Hispanic. The actual perpetrators were found in almost half of these cases.

False confessions under pressure or threat are understandable psychological phenomena. More mysterious are confessions that are false but made sincerely, and that defendants firmly believe to be true. An extraordinary article in the *New Yorker* titled "Remembering the Murder You Didn't Commit" tells the story of six innocent individuals convicted of suffocating a sixty-eight-year-old widow to death, of whom "two had internalized their guilt so deeply that, even after being freed, they still had vivid memories of committing the crime."[41] How could this be possible?

In this case it was an excess of trust in the law enforcement community that gave rise to the miscarriage of justice. The defendants were all white, and raised in small towns where respect for police was the norm. This made them vulnerable to the power of suggestion. In fact, they appeared to ask for help from officers in attempting to reconstruct the crimes of which they were accused, so that their confessions would better fit the available evidence. Only one of the accused insisted on his innocence, but he was implicated by the false confessions of his codefendants and sentenced to life in prison. His long struggle to clear his name eventually led to DNA testing of evidence from the crime scene, identification of the actual culprit, and exoneration for the entire group.

Psychologists have managed to implant false memories in experimental settings with surprising ease, including memories involving criminal events and police contacts.[42] This is done by asking probing questions that address true as well as false events, and strategically introducing new and inaccurate information. The resulting false memories can be richly detailed and are not easily distinguishable from memories of events that did indeed occur.

Memories are so central to the administration of justice that their vulnerability to the power of suggestion is disturbing. As we have seen, testimony under oath in the Ferguson case offered sharply conflicting accounts of what transpired. Whether this was due to deception induced by community norms or honest lies based on sincere but flawed recollections is impossible to say. What is clear, however, is that problems with witness cooperation extend well beyond fear, legitimacy, and the willingness of citizens to shoulder the costs and risks of assisting police. Witnesses are human, and subject to all the cognitive limitations and social pressures that this implies.

In Chapter 10 we see that witnesses are not the only fallible people in the system—judges, jurors, and lawyers also make errors, often in predictable ways.

JUDGMENT

Just as stereotypes affect decisions made by victims, offenders, officers, and suspects, they also affect judges, jurors, and parole boards when deciding the fate of defendants or prisoners. Furthermore, just as robbery offenders attempt to anticipate and exploit the stereotypes they believe certain victims to hold, prosecutors and defense attorneys face strong incentives to infer and exploit stereotypes held by potential jurors.

Juries

In 2007, two teenage sisters were molested in the bathroom of a Colorado horse racing facility, and separately identified a racetrack employee, Miguel Angel Peña-Rodriguez, as the culprit. Peña-Rodriguez was found guilty of harassment and unwanted sexual contact at trial in 2010, with the jury deadlocked on a charge of attempted sexual assault of a child.[1]

Immediately after the trial, however, two members of the jury reported that one of the other jurors had made numerous anti-Hispanic statements during deliberations, claiming in particular that in his experience as a law enforcement officer, "nine times out of ten Mexican men were guilty of being aggressive toward women and young girls." The juror in question also claimed that a Hispanic alibi witness was "an illegal" and therefore not credible.

The two jurors who reported these remarks signed sworn affidavits, which were then used as grounds for appeal. The appeal was denied in the Colorado courts on the basis of the *no-impeachment rule*—the principle that juror statements during deliberations could not be used to question a verdict once it had been entered. The Supreme Court, while recognizing the importance of the principle in protecting the final verdict and allowing for a free exchange of perspectives in the jury room, nevertheless ruled that an exception is warranted when "a juror comes forward with compelling evidence that another juror made clear and explicit statements indicating that racial animus was a significant motivating factor in his or her vote to convict."

The attitudes that the juror expressed in this case troubled a majority of the justices, to the point where they were willing to grant an exception to the no-impeachment rule. But a canny prosecutor faces strong incentives to seek out precisely this kind of juror and challenge the seating of those whose attitudes are suspected to be sympathetic to the defendant. As Randall Kennedy notes: "Just as many police officers believe that race matters for purposes of more efficiently apprehending criminals, so, too, do many lawyers believe that race matters for purposes of shaping a jury favorable to their client." He illustrates the argument using the example of a case that hinges on the testimony of a police officer:

> That prosecutor is going to want jurors who are most likely to credit the officer's version of events. In light of the poor reputation of police officers in many black communities, it would make sense for the prosecutor to take race into account in seeking as prosecution-minded a jury as possible. More specifically, in the absence of countervailing facts, it would make sense for this prosecutor to peremptorily challenge as many blacks as he could. . . . The prosecutor's

racially discriminatory conduct might well reflect intelligent strategic decision-making.[2]

By the same token, defense attorneys have incentives to exclude jurors perceived to be hostile to their client, with the result that "many attorneys, prosecutors as well as defense counsel, racially discriminate in their deployment of peremptory challenges because they reasonably believe that doing so redounds to the benefit of the side they represent."[3]

Such "strategic decision-making," coupled with an unwillingness to countenance the presence of African Americans on deliberative bodies requiring intelligence and thoughtful reflection, resulted in all-white juries in much of the American South for several decades after the abolition of slavery. And such juries were quick to convict black defendants accused of crimes against whites, even on the flimsiest of evidence, while refusing to hold whites accountable for crimes against blacks. According to James Forman, the "greatest legal injustice" of the Reconstruction era "was the failure to protect black victims of white violence."[4]

However, it was not always the case that black jurors were more sympathetic to black criminal defendants. Randall Kennedy quotes a Mississippi jury commissioner in 1910 to the effect that the few black citizens who managed to evade exclusion from juries tended to convict black defendants at higher rates, and were thus frequently challenged by defense attorneys; he also cites evidence for the belief that such jurors were more likely to inflict capital punishment.[5] Here a tension between strategic and prejudiced discrimination arises: black jurors were excluded from jury service, which was seen as a mark of status, despite the fact that their presence could have served the interests of prosecutors.

Even when defense attorneys believed that a black juror would be sympathetic to their cause, they were often reluctant to have them seated, for fear of alienating white jurors who might retaliate by being especially harsh toward their clients.[6]

A variety of factors thus conspired to sustain and entrench the norm of all-white juries across the southern states for several decades, regardless of the race of the defendant. In the case of white defendants accused of crimes against blacks, conviction was rare. For instance, in Texas: "From mid-1865 to early 1866 authorities issued 500 indictments for the murder of blacks by Anglos, but because of white attitudes no convictions resulted."[7]

Challenges explicitly based on race are no longer permissible in jury selection, though the use of certain facially neutral criteria such as prior arrest or incarceration, or subjective assessments of moral character or attentiveness, can serve as effective proxies.

Venues

Another proxy for race is location—given the extent of residential segregation that continues to prevail in American life, the pools from which jurors are drawn vary widely across jurisdictions. For instance, murder prosecutions in Los Angeles County are far more likely to be successful in suburban courthouses than in the central courthouse, where "prosecutors are more likely to face juries composed of residents of inner-city neighborhoods where skepticism about the police abounds."[8]

It was in the central Los Angeles County courthouse where the criminal trial of O. J. Simpson for the murders of Nicole Brown Simpson and Ronald Goldman played out in 1995, and where a jury that was three-quarters black returned a not-guilty verdict. In contrast, the civil trial was held in Santa Monica, and a jury that was three-quarters white unanimously found Simpson liable for the murders.[9]

There were many differences between the two trials aside from jury composition—the civil trial required a lower standard of proof, for instance, and the defendant was compelled to testify. Nevertheless, claims of egregious police misconduct were central components of the defense in the criminal case, and the success of this strategy probably required a jury that was willing to entertain doubts about police motives and practices.

Perhaps the most consequential difference between the two Simpson trials was the involvement of Detective Mark Fuhrman in the former but not the latter. Fuhrman testified that he found a blood-soaked glove on Simpson's estate, which was later paired with one left at the crime scene; the blood on the glove was matched to the victims. In response to questioning by the defense, he also testified that he had not used a racial epithet in reference to African Americans during the previous ten years. This turned out to be false:

> Several months after Fuhrman's denial, audiotapes were unearthed in which he was heard to use the N-word liberally and with obvious relish. On the taped conversations, Fuhrman offered . . . opinions and anecdotes that were not only laden with contempt for blacks but also laced with boasts that he had destroyed or otherwise tampered with evidence related to false charges he had lodged against blacks, particularly black men accompanying white women.[10]

Although the jury heard only a few selections from the audiotapes, and none that spoke to the planting of evidence, they were aware that he had lied on the stand. When asked by the defense to entertain the possibility that the considerable physical evidence linking Simpson to the murders had been planted, their prior beliefs about the likelihood of such incidents came into play.

When faced with evidence, individuals do not form beliefs in a vacuum. Even two statisticians given the same set of facts may arrive at different conclusions depending on their prior beliefs about the base-line frequencies with which particular events occur. And there are large differences in these beliefs across groups.

A 2016 survey by the Pew Research Center found that "black and white adults have widely different perceptions about what life is like for blacks in the U.S. For example, by large margins, blacks are more likely than whites to say black people are treated less fairly in the workplace (a difference of 42 percentage points), when applying for a loan or mortgage (41 points), in dealing with the police (34 points), in the courts (32 points), in stores or restaurants (28 points), and when voting in elections (23 points)."[11]

These findings are consistent with those of many other surveys. According to a Quinnipiac poll conducted in March 2017, 39 percent of whites and 66 percent of nonwhites thought that "prejudice against minority groups" was still a "very serious" problem in the United States. And a 2014 CNN / ORC poll found that 50 percent of whites and 21 percent of nonwhites agreed with the statement "The country's criminal justice system treats whites and blacks equally."[12] As Jennifer Crocker and her colleagues observed in a 1999 study of racial differences in beliefs, black and white Americans "exist in very different subjective worlds," with a "chasm . . . in the ways they understand and think about racial issues and events."[13]

This chasm was reflected in beliefs about Simpson's guilt long before evidence was presented at trial. John Brigham and Adina Wasserman tracked beliefs about the case over the course of a year. During jury selection, 54 percent of whites and 10 percent of blacks in their sample thought that Simpson was "guilty" or "probably guilty." This gap widened during the trial, with 70 percent of whites and 12 percent of blacks expressing these beliefs by the conclusion of the closing arguments. Even three weeks after the verdict, after intensive coverage of the range of public reactions, a significant gap persisted, with 63 percent of whites and 15 percent of blacks believing that he was probably or certainly guilty.[14]

Belief differences arising from life experiences naturally give rise to different interpretations of evidence, different deliberations in the jury room, and different verdicts in some cases. Just as jurors act on beliefs about law enforcement officers, prosecutors and defense attorneys act on their beliefs about these beliefs.

The Simpson case also illustrated the role of gender stereotypes in jury selection. Both sides in the criminal trial felt that women would view their arguments more favorably than men: the prosecution believed that women (regardless of race) would identify with a victim of domestic violence, while the defense speculated that black women uneasy with the interracial marriage of Simpson and Brown would be less sympathetic to the victims. Whether a different jury composition would have resulted in a different verdict given the evidence presented at trial is impossible to say, but the defense probably felt vindicated in the end.

Even before the Simpson trial transfixed a nation, there was a highly consequential trial involving four police officers accused of assault with a deadly weapon and excessive use of force for the beating of Rodney King. The officers caught up with King after a high-speed chase and were captured on video pummeling him with nightsticks and kicking him repeatedly. King suffered multiple skull fractures, a broken leg, a concussion, burns, and nerve injuries; President George H. W. Bush described the video as outrageous and sickening.[15]

The officers requested and were granted a change of venue on the grounds of pretrial publicity. The trial was held in suburban Simi Valley, where a jury composed of ten whites, an Asian, and a Latina cleared three officers of all charges and the fourth officer of the assault charge; they were deadlocked on the charge of excessive force.[16] The verdict set off six days of rioting in Los Angeles with more than 60 deaths, 2,000 people injured, 12,000 arrests, and a billion dollars in property damage. Two of the officers were subsequently found guilty on federal civil rights charges, and King won a settlement of close to $4 million from the city.

Execution

The most grave and consequential decision a jury can make concerns the death penalty. In determining whether to spare from execution a defendant convicted of a capital crime, jurors are required to weigh aggravating and mitigating circumstances that apply to the defendant, the victim, and the crime itself. And stereotypes contaminate this process too.

A dramatic illustration of this point comes from a team of psychologists led by Jennifer Eberhardt, who sought to identify determinants of sentencing severity in capital cases.[17] The researchers presented experimental subjects with photographs of forty-four black men and asked them to rate the "stereotypicality" of their features. Subjects were not told this, but all photos were of individuals who had previously been convicted of murder. The victims in all cases were white, and all defendants were "death-eligible" because of the nature of the crimes. However, some of the defendants had been spared the death penalty during the punishment phase of their trials while others had not.

The researchers found that those individuals rated as more "stereotypically black" by the naive raters were significantly more likely to have previously been sentenced to death.[18] No such effect was found among defendants with black victims, and the authors speculate that when crimes cross group boundaries the "salience of race may incline jurors to think about race as a relevant and useful heuristic for determining the blameworthiness of the defendant and the perniciousness of the crime."[19]

Decisions made by jurors are the outcome of a process of deliberation. In his book *Jurors' Stories of Death*, Benjamin Fleury-Steiner provides a window into this process, based on in-depth interviews with jurors in capital cases. These conversations reveal how some dominant members coax and cajole holdouts, sometimes using reason and sometimes mockery and ridicule. Stereotyped views of defendants are commonplace, though they occasionally lead to more merciful attitudes.

One juror explains her initial reluctance to vote for the death penalty on the grounds that the defendant was "a very typical product of the lower socioeconomic black group who grew up with no values, no ideals, no authority, no morals, no leadership, and this has come down from generation to generation. . . . I just saw him as a loser from day one, as soon as he was born into that environment, and into that set of people who basically were into drugs, alcohol, illegitimacy, AIDS, the whole nine yards. This kid didn't have a chance . . . and there are ten thousand others like him out there, which is very tragic."[20] This juror was eventually persuaded to overcome her reluctance and vote for the death penalty.

Consider the incentives that these findings create for a zealous prosecutor with political ambitions who views successful death penalty convictions as enhancing a reputation for toughness.[21] Such a prosecutor will challenge the seating of jurors who are stereotyped as being inclined to spare defendants from execution. But if this is not entirely possible—because, say, the prosecutor is precluded from using blatant racial profiling—he would want jurors who appear to have the power to pressure and persuade holdouts, and holdouts who are vulnerable to such tactics. Defendants with ample resources will hire attorneys and jury consultants to counter this strategy.

Jurors are tasked with using the information available to determine what the accused may or may not have done in the past. Judges at bail hearings, in contrast, need to predict how a suspect will behave in the future. And stereotypes can shape these predictions too in systematic ways.

Bail

A judge considers two key factors when deciding whether to release a defendant awaiting trial: the likelihood that the defendant will fail to appear in court, and the likelihood that the defendant will commit an offense while free. Ideally, judges should release those for whom these probabilities are low, and keep in custody only those for whom they are high. But on what basis can such determinations be made?

The judge has information that is specific to both the case and the defendant, such as prior involvement with the justice system, employment and marital status, and the current charge. Demographic information is also available, such as age, ethnicity, and gender, as well as less easily quantifiable attributes such as demeanor and patterns of speech. All these factors affect the judge's beliefs and decisions.

As with police stops, one can ask whether judges engage in disparate treatment discrimination, in the sense that their decisions are contingent on defendant race (holding other attributes constant). As before, such discrimination can be prejudiced or strategic. If strategic, then race is taken into account only to the extent that it serves as a proxy for risk; if prejudiced, then a white defendant may be released even if a black defendant perceived to be equally risky is held in custody.

If one could identify the set of defendants on the "margin of release"—those who barely meet a judge's criteria for release—one could look at the pretrial behavior of these individuals to see whether it differs systematically by defendant identity. If the marginal white defendants end up fleeing or offending during the pretrial phase at higher rates than the marginal black defendants, we may conclude that leniency is shown toward whites relative to blacks with similar risk profiles. This is precisely the hit-rate test for contraband recovery that has been used to determine whether police stops are motivated by prejudice rather than strategic discrimination.

But to conduct such a test convincingly—and avoid the problem with the hit-rate test that we previously discussed—one needs to identify those on the margin of release. Recent studies have attempted to do precisely this, using the fact that judges vary in leniency to identify those defendants who are on the borderline.[22] The idea is roughly the following: as one moves from one judge to a slightly more lenient one, the defendants released by the latter who would have been retained by the former—based on a statistical model fitted to judge behavior in relation to defendant characteristics—are on the margin of release at the specified level of leniency. Aggregating across all levels of leniency then gives us a pool of defendants on the margin of release. One can then look for bias by assessing whether the likelihood of rearrest before trial varies by defendant race within this pool.

The data for one of the recent studies come from two counties—Philadelphia and Miami-Dade—with very different institutional structures for dealing with bail hearings. Defendants in Philadelphia typically face full-time bail judges who make thousands of bail decisions a year, while those in Miami-Dade are more likely to confront trial judges who handle bail hearings only on a part-time basis.

The authors find that among defendants on the margin of release, whites are significantly more likely to be rearrested during the pretrial period. This suggests that, on average, judges treat white defendants with greater leniency, releasing some high-risk white defendants who would have been retained if they were black. The disparity in rearrest is greatest for drug crimes but also arises for property and violent crimes.

Furthermore, the bias is concentrated among the less experienced part-time judges of Miami-Dade rather than the full-time bail judges in Philadelphia, and does not seem sensitive to the racial identity of judges. This latter fact leads the authors to conclude that it is not racial animus that gives rise to the disparity but rather "incorrect inferences of risk based on defendant race due to anti-black stereotypes, leading to the relative over-detention of black defendants at the margin."[23]

Judges face the risk of backlash from the media, citizens, or voters if a released defendant commits a serious offense while awaiting case disposition. If this backlash is especially great when the defendant is black, Hispanic or a non-citizen, judges may apply identity-contingent standards of release for entirely instrumental reasons. That is, judges will tend to show less leniency towards those whose subsequent crimes invite the greatest public scrutiny and outcry, regardless of their own ethnic or racial identity.

Bail setting has consequences. Aside from the costs of being held in jail while awaiting trial, being denied bail weakens a defendant's bargaining power and makes it more likely that the defendant will eventually end up in prison. Defendants who had to post bail were more likely to plead guilty than essentially similar defendants who did not have to post bail, according to two recent studies.[24]

If inexperienced bail judges make risk assessment errors that vary systematically across groups, then perhaps they also make serious errors along other dimensions, even for defendants belonging to the same group. Recent advances in machine learning are starting to allow for systematic explorations of such questions.

Algorithms

In 1996, IBM's Deep Blue became the first computer to beat a reigning chess champion under standard tournament time controls, defeating Garry Kasparov in the first game of a six-match series. Kasparov came back to win the series, then lost the rematch a year later.

But even as algorithms became capable of mastering strategically complex games, there were simple tasks at which they could not compete, even with young children—such as identifying sarcasm or determining whether an animal in a photograph is a cat or a dog. This started to change with rapid advances in machine learning.

Consider, for instance, the problem of classifying a large number of images, each of which is a cat or a dog. The data corresponding to an image are just pixels with characteristics such as brightness, color, and location in a two-dimensional array. How might one program a computer to accurately distinguish between images of cats and images of dogs? One can start with a subset of images—called a training set—for which the correct answer is provided to the computer. With these data the algorithm fits a function mapping image properties to one of the two categories (or more generally, to a probability distribution over the two categories). This is done by working within a class of functions and tuning various parameters to minimize classification error. A second set of images—the test set—is then used to assess performance out-of-sample; this requires classification of images to which the algorithm has not previously been exposed.[25]

The process is similar in some respects to human learning—children make classification errors, are corrected, and learn to classify correctly over time. But relative to machines, most humans manage to achieve high levels of accuracy using a very small training set, drawing on capacities that it is not yet possible to encode. Nevertheless, humans are also subject to biases, and in the case of bail decisions, we can compare the performance of judges to that of algorithms.

An interdisciplinary team of researchers has attempted to make this comparison, using data from more than 550,000 bail decisions in New York City over the period 2008–2013.[26] About 400,000 of the defendants in these cases were released, and for this subset one can observe whether they were rearrested before case disposition or failed to appear in court as required. The machine learning algorithm can be configured to assign to each of these defendants a probability of crime risk (or of failure to appear) based on the characteristics in their case files, which are available to judges. The model does not use information on race, gender, or any demographic characteristic other than age. However, it may use information that is correlated with race, that in fact has nothing to do recidivism or flight, but will act as a proxy for race if it is included in the algorithm.

Given the output of the model, the authors then ask the following question: Relative to the most lenient judges, do stricter judges simply apply a more demanding standard for release (based on crime risk), or do they release an entirely different set of defendants? Remarkably, the authors find that stricter judges "do not simply jail the riskiest defendants; the marginal defendants they select to detain are drawn from throughout the entire predicted risk distribution."

These effects are large. Compared with the most lenient judges, stricter judges increase detentions by 13 percentage points and reduce crime by 19 percentage points; by choosing a different set of defendants for release, they could achieve the same crime reduction with just 6 percentage points of increased detention, or reduce crime by 33 percent while maintaining their rates of detention.

These estimates refer to policy changes affecting only the pool of individuals who were released, since we cannot observe how the detained defendants would have behaved if they had, in fact, been released. If one were to predict their crime risk based on their case characteristics using the same model that is fitted to released defendants, and release individuals strictly in order of predicted crime risk, the authors estimate that there would be 25 percent fewer crimes under current release rates, or 42 percent fewer detainees under current crime rates. And for this particular sample, release based on predicted crime risk would reduce rather than exacerbate racial disparities.

Of course, it is possible that those whom judges detain differ systematically from those who are released, in ways that judges can discern but the algorithm cannot. Nevertheless, it appears that judges detain many defendants with low crime risk and release many with high crime risk. What could account for this? Using machine learning methods to predict the behavior of judges, the authors find that decisions appear to depend on extraneous factors that are treated as informative about crime risk when in fact they should be ignored. That is, the decisions are too variable and are contaminated by noise.

This finding is consistent with earlier studies showing that judicial decisions can be affected by such factors as tiredness, hunger, or mood. As one analysis of the effects of meals and breaks on parole decisions in Israeli courts concluded, "Legally irrelevant situational determinants—in this case, merely taking a food break—may lead a judge to rule differently in cases with similar legal characteristics."[27] Along similar lines, it was found that in the weeks after football games that Louisiana State University (LSU) lost in an upset, juvenile court judges in Louisiana imposed harsher sentences on defendants. This was especially true for black defendants and for judges who were LSU alumni.[28] These are supposed to be deliberate, thoughtful decisions by educated professionals, and yet they exhibit a shocking level of arbitrariness and sensitivity to physiological and emotional states.

The pursuit of justice is contaminated by human biases and frailties, and algorithms can bring some of these to light. But algorithms themselves are subject to objections and pitfalls. To begin with, it is not really crime risk that the algorithm is predicting; it is the likelihood of arrest, and this is only loosely connected to actual offending. As we saw in Chapter 3, some crimes such as robbery result in a much greater likelihood of arrest than others such as burglary or motor vehicle theft. But it is impossible to train an algorithm on actual offending data, since this is not observed.

Algorithms also may not be race-blind, and because of their construction it may be hard to tell whether they are. How can they be race-sighted if they do not use information about race explicitly? By using information that is correlated with race but not otherwise correlated with crime. For instance, African Americans are more likely to smoke menthol cigarettes than whites, and less likely to smoke non-menthol brands.[29] If blacks are more likely to be arrested than whites on average, and an algorithm has information about cigarette brand, it may reward non-menthol smokers and penalize menthol smokers. Menthol cigarettes almost certainly do not cause crime. Their use in an algorithm would be a way of discriminating against individuals based on characteristics of a group to which they belong, and hence a violation of the rights of black civilians.

Defendants have a right to be judged as unique individuals rather than simply a constellation of characteristics. Two individuals with identical case files are not the same person, even though an algorithm would predict that they have the same crime risk. And any changes in release decisions that are informed by an algorithm will result in the detention of some who would otherwise have been released, and among these will be some who are actually innocent. Such individuals—who are innocent and would have been released were it not for the algorithm—could well have grounds for legal recourse.

Compounding

After setting bail, prosecutors decide what charges to bring and what sort of bargains to offer. These are probably the most crucial steps on the path to prison, but little is known about them because research requires detailed internal information from prosecutors' offices. The meager research available suggests that race matters in charging and plea-bargaining decisions, but not all studies have found racial effects at this stage.[30]

The best research in this area relies on complete histories from arrest to sentencing in the federal system.[31] It finds that black defendants are much more likely to be charged with crimes carrying mandatory minimum sentences, holding all the relevant information at arrest constant. Juries that are entirely white convict black defendants more often, and white defendants less often, than juries with at least one black member.[32] This is the kind of phenomenon that creates incentives for racial profiling in jury selection, as we have seen.

Most research has concentrated on sentencing, because that is the step for which the best data are available. The National Research Council summarizes this research as follows: "Blacks are less likely than whites to be diverted to non-incarcerative punishments. . . . Overall, when statistical controls are used to take account of offense characteristics, prior criminal records, and personal characteristics, black defendants are sentenced somewhat but not substantially more severely than white."[33] Even though sentencing usually occurs after most of the important decisions have been made, and so is often a formality, anticipations of what a judge might do at this stage can affect bargaining between prosecutors and defendants at an earlier stage.

All in all, the studies of disparate treatment in the criminal justice system indicate that from arrest to release from prison, blacks fare worse than whites at many different steps, though not necessarily each step. That there are many steps means that these disparities are compounded. Small disparities at many steps can result in large disparities overall.

In their study of the federal pipeline from arrest to sentencing, Marit Rehavi and Sonja Starr illustrate how this happens.[34] Overall, a black person with the same relevant characteristics and case facts as a white person can expect a 13 percent longer sentence when the two of them are arrested. But even the step with the greatest racial disparity—whether the charge is for a crime that carries a mandatory minimum sentence—accounts for only about half of this disparity.

Compounding occurs over longer periods of time too. Blacks are more likely to come out of these processes with convictions than otherwise identical whites. Prior convictions lead to worse treatment in the future at every step of the way. The work cited here treats prior conviction as relevant, racially neutral information. But it is not racially neutral in the long run, since the likelihood of prior conviction is itself not independent of race.

The majority of cases, however, never go to trial. Trials matter not because they are frequent but because beliefs about what is likely to happen at trial affect decisions and bargains reached at earlier stages.

Plea Bargains

Among those charged with crimes, a truly negligible proportion are sent to prison (or spared from prison) as a result of a jury trial. Trials are what happen on television and in the movies, not what happens in twenty-first-century America. In the nation's seventy-five largest counties in 2009, only 2 percent of those arrested on a felony charge were convicted in a trial, and only 1 percent were acquitted in a trial.[35] Most criminal cases are resolved by plea bargaining—negotiations between prosecutors and defendants, or defendants' lawyers. Why, then, should anyone care about criminal trials except for their participants?

The main reason is that trials are the fallback option if plea bargaining negotiations fail. In these talks either party can force a jury trial by rejecting the other side's offer, and so each has to compare the other's current offer with what they expect will happen if the case were to go to trial. Like the moon moving the tides even though it is nowhere near the ocean, trials can move plea bargain outcomes even if they rarely occur.

The fact that few cases go to trial adds an additional layer of uncertainty to the criminal justice system. Not only are judges and juries uncertain of the facts on which they are supposed to base their verdicts and sentences, but defendants and prosecutors are uncertain about how the judges and juries would handle their doubts if a trial were to occur. Beliefs about the beliefs of others determine who goes to prison and how long they stay there.

How, then, do prosecutors arrive at their beliefs about what would happen if their cases went to trial? Perhaps, as economists tend to assume, their expectations are tethered tightly to the meager evidence the few trials that actually occur can provide.[36] If that is the case, then the issues we have discussed in this chapter have direct relevance to all of the plea bargains that are struck and all of the charging decisions that are made. Alternatively, expectations might be concocted from rumors, wild stories, popular movies, and moods of pessimism and optimism. Then this chapter would be only about the sliver of cases that actually go to trial.

Most likely, both sorts of expectations are at work, with repeat players like prosecutors and experienced defense attorneys influenced quite heavily by trial outcomes, and poorly represented defendants adrift on a sea of speculation, stereotypes, and mood swings.

Summing Up

Chapters 8 and 9 showed that courts make errors; sometimes innocent people are convicted, and sometimes guilty people are not even tried. All of the actors involved in the process—witnesses, police, prosecutors, defense lawyers, juries, and judges—are fallible and act on stereotypes. Is there a markedly better system? We believe there is, and so we offer a few suggestions for improvement in Chapter 12.

Whether or not it can be improved, every year this error-prone system puts a large number of people in jail and prison, many of them for long periods of time. Usually the possibility of being wrong results in decision makers being cautious and reluctant to take drastic and irreversible actions—prudent individuals, for instance, generally don't bet their life savings on the outcome of a baseball game when they don't even know for sure who the starting pitchers are. Is our criminal justice system sufficiently reliable to justify the savage punishments that it imposes? The question is worth contemplating while reading Chapter 11, which looks at jails and prisons.

chapter 11

PUNISHMENT

In 2010, the incarceration rate for African Americans in the United States was 2,207 per 100,000 population, and the corresponding rate for Hispanics was 966.[1] Such rates are unprecedented in world history. We have become, in Glenn Loury's words, a nation of jailers.[2]

Figure 11.1 shows incarceration rates around 2010 for the United States as well as the other thirty-four members of the Organization for Economic Cooperation and Development (OECD), a collection of the world's high- and middle-income countries. We have also added Rwanda, Russia, Cuba, and Belarus because, with the exception of the United States, they have the highest incarceration rates in the world among countries larger than New York City. And we have added the rates for three American subpopulations—blacks, whites, and Hispanics.

The rates for the United States as a whole, and especially for black and Hispanic Americans, are extraordinary. Hispanic Americans were about five times as likely to be incarcerated as Mexicans, and about six times as likely as Spaniards. African Americans were almost four times as likely to be incarcerated as Rwandans, nineteen times as likely as Canadians, and thirty-eight times as likely as Japanese.[3]

Even whites in the United States were incarcerated at rates outside the bounds of international norms. At 380 per 100,000, their incarceration rate was higher than that of any other OECD country, and behind only Rwanda, Russia, Cuba, and Belarus among large countries in the world.

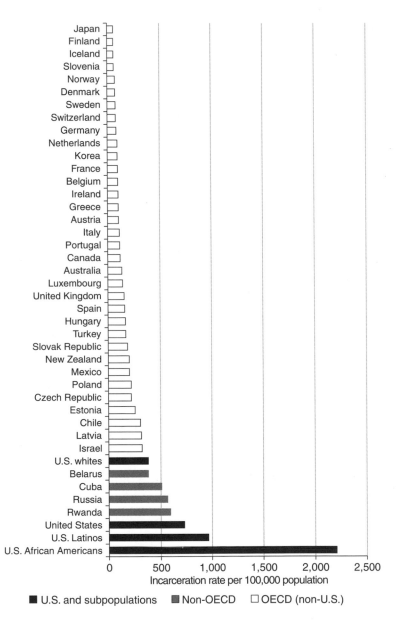

Incarceration rate per 100,000 population

■ U.S. and subpopulations ■ Non-OECD □ OECD (non-U.S.)

FIGURE 11.1. Incarceration rates for OECD and selected other countries around 2010 (number incarcerated per 100,000 population). Data are from 2010 for all countries except France (2008); Belarus, Israel, Canada, and Greece (2009); Russia, Chile, Estonia, Czech Republic, Poland, New Zealand, Turkey, Spain, Portugal, Italy, Ireland, Denmark, Norway, Iceland, Finland, and the UK (2011); and Cuba (2012). Source: Walmsley (2011) for all countries except the United States (Wagner, 2012), Cuba (Walmsley, 2013), and authors' calculations for US non-Hispanic whites.

It wasn't always this way. In 1972, the U.S. incarceration rate was 161 per 100,000, much like that of an average OECD country, and it had been around that level for over forty years.[4] The white incarceration rate in 1972 was around 115 (like Portugal or Italy in 2011), and the black incarceration rate was around 525 (like Cuba in 2012).[5] Then followed four decades of spectacular growth in the prison population that took the country well outside the bounds of international norms.[6]

This particular manifestation of American exceptionalism is not driven by extraordinary rates of criminal offending. In 2011, per capita index crime was not much different from that of 1972.[7] Among the thirty-five OECD countries in 2011, the United States ranked third in murder, fourth in rape, eighth in robbery, sixteenth in assault, thirteenth in burglary, and tenth in motor vehicle theft.[8] Only in incarceration did the United States lead this group. Even the Rwandan rate—bloated in the wake of a catastrophic genocide—is well below that in the United States.

What, then, drives such high rates of incarceration? If you looked at the other four high incarceration countries (Rwanda, Russia, Cuba, and Belarus), you would not think about wealth or urbanization or family structure or out-of-wedlock births. You would think about politics and ethnic discord. That is probably the right way to think about incarceration in the United States too.

The 1970s television detective series *Baretta* popularized the phrase "Don't do the crime if you can't do the time." This suggests that crimes are somehow linked to times in a natural, obvious, and almost automatic way: for every crime, there is a corresponding "time" in prison. There is, in practice, no such correspondence.[9] Incarceration rates vary so much across time and space because the link between crime and punishment differs so greatly.

Anders Behring Breivik, for instance, killed 77 people, mainly children, and injured over 400 in a pair of attacks in Norway in 2011. He was sentenced to twenty-one years in prison with parole eligibility in ten years, although his imprisonment could be extended in five-year increments if he is still considered dangerous. This was the maximum penalty in Norway in 2011. In contrast, under the Violent Crimes and Law Enforcement Act in the United States, someone who has been convicted of a robbery in federal court and who has two previous convictions for serious violent or drug crimes must receive a sentence of life imprisonment.[10] In 2008, 134,000 American prisoners were serving life sentences, 40,000 of them without possibility of parole.[11] Except for Terry Nichols (one of the Oklahoma City bombers who is serving 161 consecutive life sentences), none of them has as much blood on their hands as Breivik. The differences across time and space in normal punishment for less serious crimes are just as great.

Governments determine what activities are treated as crimes, who is arrested, and what happens to them after they are arrested. They determine how much "time" gets assigned to each crime. Because different governments do this in different ways, incarceration rates vary. To understand incarceration, one must look at how governments behave, rather than how citizens behave. That's why Rwanda, Russia, Cuba, and Belarus stand out in international comparisons.

In the United States, many important government functions are decentralized, and the criminal justice system is no exception. Public opinion matters, voters' choices matter, politicians' attempts to manipulate public opinion matter, laws matter, policies matter, and the idiosyncratic actions of millions of government employees including police officers, prosecutors, judges, corrections officers, and parole board members also matter. Somehow, in a complex way, this multitude of actors assigns "times" to crimes. The outcome is not necessarily what any single individual wants, or even what people would agree on if they could decide collectively.

Few of these actors are race-blind, even though almost all of them profess to be. As we have seen, most Americans respond to racial markers in much of what they do, and the implementation of criminal justice necessarily reflects this. Because the relationship between attitudes and outcomes is complex, simple stories about racism cannot account for the big picture. After all, the African American incarceration rate was probably more than four times as high in the year that Americans elected a black president as it was in the years when blacks had to sit in segregated compartments on trains and drink from separate water fountains. On almost all measures, white attitudes toward blacks were improving during the years when black (and indeed white) incarceration was skyrocketing.

Why the incarceration rate in the United States started rising in 1973 and continued to rise for almost four decades thereafter is not an easy question to answer. Major events like the Industrial Revolution and the Civil War rarely have single causes; rather, many different strands of history, all of them necessary for the event, interact in a manner never encountered before. So it is with mass incarceration. Telling this story is beyond the scope of this book, and various pieces of the puzzle have been assembled by others.[12]

The racial stereotypes that we concentrate on in this book, however, were certainly implicated in this rise. These stereotypes have been around for generations, even as the country had a much smaller prison population, and so they were not solely responsible. Nor can they directly explain the very high incarceration rates of white Americans relative to international norms. But without them the story would have been different and incarceration would probably be a lot lower today.

To show how they have operated, we return to our distinction between disparate treatment and disparate impact. In this context, disparate treatment is about how officials—prosecutors, judges, and parole boards in particular—treat the individual defendants and prisoners who come before them. Disparate impact is about how policies, laws, and government budgets are made. Disparate impact is a much more serious problem than disparate treatment, although both types of discrimination are commonly present. A major part of this chapter is about documenting disparate impact (just as Chapter 10 concentrated on disparate treatment) and the enormous costs associated with it.[13]

Talking about incarceration is challenging because there are varying views of the purpose that incarceration is meant to serve. As we mentioned in Chapter 2, there is no agreement over whether crimes are activities that are merely prohibited or intrinsically wrong. This distinction is tied to the important philosophical question of whether the suffering of legitimately and appropriately sentenced prisoners is a feature of the system (the retributivist view) or a bug (the consequentialist view). This question is particularly important in thinking about disparate impact. Having two different goals for incarceration also greatly confuses debates and discussions, and often leads to policies that cannot be justified by either goal.

We begin with an overview of incarceration in the United States: its component parts, how they fit together, and why the system grew so large. Then we look in more detail at retributivism, consequentialism, and mixed systems, and what they imply. We then examine the role of racial stereotypes in holding this system together, and conclude by considering how the costs of the incarceration boom may be enumerated.

Crime and Time

Criminal justice in the United States is a complex, decentralized operation where key decision makers often have only vaguely specified incentives. Nobody decides how many people will be incarcerated. In fact, no individual acting alone decides whether any specific person will be incarcerated, or for how long.

American adults who are accused or convicted of having committed crimes get incarcerated in three kinds of places: jails, state prisons, and federal prisons. In addition, some adults are incarcerated in Indian country jails, military facilities, and immigration detention centers.

Figure 11.2 shows the staggering fivefold increase in the incarcerated population from 1978 to 2009 by type of institution, and the modest decline since then. This figure shows the raw numbers, but a similar picture emerges if one looks at incarceration rates, to allow for population growth. Over the three-decade period starting in 1980, the rate at which Americans were incarcerated increased by a factor of four.

Jails are run by counties or cities and hold people who are awaiting trial as well as people who are serving short sentences for minor crimes. In 2015, on an average day, more than 700,000 people were in jails—60 percent of them awaiting trial, meaning that they had not been convicted of any crime. About 35 percent of the people in jail were African American and 15 percent were Hispanic. Jails involve a large transient population: the number of people admitted to jail in the year was about fifteen times the average daily number of prisoners.

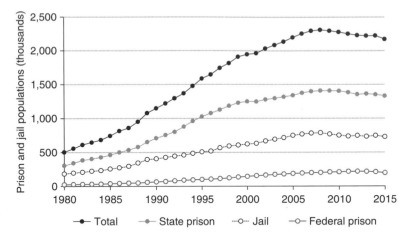

FIGURE 11.2. Prisoners under the jurisdiction of state or federal correctional authorities at the end of the year, 1978–2016, in thousands. Source: National Prisoner Statistics Program, Bureau of Justice Statistics.

Federal prisons hold people who have been convicted of committing federal crimes. These are a specific subset of activities with some connection to interstate commerce that Congress has decided to criminalize. Most of the index crimes are not federal, except for some unusual variants—murder in general is a state crime, for instance, but the murder of a postal worker is a federal crime.

Because federal prisons deal with only a specific subset of crimes, they do not hold a lot of prisoners relative to the states. To provide some context, the state prisons of Georgia and Texas combined to hold more prisoners in 2015 than the entire federal system. Relative to their size, federal prisons receive a disproportionate amount of attention because policies are set in Washington by people who are frequently in the news for other reasons.

Federal prisons have rapidly expanded in the past few decades, much faster than any other part of the criminal justice system. While the jail population expanded fourfold between 1980 and 2015, the federal prison population expanded eightfold. Part of the reason for this growth is that Congress enthusiastically created new federal crimes, and part is from the expansion of the War on Drugs. Figure 11.2 also illustrates the time trend of the federal prison population. The major part of the growth has come from a rapid increase in the number of drug prisoners, who are now a majority of federal prisoners. Despite this growth, federal prisoners still remain a relatively small minority of total prisoners. Most federal prisoners are members of minority groups: in 2017, 38 percent of federal inmates were black and 33 percent were Hispanic.

State prisons are the largest form of incarceration, holding about a million and a half prisoners in 2015—more than jails and federal prisons combined. They hold people convicted of major crimes, including most of the index crimes. About half of state prisoners have been convicted of violent index crimes; the rest are about equally split between property crimes and drug crimes, with a small number being held for other offenses. Although some people stay in prison for decades, around 45 percent of the state prisoners present at the start of a year are released before the end.[14]

Figure 11.2 shows that the state prison population grew quickly at the end of the twentieth century, slowly in the beginning of the twenty-first century, and dipped slightly after the Great Recession. There were about four and a half times as many state prisoners in 2015 as in 1980. An increase in drug prisoners has been part of this story, but the rise in prisoners convicted of violent crimes has been greater in absolute terms; the popular impression that prisons are full of drug offenders may arise from a misguided emphasis on federal prisons.

In addition to the people who are behind bars, several million people are "under the supervision of the correctional system." They are treated as less than full, free citizens, but most of their daily movements are under their control. In 2015, 3.8 million people were on probation and 870,000 were on parole. Probation is an alternative to a prison term for people who have been convicted of a crime; those on probation have to live for a period of time under restrictions that might include community service, staying away from various people and places, and checking in with a probation officer regularly. About half of probationers were convicted of misdemeanors (minor crimes) and half were convicted of felonies (major crimes including index crimes).[15]

Parole is like probation, but it follows a spell in prison rather than substituting for one. People who violate their conditions of probation or parole can be sent to prison, even if the violation—such as purchasing alcohol—is not itself a crime.

The number of probationers and parolees has also been rising, but not quite as fast as the incarcerated population: the probation population grew 3.4 times and the parole population grew 3.9 times between 1980 and 2015. Probationers and parolees are also disproportionately black and Hispanic, but less so than incarcerated populations: in 2015, African Americans represented 30 percent of probationers and 38 percent of parolees, while Hispanics were 13 percent of probationers and 16 percent of parolees.[16]

Cities and states also impose many different fees and fines on people who have been convicted of crimes (or even just arrested, in some cases). These charges include fees for the expense of jail incarceration, fees for the use of public defenders, fees and surcharges for court costs and for probation supervision, punitive fines levied at sentencing, and restitution awards paid to specific victims or victim compensation funds. Landlords are also sometimes fined if police have to respond to their properties. Arrearages are common, and enforced at substantial interest rates. One study of people who were convicted of felonies in Washington state found that median outstanding debt among those who had debt to the legal system was about half of what they were likely to make in a year of full-time work.[17]

Collecting money from felons is a relatively recent practice in the United States, although it was common in the early twentieth-century South, combined with profit-making prisons and work camps.[18] The proportion of convicted felons with fines imposed at sentencing rose from 11 percent in 1991 to 34 percent in 2004—another dimension in which the nation has become more punitive.[19]

Finally, for anyone convicted of a felony, whether or not incarcerated, there is also a series of punishments and losses that don't involve confinement or supervision (and so they are not expensive to the government). Michelle Alexander describes these punishments this way:

> Once you're labeled a felon, the old forms of discrimination—employment discrimination, housing discrimination, denial of the right to vote, denial of educational opportunity, denial of food stamps and other public benefits, exclusion from jury service—are suddenly legal. As a criminal, you have scarcely more rights, and arguably less respect, than a black man living in Alabama at the height of Jim Crow.[20]

Those are the pieces. We next describe how they fit together.

Paths to Prison

For most people, the point of entry into the criminal justice system is an arrest by a police officer or a federal marshal. Arrest usually means that a police officer believes you have committed a crime, and places you in custody so that you cannot avoid trial and punishment. Arrest is not itself intended to be punishment; it is a way to keep you from fleeing. It is based on the officer's subjective judgment and the guidelines of the police department.

In 2015, close to eleven million people in the United States were arrested, but less than one-third of them for the type of crimes that typically result in state prison sentences—two million for index crimes and a million and a half for drug crimes. The majority of index crime arrestees were charged with theft (1.2 million). Most people were arrested for less serious crimes, with the largest numbers being for simple assault and driving under the influence (both about 1.1 million). More people were arrested for vandalism than for murder, robbery, and motor vehicle theft combined.[21]

After you are arrested, you decide whether to plead guilty. If you plead guilty, a judge decides whether to fine you or hold you for sentencing. If you plead not guilty, the judge decides whether to dismiss the charges against you, let you go on your own recognizance until the trial, hold you on bail, or hold you without bail. This process is called arraignment. Arraignment judges have much discretion, as we saw in Chapter 10.

For most people who are arrested, punishment is a fine or a short stay in jail. Although 3.5 million people were arrested on index crime or drug charges in 2015, fewer than 400,000 entered state prison as new court commitments, and about a million entered probation.[22] Still, every arrest creates a record that is available online.

For serious crimes, the prosecutor is the key actor after arraignment. Every county in the nation has a prosecutor, and in almost all states prosecutors are elected directly. For federal crimes, the U.S. attorneys for different jurisdictions act as prosecutors; these individuals are appointed by the president. Most prosecutors have staffs—assistant prosecutors and investigators—and in large counties, prosecutors have very large staffs. Ostensibly, the prosecutor's job is to present the case against anyone who has been accused of a crime in the county, and then let juries and judges decide whether the person is guilty, and if so, how he should be punished. But in fact, the prosecutor has much more discretion. For instance, a prosecutor can decide to dismiss the case against someone who has been arrested and charged with a crime. Or she can decide to charge the person with a different crime.

The most important discretionary power that a prosecutor has is plea bargaining. This is a negotiation between the prosecutor and the defendant. The prosecutor agrees to ask for a certain kind of sentence if the defendant agrees to plead guilty to a less serious crime than the one with which he has been charged. A plea bargain is a compromise and a mutual insurance pact: the prosecutor gets a case resolved without a trial and without the possibility of losing, and the defendant gives up the prospect of walking free after a trial for the certainty that he won't be convicted of the more serious crime.

Plea bargains are how most cases are resolved, and how most people go to prison; contested trials and decisions by juries and judges are rare. Almost 95 percent of the cases that prosecutors choose to pursue end with a guilty plea. Such deals are appealing to prosecutors because they can allow cases to be resolved quickly and with much less strain on limited prosecutorial resources.[23] As a result, you should be skeptical of the crimes that prisoners are supposed to be in prison for. In almost all cases, these are the crimes that closed the deal between prosecutor and defendant, not the crimes that a jury solemnly and scrupulously decided that the defendants were guilty of beyond a reasonable doubt.

The sentences that prisoners receive therefore depend on bargaining outcomes, which in turn depend on the bargaining power of the two parties. What determines bargaining power? There are a number of factors that mattered during the incarceration boom.

The prosecutor's bargaining power is greater if she can credibly threaten more serious punishments at a trial. So if the defendant's case is weak against the more serious charge, or if the punishment for the more serious offense is more severe, the defendant is more likely to agree to a disadvantageous plea bargain. When more offenses are made capital crimes, for instance, defendants who can be threatened with being charged with these offenses will accept longer sentences on other charges. As John Pfaff observes: "Using a gun during a drug deal can result in mandatory minimums up to thirty years under a particular statute. A prosecutor, however, can tell a defendant that if he pleads guilty to just the drug charge, the prosecutor will make the gun disappear. The threat of thirty years is enough to terrify most defendants into agreeing. So even if the mandatory is rarely imposed, it is used much more often."[24]

The prosecutor's bargaining power is greater if the defendant has a poor or overworked lawyer, because such a lawyer is more likely to lose a trial on a more serious charge. So cuts to funding for public defenders are likely to result in more disadvantageous plea bargains for defendants.

The prosecutor's bargaining power is greater if the defendant is in jail rather than out on bail. If the defendant holds out for a trial, he will have to sit in jail for a long time because trials don't happen right away. If he agrees to a plea bargain, the prosecutor can agree to credit jail time against his prison sentence, and he may even go home immediately—but with a record of his conviction.

Finally, prosecutors with larger staffs relative to their caseload have greater bargaining power. The cost to the prosecutor of going to trial is greater when she has a larger caseload, and so she will be willing to give up more in order to avoid a trial. Defendants who accept plea bargains rather than go to trial weaken the bargaining power of other defendants. For this reason, when the number of prosecutors increased but crimes decreased in the 1990s and early 2000s, the position of defendants worsened. This is one channel through which lower crime can result in increased incarceration.

After a plea bargain has been agreed to, or a jury has found the defendant guilty, a judge decides what sentence to impose. Judges can sentence a convicted defendant to probation or to a prison term of a specific length, as well as set other conditions, such as restitution. (On some rare occasions, a convicted defendant may be sentenced to be executed, for which the procedures are somewhat different.) Before sentencing, both the prosecutor and the defendant's lawyer can present arguments to try to influence the judge, and the prosecutor's arguments, especially if they lean toward leniency, usually carry great weight. Judges usually have some discretion in sentencing, but today are often bound by rules set by legislatures (mandatory minimum sentences for crimes, for instance) and by sentencing guidelines. The sentencing guidelines are often based on predictions about recidivism; some use proprietary algorithms to predict who is more likely to be rearrested.

The final actors in determining the size of the prison population are parole boards. Prisoners petition them to be released before the end of their sentences. Usually these boards have some discretion in their decisions, but different states have different rules. In making their decisions, parole boards generally consider the petitioner's behavior in prison, the seriousness of the original crime, and the likelihood of rearrest.

It is this complex and decentralized process, involving chains of events with many regional variants, that determines who gets incarcerated and for how long.

Mass Incarceration

The number of people held in jails and prisons will increase if people either arrive more quickly or leave more slowly. The incarcerated population rose because both phenomena occurred. The relative importance of quicker entries and slower exits varied with institution, decade, and type of crime.

Jails have been less studied than prisons. Between 1983 and 2015 (the period for which good data are available), slower exits—that is, longer stays—were the predominant force raising the population. The average stay in jail rose from about ten days to more than twenty-four, while annual admissions grew by about 35 percent (from about eight to eleven million). Longer stays appear to be due mainly to more inmates awaiting trial. The proportion of convicted inmates in jail on an average night fell from 47 percent to 37 percent.[25]

For state prisons, the opposite appears to be true: faster entries were generally a more powerful force than slower exits. But the story depends on which crime is being studied and in which decade.

Almost uniformly, however, greater police efficiency in solving crimes contributed almost nothing to the rise in prison population. For each of the index crimes, the ratio of arrests to reported crime has been essentially constant, at least since 1980.[26] Since reported index crime fell after 1990, the number of index crime arrestees fell in tandem. If you looked only at index crime arrestees, you would have expected prison population to have fallen after 1990.

But that is not what happened, for at least two reasons. First, drug arrests rose substantially; arrests per capita in 2009 were more than twice arrests per capita in 1980. Second, for all crimes, prison commitments per arrest rose substantially after 1980. Between 1980 and 2010, for every hundred arrests, the rate of commitment rose from forty-one to ninety-two for murder, from two to nine for drug offenses, from eight to thirty for sexual assault, and from four to fourteen for aggravated assault. Rates of commitment for the other index crimes also rose substantially.[27]

For drug crimes, the increase in commitments per arrest compounded the increase in arrests to produce a large percentage increase in the rate at which drug arrestees entered prison. But this rate started at a very low level. For the index crimes, commitments increased too, but since arrests did not rise, the overall percentage increase was smaller. The main reason why the state prison population rose over the entire period was that people entered prison faster.

What about exits and time served? Mechanically, it appears that time served for drug crimes changed very little. The average time served for drug crimes (between a year and two years) is shorter than the average time served for other crimes, and so by itself the rise in the proportion of prisoners being held for drug crimes should have reduced average time served and increased exit rates.

We should be careful here: we want to concentrate on exit rates—the proportion of prisoners who leave each year—not on time served, although the two concepts are obviously connected. The reason is that with state prisoners we cannot know much about time served because a substantial number of prisoners are serving very long sentences; 15.2 percent of newly sentenced entering prisoners for violent crimes carried sentences over twenty years in 1991, and the corresponding figure was 14.2 percent in 2011.[28] We don't know how long those who are in prison today will eventually serve. However, to explain how and why the prison population has changed, all we need to know is historical exit rates, not what time served will actually be. This distinction is not useful with jails, where time served is measured in days and months, but it is useful with prisons, where time served is sometimes measured in decades.

For the index crimes, exit rates fell noticeably for violent crimes, specifically murder and sexual assaults, especially in the 1990s.[29] For the other index crimes, exit rates were fairly stable, maybe trending down a little. Thus the main driver of the rising state prison population has been faster entries, except for violent crimes in the 1990s. The mechanical effect of slower exit rates has been noticeable but smaller.

Notice the word "mechanical." In a time of rising entry rates, we would expect faster exit rates; and even stable exit rates suggest very strongly that as time passed, identical crimes were being treated more and more harshly.

To be concrete, consider burglary, a serious crime where exit rates appear to have declined modestly from 1984 to 2009.[30] For every one hundred arrests, four people were sent to prison in 1984 and nine were sent to prison in 2009. Suppose the people arrested for burglary were about the same in 2009 as in 1984 in terms of both background characteristics relevant for sentencing and the seriousness of the burglary. Then it is reasonable to suppose that the 4 percent of arrested burglars sent to prison in 1984 committed the most serious burglaries. The next 5 percent—the burglars who would not have been sent to prison in 1984 but were sent to prison in 2009—probably committed less serious burglaries or had less problematic records, at least on average. We would expect, then, that this swing group of 5 percent, when they went to prison in 2009, would serve less time than the hard-core group of 4 percent who went to prison in 1984. Thus, average time for burglars who entered prison in 2009 should be less than that for burglars who entered in 1984, because the former are a less hard-core, less carefully selected group on average.

That is, if sentencing and release policies do not change to become more severe, then exit rates should rise whenever prison entry rises. The fact that exit rates did not rise, even for drug crimes, suggests that across the board, prison time grew, holding constant the severity of the crime. Prisons were flooded with relatively soft-core criminals, but exit rates on average continued to be those that only hard-core criminals had experienced a few decades earlier.

The story is similar for federal prisons, except that the role of drug, weapon, and immigration crimes is much more prominent, and the creation of new federal crimes adds a twist. The rate at which drug, weapon, and immigration cases were brought to U.S. attorneys (the equivalent of arrests) rose substantially, but the rate for other kinds of cases did not. For all types of cases the proportion in which the defendant went to prison rose substantially. Thus, on the front end, the picture is similar to that of state prisons. But for exit rates, the pattern reverses: exit rates of drug, weapon, and immigration cases fell substantially, while those for other types of cases were close to stable. The federal government became more strict in both dimensions—entry and exit—with drugs, weapons, and immigration.[31]

For parole, the numbers rose approximately in tandem with the state prison population, as one would expect.

Finally, for probation, the story is once again primarily one of more entries. Between 1981 (the first year for which reliable data are available) and 2015, the number of entries increased a little less than threefold, and the population on probation increased a little more than threefold.[32] The proportion of probationers being supervised for felony offenses appears to have remained fairly stable at around half for this period. Thus it appears that the number of probationers who were never seriously at risk of going to prison—those charged with misdemeanors—roughly tripled in the period, rising to about two million (almost as large as the entire incarcerated population).

The incarceration rate understandably attracts the greatest public scrutiny, but the reach of the correctional system expanded along other dimensions too, and more widely than most people realize.

Intentions and Results

Why did so many more people get sucked into the correctional system? And why did many stay longer? The official story emphasizes a series of laws that individual states and the federal government adopted, starting around 1968. These legislative actions clearly mattered, but not always in the manner intended.

The earliest—and most subtle—changes were restrictions on the discretion of judges and parole boards. Under what is called the indeterminate sentencing regime, which prevailed in the 1950s and 1960s, judges had considerable discretion in setting sentences. The sentences they set gave wide ranges for time to be served, and parole boards had considerable discretion in determining how long people would stay in prison. The ostensible goals of this regime were to tailor the penalty to the person and the crime, to provide incentives for prisoners to rehabilitate themselves, and to allow rehabilitated prisoners to return home as soon as possible. An unstated goal was to contain the size of the prison population. Prison population per capita stayed in a narrow band during the regime of indeterminate sentences.[33]

Indeterminate sentencing came under attack from both the left and the right in the 1970s. For the left, the problem was that discretion was really a mask for favoritism and discrimination, racial or otherwise. For the right, the problem was that discretion let weak judges and weak parole boards shorten prison spells too much. The result of this unhappiness was a series of laws, both state and federal, that constrained judges and parole boards: grids to tell judges what sentence they should impose, guidelines for parole boards, mandatory minimum sentences for certain crimes, and truth-in-sentencing laws (criminals had to serve a fixed fraction, usually 85 percent, of their sentences before being eligible for parole), for instance. Most states had enacted some or all of these measures by the mid-1980s. The federal government enacted many of them, and went so far as to abolish parole for federal prisons in 1984.

Starting in the 1980s, a series of laws to increase sentence length more directly was adopted. "Three-strikes" laws, in which an individual's third conviction for a serious crime had to be followed by a long sentence with little chance for parole, were the most popular of these. The expectation, roughly, was that people convicted of three serious crimes would die in prison. There were also laws that added penalties for compound events — for instance, committing a crime with a gun carried penalties far beyond those for committing the same crime without a gun. Sentences for many specific crimes, especially those involving drugs, were also increased, and capital punishment returned in many states.

Legislatures also allocated resources to help put more people in prison. The budget of the federal Drug Enforcement Administration grew from $321 million (in 2007 dollars) in 1972 to $2.35 billion in 2007.[34] The number of line prosecutors (lawyers who work in a prosecutor's office and can bring cases) rose from 17,000 in 1970 to 30,000 in 2007, with most of the gain coming after 1990. Meanwhile, real spending for public defenders increased at a much slower rate than felony case filings, and the number of judges also grew at a much smaller rate.[35]

Not all these changes have worked in the way they were supposed to. The major result of determinate sentencing has been greater power for prosecutors. Because judges and parole boards can now influence time served to only a small extent, the key steps in determining prison time are setting the charges and reaching the plea bargain. The prosecutor controls both of these steps. Prosecutors exercise these powers in most jurisdictions without guidelines, without transparency, and without any outside review. Determinate sentencing (helped by the many new possible charges on the books) has not eliminated discretion; it has just changed who exercises it (prosecutors rather than judges and parole boards).

Because discretion remains in the system, prosecutors have been able to determine how other reforms have played out. For instance,

New York State adopted draconian drug control laws in 1973, but the number of people admitted to New York prisons on drug charges barely moved until 1984, when some prosecutors decided to start enforcing those laws.[36] And California prosecutors often got around the unduly harsh punishments imposed by that state's three-strikes law by downgrading charges.[37]

But that does not mean that the legislative changes were meaningless. Instead, the lawmakers created new tools, and when the time came, prosecutors used those tools as they saw fit. The possibility that defendants who did not accept plea deals could end up with much more severe sentences improved the bargaining power of prosecutors. Defendants settled for less, because they avoided more. For instance, defendants who ended up with longer sentences because of truth-in-sentencing laws were mainly those who pleaded to lesser crimes but who could have been sentenced to crimes that these laws covered.[38]

Thus, the effect of the laws was not so much that people who committed the particular crimes they spotlighted were punished more severely, but that people who committed crimes that might plausibly be portrayed as those crimes were punished more reliably and harshly. The laws frightened those people, and they were induced to plead guilty to lesser crimes. Laws that were designed primarily to increase the time served of a small number of people who were already going to prison instead cast a wide shadow of fear, and so increased the number of people entering both prison and probation. The laws were advertised as a way to concentrate extremely severe punishment on a narrow set of targets; instead, they spread more modest punishment over a much larger population.[39]

Why did lawmakers give prosecutors these tools? And why did prosecutors decide to use the tools in the manner that they did? These are really challenging historical questions for which we do not have complete answers.

The proximate answer is that a large proportion of voters responded favorably to politicians who could promise credibly to get tough on crime, and unfavorably to those who were seen as soft. In the late 1970s and early 1980s, over 80 percent of both whites and blacks thought that their local courts were not harsh enough when dealing with criminals. Even in 2014, after peak incarceration rates had been reached, 59 percent of whites, 53 percent of Hispanics, and 51 percent of blacks felt this way.[40]

These survey results suggest a level of uniformity across groups, but mask substantial differences in attitudes about just how much harsher the system should have been, or which specific policies were favored. The push for a more punitive justice system was fueled, in part, by racial attitudes, and much of the rhetoric was tinged with racial overtones. According to the National Research Council, "A sizable body of research supports the thesis that public opinion on crime and punishment is highly racialized. Whites tend to associate crime and violence with being black and are more likely than blacks to support harsh penal policies. Whites who harbor racial resentments are especially likely to endorse tougher penal policies and to reject claims that the criminal justice system discriminates against blacks. Blacks are much more likely than whites to say the criminal justice system is racially biased and much less likely to endorse capital punishment and other tougher sanctions."[41]

These sentiments were galvanized politically in the wake of the civil rights movement, according to many historians, and southern politicians tried to reframe "the civil rights movement as a law-and-order issue," rather than an issue of race.[42] Shortly thereafter, Richard Nixon's Republican Party adopted "law and order" as the key element of its southern strategy, which attempted (successfully) to win the allegiance of formerly Democratic whites who saw that party's support of civil rights legislation as a betrayal. "Law and order" was a way of wrapping Martin Luther King Jr.'s philosophy of civil disobedience, the urban riots, and routine index crime into a single thought. As Michelle Alexander puts it: "Proponents of racial hierarchy found they could install a new racial caste system without violating the law or the new limits of acceptable political discourse, by demanding 'law and order' rather than 'segregation forever.'"[43]

Moreover, tough-on-drugs policies were added to this mix because crime was traditionally a state and local issue. National politicians needed something to demonstrate the resolve of the federal government, and drugs, where the federal government had long played a role, gave them the opportunity they were looking for.[44]

However, the shift toward a more punitive criminal justice system cannot be understood solely as a means, conscious or unconscious, for disgruntled whites to try to undo the successes of the civil rights movement. Three facts get in the way of this simple story.

First, crime rates across all major categories were rising sharply in the 1960s and 1970s. The 1960s, moreover, were a time of falling prison populations, even though arrests were on the rise.[45] It is not surprising that more punitive policies would be implemented in response to a crime wave.

But rising crime is only a small piece of the story of why criminal justice became more punitive. The link between actual crime and public opinion is very weak. Consider the following: by 2016, index crime in the United States had been declining for almost a quarter of a century, and the decline had been uninterrupted except for occasional minor blips. Yet during this long decline in crime, around two-thirds of Americans almost always believed that crime was going up.

According to polling by Gallup on the question: "Is there more crime in the US than there was a year ago?" only in 2000 and 2001 did a majority of people not think that crime was rising.[46]

The second fact is that many African Americans, undoubtedly a majority on many specific issues, supported harsher punishment. We have already seen the polling data on opinion about local courts. Consider James Forman's account of what he found in the archives of the Washington, DC, city council:

> Letters from black citizens, neighborhood association newsletters, and the pages of the black press from the last forty years describe astonishing levels of pain, fear, and anger. In 1968, a group of black nationalists in DC called drug dealers "black-face traitors of our people who sell dope to our young boys and girls and make whores and thieves of them." A decade later, a black DC neighborhood association circulated a flyer promoting ways to defend homes from break-ins: the list included guard dogs, security alarms, wild snakes, and . . . fishhooks strung around doors and windows to puncture the flesh of would-be burglars. By the 1980s and 1990s, the files of DC council members were crammed with letters from scared constituents, complaining that "we feel like prisoners in our homes, strangers on our own streets," and begging for more police action.[47]

Between 1980 and 1997, when Washington began to hand over its sentenced felons to the federal government, elected officials in Washington were almost all black, reflecting the majority of the electorate. During this time, its per capita number of sentenced prisoners rose almost four times faster than the rate at which the per capita number of sentenced prisoners was rising nationally.[48]

Third, white incarceration rates also rose sharply, and by 2011, white Americans were incarcerated at a rate exceeding the overall incarceration rate of all other OECD countries. This does not accord well with the idea that mass incarceration was an attempt to recover any loss of white privilege attributed to the civil rights movement.

These three considerations suggest that no straightforward account of the rise in mass incarceration is adequate. The move to greater incarceration was not a result of a single decision or even a small set of identifiable decisions made around 1970. Instead, it was a continuing series of actions by legislators and prosecutors that unfolded over a generation.

It was not until 1994 that Congress passed the Violent Crime Control and Law Enforcement Act; it added sixty new death penalty offenses, eliminated funding for prisoners taking college courses, brought a three-strikes law to the federal system, created fifty new federal offenses, and set aside $8.7 billion for prison construction by states that passed truth-in-sentencing laws. And it was only after 2007 that the number of people entering prisons started to go down.[49] Babies born at the time of the March on Washington were in their thirties when the Violent Crime Control Act was passed, and in their forties when the rate of admission to prison finally turned around.

These historical and empirical realities suggest that we have to look at a series of questions—not just why the trend began but why it continued for so long. The beginning of the mass incarceration regime, which has received the most attention, is in some ways the easiest part to explain. It seems like an unusual moment of consensus in American history. The indeterminate sentencing regime of the 1960s was arbitrary, opaque, and probably discriminatory, but also incapable of handling the rise in crime, especially in urban neighborhoods. Astonishing as it may seem, segregationists, a large part of the black community, and legal scholars managed to simultaneously agree on the need for change and the direction of change. Sometimes people who disagree violently about one thing happen to have a common interest in something else. It is not at all surprising that when these three groups agreed on something, it began to happen.

Nor is it surprising that the agreed-upon change began to produce unintended consequences—the ascendancy of prosecutors, the removal of any discretionary apparatus to constrain prison population growth, the rise in prison commitments and in probation as defendants sought insurance against harsher penalties, and a white incarceration rate that matched that of Belarus.

The major puzzle about the rise of mass incarceration is not that the process started but that it continued for so long and hence drove incarceration so high. It did not just correct the excesses of the 1960s; it obliterated any resemblance to the American past or to any other comparable nation. Even after crime had been falling for fifteen years, prison admissions were still going up.

Persistence, then, is the big puzzle. To tackle this puzzle, we have to step back and address the very basic question of why people are incarcerated at all.

Retribution and Consequentialism

To think about why this long rise in incarceration persisted and whether it pushed the country to levels beyond anything that might be considered proper, we have to understand why governments would ever want to punish any of their citizens. We also look at how attempts to administer a criminal justice system according to these principles can go awry.

Philosophers and legal scholars generally give two kinds of answers to this question, although the answers come in many shades and sometimes blend together. The first is retributivism: people who commit serious crimes deserve proportionate punishment, and it is intrinsically good that they be legitimately punished. The other is consequentialism: people should be punished if and only if the beneficial consequences of the punishment are large enough to offset its costs, both to the government and to the people punished. The purportedly beneficial consequences are incapacitation (people in prison usually cannot commit crimes against people outside), deterrence (the punishment of some leads others to think that they are likely to be punished if they commit crimes), and rehabilitation (people will emerge from prisons reformed in ways that lead them to commit fewer crimes). Retributivism is backward-looking (people should be punished because of what they did in the past), while consequentialism is forward-looking (people should be punished because of what they and others might do in the future).

Retributive theories of punishment hold that certain acts are so terrible that they cry out for punishment. Punishing the perpetrators and censuring them is a way of undoing some of the evil of the crime. Every crime has an appropriate and deserved punishment attached to it that depends on the crime's severity. Punishing the perpetrator either more or less harshly than that is unjust (as is punishing someone who has not committed a crime in this sense), but the just punishment that the perpetrator receives is not seen as a cost to society. On the contrary, it is viewed as a benefit.

In retributive theory, not every act with harmful consequences requires punishment and censure, and not every prohibited act rises to the level of a crime. A retributive government, for instance, can decide that levying library fines for overdue books and denying driver's licenses to the visually impaired are wise policies without judging that either delinquent borrowers or the near-blind are criminals who should be censured and whose suffering as a result of these policies can be either ignored or exulted in. When thinking about these policies, the hardships imposed on delinquent borrowers and the visually impaired are viewed as costs to society, but the hardships imposed on burglars and thieves are a benefit. A retributive theory, then, has to be explicit about what makes burglary and larceny different from delinquency in the return of library books.

A consequentialist theory, by contrast, makes no qualitative distinction between overdue library books and burglary; the difference is simply one of degree. Some activities impose costs on the rest of society, and sometimes the cheapest and most effective way of discouraging those activities is to threaten their perpetrators with punishment. Unfortunately, the threat sometimes fails and people continue to engage in the activity. The government must then carry out its threat to maintain credibility. For a consequentialist, the sufferings of both delinquent borrowers and burglars are a cost, not a benefit, and must be accounted for as such when evaluating policies. Moreover, the losses that must be considered include not only the fines that actual delinquent borrowers pay but also the pleasure that deterred would-be delinquent borrowers miss out on when they cannot finish the book and find out how the story ends. Similarly, for strict consequentialists, the costs of laws against burglary include the disutility imposed on deterred offenders who refrain from acquiring the property of others.

Retribution and consequentialism do not exhaust all possible theories of punishment, but it is important to note that current practices in the United States accord with neither. Retribution does not countenance locking people up because the authorities think that they might commit a serious crime—as we do now when people are incarcerated for possession of burglary tools, for instance—or extending the prison sentences of those who are thought to be likely to recidivate. Strict consequentialism requires that we think about burglars the same way we think about delinquent borrowers, but almost nobody does.

Among those who think seriously about reasons for punishment, retributivism is probably the dominant theme. Criminal trials are backward-looking, not forward-looking, and most people would recoil from executing an innocent person even if such an act would save lives in the aggregate, for instance by deterring others from killing. Retributivism may sound like revenge to some people, but it is not. As George Fletcher puts it, retribution "is not to be identified with vengeance or revenge, any more than love is to be identified with lust."[50]

Two weaknesses in retributivism, however, can make it hard to apply in twenty-first-century America.

The first weakness is that retributivism has no obvious way of specifying the appropriate punishment for each crime—no principles to match crimes with times, in the words of the *Baretta* theme song. There is some sense about relative punishments—murder should be punished more harshly than theft—but even that is imprecise. Should the punishments for murder be ten times or a thousand times as harsh as those for larceny?

Note that we are talking about the total punishment for various crimes, not just the number of months in prison. Prison conditions differ from state to state and within states, and from establishment to establishment. Current practice also prescribes a wide array of post-prison punishments: periods of parole supervision, fines, loss of voting rights, and prohibition from practicing certain occupations, from receiving certain government benefits, and from living in certain neighborhoods. Conditions of probation also differ. Punishments like these are not inconsistent with retributivism, but they make the job of specifying what is appropriate even more daunting.

The second weakness is that the public disregard of the criminal's well-being can be misinterpreted and lead observers astray. The problem is disentangling the criminal from the crime.

Retributivism argues only that the criminal's suffering caused by appropriate punishment for an actual crime can be disregarded. Indeed, philosophers are clear that only deliberate punishment for the sake of retribution has ethical merit. A wrongdoer who is afflicted with a serious disease after committing a crime should be punished just as much as one who is not afflicted, and a medical intervention that would have prevented the wrongdoer's disease is just as valuable as an intervention that would have prevented an innocent person's disease.[51]

But the temptation is great to sidestep this philosophical subtlety and attach the disregard to the criminal instead of the crime. So if, for instance, prisoners have to subsidize the state government by paying exorbitant prices for phone calls in addition to serving appropriate sentences for their crimes, the temptation is to ignore the costs to prisoners in a cost-benefit analysis of the phone scheme. After all, it is often said, they wouldn't have to pay the phone bills if they didn't do the crime, and they chose to do the crime.[52]

This tendency to conflate the criminal with the crime is exacerbated in the United States by the history of race. Historically, many sufferings of some groups of people have not been seen as serious social costs—witness, for instance, the Tuskegee experiment and Japanese internment during World War II. In a society with a history of ignoring the sufferings of certain groups of people, any costs imposed on a convict—regardless of whether they arise from carefully calibrated punishments for a specific crime—can come to be seen as justified by retribution.

These two factors—the indeterminacy of just punishment, and the conflation of the criminal with the crime—imply that the maintenance of a strict retributive regime in the United States today would be very challenging.

Next consider consequentialism. The ideas of consequentialism are also common in discussions of incarceration. If you ask an ordinary person why the government punishes criminals, she may very well say that if we didn't do this, crime would be rampant. Still, implementing punishments based solely on consequentialism in the United States today would also face some serious problems.

The first difficulty is that the correct punishments are hard to calculate because they rely on forecasts of possible futures. A consequentialist judge deciding whether to sentence someone to six months in prison or twelve months of probation would have to forecast how the world would evolve in both scenarios, and decide in which scenario expected social welfare was greater. This calculation is beyond the ability of any statistician. The same sort of problem would confront a prosecutor, or a legislator setting prescribed standards for different crimes.

Consequentialists also have to pick winners and losers, while retributivists do not. Any decision a consequentialist judge, prosecutor, or legislator makes will make some people better off (maybe because future crimes against them are averted) and some people worse off (maybe because they or their family members go to prison). Implicitly they have to decide whose future well-being matters more, and the changes in well-being at stake can be substantial.

Thus, a consequentialist regime faces many of the same temptations and dangers that a retributive regime faces.

Like almost all systems in the world, the American criminal justice system is neither purely retributive nor purely consequentialist. Instead, it contains elements of both approaches. That's not logically impossible. For instance, most retributivists consider retributive punishment only one of many desirable goals; if mercy is another important goal, then shortening a sentence below the retributive length for the sake of mercy could sometimes be a sensible compromise between these goals. Shortening prison spells through parole as a way of maintaining order in prisons could be a similar compromise.

But in two areas, retributivism seems to allow no compromise: the prohibitions on knowingly punishing the innocent, and on punishing the guilty more than the appropriate amount. The prohibition of "cruel and unusual punishment" codified in the Eighth Amendment to the U.S. Constitution—and previously in the 1689 English Bill of Rights—reflects the latter concern. Consequentialist reasons can reduce punishments, it seems, but not increase them.

Retributivism, however, does not prohibit governments from taking adverse actions against innocent citizens; it prohibits only punishment. Governments can levy taxes on innocent people, prohibit drivers from parking near hydrants, require borrowers to return library books within two weeks, and deny driver's licenses to the visually impaired, for instance. These are merely adverse actions. What makes adverse actions different from punishment? Two things: they carry no censure, and the suffering these actions cause is an argument against them, not an argument for them. So in a mixed system, governments could take adverse actions against criminals, in addition to the retribution-appropriate punishment, but these adverse actions could not carry censure, and the suffering that they cause would be a cost.

A mixed system is thus logically possible. Not everyone agrees that a mixed system is a good idea—some libertarians, for instance, would want a purely retributive system—but combining elements of retribution (backward-looking trials) and consequentialism (forward-looking sentencing and parole) can make sense only as a mixed system. But a mixed system combines and compounds the weaknesses of its two constituent parts.

Consider the first problem with retributive punishments—there is no way of figuring out what they should be in absolute terms. A pure retributive system has the feature that judges could maintain relative (if not absolute) punishments by observing other sentences, but this feature disappears in a mixed system.

To see why, consider a criminal who is convicted of robbery, sentenced to five years, and paroled in four. In a retributive system we can learn from this that the retributive punishment for robbery is five years in prison. But in a mixed regime we can learn nothing about the retributive punishment for robbery: perhaps it is ten years but shortened to four for the sake of the public budget, mercy, and order in prisons. Perhaps it is three years but lengthened to four to incapacitate a criminal. Or perhaps it is just five years. In a mixed regime, retributive punishments are even more uncertain.

A mixed system also compounds the problem of conflating the crime and the criminal. In a mixed system, prisoners sometimes suffer for retributive reasons and sometimes for consequentialist reasons. The former carries censure and is not a social cost, while the latter is the opposite. But there is no good way of telling which suffering is retributive and which is consequential. Hence the temptation to treat everything as if it were retributive—not a social cost but carrying censure—is very great.

Should punishments have become harsher when the crime wave started in the 1960s? Should they have become more lenient (or at least stopped becoming harsher) when crime started to fall in the 1990s?

For consequentialist punishments, the answer is yes in both cases. Retributive punishments should not change. To see why consequentialist punishment should change over time, suppose crime is high: many people are committing many crimes when they are not in prison because certain norms have broken down or police departments are depleted. Then the incapacitation benefits of locking up a criminal for a year are high, because he would have committed many crimes in a year if he were free. The deterrence benefits are also great, since many would-be criminals can see the punishment and adjust their expectations of the costs of offending. The social cost is no greater, and so when crime is high, consequentialist punishments should be harsh.

By the same token, punishment should have become more lenient after 1990. But a system that mixes retributivism with consequentialism has a hard time reversing itself when crime falls. Some of the problem stems from the impossibility of observing retributivist punishment separately from consequentialist punishment. Because there is no absolute standard anyone can point to for retributivist punishment, after a while "normal punishment"—whatever people get used to—starts looking like appropriate retributivist punishment. If the usual punishment for armed robbery in Alabama is ten years, and has been for a while, then an eight-year sentence will look excessively lenient to many Alabamans, even if the usual sentence in France now is four years and the usual sentence in Alabama in 1965 was six years. Ten years, for Alabamans, is the "time that goes with the crime." Even if the usual sentence in Alabama was lengthened for consequentialist reasons (which is probably why it was lengthened), few people make the distinction now, and no one can say independently what the retributivist punishment would be. The same logic applies to changes on the margin between sentences and probation.

Reductions in sentence harshness, then, are likely to generate opposition. On the other hand, the creep of retribution reduces the legitimacy of the arguments that proponents of leniency can make. Those arguments are primarily consequentialist: harsh punishment imposes costs on prisoners and their families that are greater than the crime reduction benefits that it brings. If the sentences are deserved on retributivist grounds, then this suffering can and must be ignored ("they did the crime so they must do the time"). Retributivist creep makes it easy for the opponents of leniency to ignore the proponents.

Retributivism constrains family, friends, and prisoners from lobbying for leniency in another way too. Retributive punishment carries censure with it. Being a prisoner, in the retributive view, is shameful, and friends and relatives of prisoners often face guilt by association. People who are stigmatized are often reluctant to march in the streets, testify before councils and committees, go on talk shows, and write letters to the media. By contrast, those who lobby for harsher punishments, including crime victims, are not constrained by shame.

Another reason why the harsh punishments that crime waves create are difficult to reverse is that the public has a hard time learning that crime is falling. We have already seen that for a quarter century after crime started to fall in the 1990s, a majority of Americans still believed that it was going up.

The incentives faced by major criminal justice actors such as prosecutors, judges, and parole boards are yet another reason why the process of re-setting punishment after the end of a crime wave is slow. These actors have incentives to err on the side of strictness, not on the side of leniency. A parole board that keeps someone in prison for an extra year or two may do him great harm but will not get into trouble for doing so; a parole board that releases a prisoner who commits a horrendous crime faces serious scrutiny and condemnation. A drop in crime creates a period of uncertainty, so these criminal justice actors will react more slowly to a drop in crime than to a rise in crime.

Hence there are many, mainly nonracial, reasons why the trend toward greater punishment did not reverse immediately in the 1990s. These reasons apply in most developed countries, since mixing retributivism and consequentialism is common. These countries have also experienced crime waves. But no other country ever went on a punishment binge as long and powerful as the United States did. Something peculiarly American must have been at work.

Racial Stigma

The last, and probably the most distinctive, piece in this puzzle is stigma, which we have discussed in earlier chapters.

One effect of racial stigma is that the dispropotionately black prison population is viewed as an unsurprising occurrence (like a snowstorm in New York in February), not a shocking condition that demands immediate redress (like a plane door that opens in midflight). Glenn Loury makes this point in *The Anatomy of Racial Inequality:*

> Dramatic racial disparity in imprisonment rates does not occasion more public angst . . . because this circumstance does not strike the typical American observer at the cognitive level as being counterintuitive. . . . It can be accounted for by a narrative line attributing the outcome to the inadequacies of the persons who suffer the condition, not to any as yet undiscovered problems with our own social organization. . . . If there were a comparable number of young European-American men on beer-drinking binges, or anorexic teenage girls starving themselves to death, and if these were situations in which the same degree of human suffering was engendered as is being produced in this case, it would occasion a profound reflection about what had gone wrong, not only with THEM, but also with US.[53]

The effects of stigma are measurable. The psychologists Rebecca Hetey and Jennifer Eberhardt examined how attitudes toward harsh sentencing vary based on perceptions of the degree to which punishment involves racial disparities. In one experiment, subjects in California were shown a sequence of mug shots of actual prisoners but exposed to different ratios of black to white faces: 25 percent of prisoners were black in one treatment and 45 percent in the other. They were then asked to rate the punitiveness of the California three-strikes sentencing law, which at that time mandated a sentence of twenty-five years to life for anyone convicted of a felony if they already had two prior convictions for serious felonies. Finally, they were given the opportunity to sign a petition in support of an amendment to the law that would require the third felony to also be serious or violent. Signed petitions were actually delivered to the attorney general to be counted, and the amendment did in fact pass in 2012.

There were dramatic differences across treatments in the willingness of subjects to sign the petition: more than half signed in the less-black treatment (where three-quarters of faces were white), but just 27 percent signed in the more-black treatment.[54]

In a related experiment, New York City residents were given information about the racial composition of the inmate population (40 percent of prisoners were black in one treatment, and 60 percent in another). They were then informed about a recent ruling finding the city's stop-and-frisk policy unconstitutional, surveyed about crime concerns in the wake of the ruling, and offered the opportunity to sign a petition in support of ending the program. Those who received information about a higher black inmate population were significantly less likely to sign the petition, and expressed considerably greater concerns about crime in the wake of the ruling. The authors concluded that "exposing people to extreme racial disparities in the prison population heightened their fear of crime and increased acceptance of the very policies that lead to those disparities."[55]

In our narrative of American incarceration, stigma operated at several stages, and possibly on both retributive and consequentialist arguments. With consequentialist arguments, the connection is straightforward. Recall that consequentialism has to weigh benefits and costs to different people. To the extent that those who suffer from tougher policies are stigmatized, these sufferings are less salient and so count for less in public discussions than the benefits of lower crime that are spread more broadly. Similarly, a crime-fighting strategy that relies on more and better-trained police who deter crime by their presence is paid for almost entirely by taxpayers, but a large part of the costs of a crime-fighting policy that relies on prisons is paid for by stigmatized people, whose sufferings matter less in public discussions than those of taxpayers. Thus stigma made punitive policies attractive when crime rose.

When crime fell, retribution interacted with stigma to keep incarceration rising. As the public got used to the harsh sentences put in place during the crime wave, they began to appear normal and retributively just. To question them would have required a step back and some historical perspective, in light of which they could be seen as aberrations. This is precisely the sort of cognitive effort that stigma prevents. So retributivism and stigma reinforce each other.

While the sharp increase in incarceration rates was felt with disproportionate force in black communities, it also caused white incarceration rates to rise to levels never before seen in democratic countries. Why did this not ignite moral outrage? We offer three possible reasons.

Since many aspects of the criminal justice system are required to be color-blind, whites had to be formally subjected to the same punishment standards imposed on blacks and Hispanics. The robbery sentence that seemed just for a black offender also had to be imposed on a white one, even if it was very different from sentences in the rest of the world. People do not seem to have an independent sense of what proportion of a society should be incarcerated under a just system, and comparisons of contemporary white incarceration with Europe, Canada, or the 1960s in the United States have seldom been made.

In his book *Just Mercy*, Bryan Stevenson discusses the execution in 1944 of George Stinney, a fourteen-year-old black boy falsely accused of killing two girls and convicted by an all-white jury after a mockery of a trial. Five feet two inches tall and weighing just ninety-two pounds, Stinney was too small for the electric chair and had to sit on a Bible so that electrodes could be attached to his slender frame. Stevenson uses this case to make the following point:

The Stinney execution was horrific and heartbreaking, but it reflected the racial politics of the South more than the way children accused of crimes were generally treated. It was an example of how policies and norms once directed exclusively at controlling and punishing the black population have filtered their way into our general criminal justice system. By the late 1980s and early 1990s, the politics of fear and anger sweeping the country and fueling mass incarceration was turning its attention to children.[56]

This process of a gradually increasing scope is part of the explanation for the fact that even white incarceration rates in the United States now lie well above international norms. Paul Butler argues that the "most problematic practices of American criminal justice . . . are best understood as measures originally intended for African American men."[57] But original intentions notwithstanding, these practices have inevitably drawn other communities into their orbit. Over the first decade of this century, for instance, the incarceration rate for white women rose by a staggering 50 percent, even as the corresponding rate for black women was declining.[58]

The second reason is less direct. As Khalil Muhammad documents in depth in *The Condemnation of Blackness*, the association of criminality with racial essentialism dates back to at least the 1890 census in the United States. This sentiment can lead some prosecutors and parts of the public to view white offenders as traitors to the race, damaging its reputation, and thus deserving of especially harsh punishment.[59] In fact, some of the longest sentences for drug crimes are now handed down in rural and predominantly white counties.[60]

Third, notice that the public opinion experiments manipulated white opinion about prison reform by changing the proportions of whites and blacks among prisoners, not by changing the number of white prisoners or the incarceration rate of whites. The public, most of which has little connection with prisoners, may infer from the overwhelming proportion of blacks in prisons and jails that the number of whites in prisons and jails is small (which it is, relative to the white population of the United States but not to the prison populations of other prosperous and democratic nations). It is conceivable that the response would have been quite different if the experimenters had provided information about the incarceration rate of American whites relative to, say, the incarceration rate in Canada.

Counting the Costs

Mass incarceration matters. The costs are very large, even if one does not account for the suffering of convicted prisoners. Many different groups in society bear these costs.

Taxpayers pay tens of billions of dollars to operate correctional institutions, plus several billion more for food stamps, public assistance, and foster care for the families of prisoners who have lost income and support. In 2007, more than half of all prisoners had minor children.[61] For affected families, parental incarceration causes increases in teenage crime, pregnancy, and unemployment.[62]

There are tens of thousands of wrongly convicted prisoners incarcerated at any point in time, and several hundred thousand jail inmates, many of whom have not been convicted of anything.[63] There is no retributive justification for their detention (though there may be consequentialist reasons for it).

Many prisoners are being held for pretextual crimes, activities that probably should not be crimes, and activities that are not so heinous that they call for retribution. For instance, over 300,000 prisoners were held on drug charges in 2015 in state and federal prisons.[64] There may be consequentialist reasons to imprison these people, but nothing about the crimes seems to call for retribution.

People who have served their time in prison but remain on sex offender registries face difficulties in housing, employment, and maintaining normal relationships. Around 800,000 people were on sex offender registries in 2017, including about 1 percent of black men.[65]

Former prisoners are noticeably less likely to be employed because of their prison experience.[66] These losses cannot be considered retributive on standard theory because punishment should be administered by the state, not by vigilantes or employers. Even if employers are engaged in strategic rather than prejudiced discrimination, the costs that their behavior imposes on former prisoners cannot be ignored.

All these costs, moreover, assume that current sentencing practices in the United States are retributively appropriate. If, on the contrary, we were to assume that American sentencing practices in 1972, or practices in Western Europe today, were the retributive norm, then we would find that over 1.5 million people were incarcerated for consequentialist reasons, and so their hardships would be a social cost, too.

Thus the social costs of mass incarceration are great, however you want to handle the controversial interpretations. The benefits, on the other hand, are meager at currently prevailing levels of incarceration. Magnus Lofstrom and Steven Raphael summarize the basic picture as follows: "There is fairly strong evidence . . . that incarceration can have sizeable effects in reducing crime, operating largely through physical incapacitation. These effects, however, diminish with scale. . . . While increases in incarceration during the 1980s likely suppressed peak crime rates in the 1990s, the decline in crime since that time corresponds to a period of rapid growth in incarceration levels for which there is little evidence of an appreciable impact on crime."[67]

This skepticism about the crime-reducing effect of additional prisoners beyond the 1990 level has received some confirmation from prison reform in California. Forced by federal court rulings and a tight state budget, California reduced its prison population by 13 percent in 2011. This reduction was offset in part by a rise in jail population, but overall the reform cut the incarcerated population back to the levels of the early 1990s. The reform resulted in no noticeable change in violent crime in California, relative to the trend in other states, and only a small increase in property crime—about 1.2 property crimes per prisoner-year, mainly motor vehicle thefts.[68]

Most of this work looks at the immediate effects of incarceration on crime, but there are long-term effects too. Prison changes people. It could deter them from future crimes, or it could harden them, teach them how to be more effective criminals, and turn them into jobless pariahs whose only friends are ex-convicts. The older empirical work generally showed that incarceration was mildly criminogenic.[69] Two recent papers examining counties with large minority populations—Harris County, Texas, and Cook County, Illinois—have found substantial criminogenic effects, so large that they offset any reduction in crime while in prison.[70]

In short, the rise in mass incarceration since around 1990 has been a disaster, not only for black and Hispanic Americans but also for large numbers of whites. And the current political climate gives no reassurance that the rise in incarceration will not resume. Stereotypes and stigma have enormous material consequences.

chapter 12

JUSTICE

To this point, we have dealt primarily with the world as it happens to be. We conclude by asking how it could be made better.

Generalized Aggression

There is a paradox in the working of the American criminal justice system, which is harsh beyond measure in some respects and yet offers little protection against violent crime in the most afflicted communities. As Jill Leovy notes in *Ghettoside,* "The perceived harshness of American criminal justice and its fundamental weakness are in reality two sides of a coin, the former a kind of poor compensation for the latter. . . . It hauls masses of black men through its machinery but fails to protect them from bodily injury and death. It is at once oppressive and inadequate."[1]

As we observed in Chapter 3, if people can be killed with impunity, they have an incentive to kill preemptively. Those who are feared thus have good reason to fear, and those who are afraid are also dangerous. Breaking this cycle of cascading fear requires increasing clearance rates for violent crimes. To quote Leovy again, "Where the criminal justice system fails to respond vigorously to violent injury and death, homicide becomes endemic."[2]

Low clearance rates for serious offenses with black victims have been pervasive in American history. As Randall Kennedy writes:

"Deliberately withholding protection against criminality (or conduct that should be deemed criminal) is one of the most destructive forms of oppression that has been visited upon African-Americans."[3] This "racially selective under-protection" itself arises, in part, because witnesses and even victims are deeply reluctant to cooperate with law enforcement officials:

> The communities most in need of police protection are also those in which many residents view police with the most ambivalence, much of which stems from a recognition that color counts as a mark of suspicion relied upon as a predicate for action—stopping, questioning, patting down, arresting, beating, and so forth. This causes people who might otherwise be of assistance to police to avoid them, to decline to cooperate with police investigations, to assume bad faith or dishonesty on the part of police officers, and to teach others that such reactions are prudent lessons of survival on the streets.[4]

Some have argued that harsh policing tactics are a necessary component of an effective policing strategy in high-crime areas, and that in the absence of such strategies the degree of underprotection would be even more severe.[5] But, as we saw in Chapter 6, recent estimates indicate that the majority of the more than half-million annual stops in New York City during the peak years of the stop-and-frisk program were predictably unproductive—most weapons could have been recovered with a much smaller but more carefully targeted use of the policy.[6] And indeed, the city's murder rate has fallen to levels not seen since the 1950s, even as the incidence of street stops has dropped to less than 2 percent of peak rates.[7]

Similar trends are evident in Oakland, where a concerted effort to prevent retaliatory killings and improve community relations appears to be paying dividends in greater witness cooperation and lower rates of violent crime.[8] Whether such strategies can be successfully adapted to conditions in Baltimore or St. Louis, where murder rates remain close to historical highs, remains to be seen.

The National Academy of Sciences recently reviewed much of the literature on proactive policing and reached some conclusions about what works.

One of the most important findings is negative: we really don't have any good evidence on whether any specific strategy reduces crime on a citywide basis, and we know very little about long-run impacts. But we do know several strategies that reduce crime in a neighborhood in the short run, and most of them either do not harm or somewhat improve community attitudes towards the police.

None of these effective policies involve generalized aggression: "Policing programs relying on a generalized approach to misdemeanor arrests . . . have not shown evidence of effectiveness. This caveat, combined with research evidence that documents negative individual outcomes for people who are the subject of aggressive police enforcement efforts, even in the absence of clear causal interpretation, should lead police executives to exercise caution in adopting generalized, aggressive enforcement tactics."[9]

What are these effective strategies? They include "situational crime prevention measures, such as repairing fences, installing or improving lighting, and erecting road barriers . . . conducting community surveys and other forms of citizen outreach . . . improving recreational opportunities for youth . . . code enforcement, aesthetic community improvements . . . and nuisance abatement" as components of a suite of proactive policing initiatives that have been found to improve community relations while modestly reducing crime.[10]

In addition, hot spots policing and closed circuit television reduce crime in many studies, rarely harm community satisfaction, and sometimes improve it. Careful and targeted stops focused on high-risk repeat offenders also reduce crime. Finally, focused deterrence—programs like Operation Ceasefire that target groups of repeat offenders or gang members and blend strict law enforcement, community mobilization, and social services—also reduces street crime, possibly even in the long run.

In Chapter 4, we discussed recent work on the concentration of murder in social space, which allows individuals at high risk of homicide involvement to be identified with considerable precision. One implication of this research, as the authors note, is that we ought not to adopt "sweeping policies and practices based purely on categorical distinctions such as race and ethnicity and, instead, opt for interventions and policies that consider the observable risky behavior of individuals."[11]

Dignitarian Insults

The motto of the New York Police Department, emblazoned on its patrol cars, is "CPR—Courtesy, Professionalism, Respect." These are worthy goals, and a great deal can be achieved by pursuing them vigorously and consistently, not just in New York but across all jurisdictions. There is little cost in treating even suspected felons with the deference that one would accord a superior officer, apologizing for taking up their time, and using respectful salutations such as "Sir" or "Ma'am." If they are guilty of an offense, the courts will assign blame and inflict punishment; nothing is gained by unnecessary roughness at the hands of an officer.

It is essential that the training of officers include ample attention to the role that police have played historically in enforcing discriminatory laws. To quote Randall Kennedy again:

For a long time, criminal law—not simply the biased administration of law but the law itself—was the enemy of African-Americans. In many places, for several generations, it was a crime for blacks to learn to read, to flee enslavement, or to defend themselves, their families, or their friends from physical abuse. It was a crime, in sum, for blacks to do all sorts of things deemed to be permissible or admirable when done by others.[12]

This is part of the "historical mistreatment of communities of color" and resulting "cycle of mistrust" that Terrence Cunningham, president of the International Association of Chiefs of Police, acknowledged and apologized for in a 2016 speech.[13] All of this can be done without sacrificing crime-fighting ability.

In addition, police departments must put a stop to what the political philosopher Ajume Wingo has called "dignitarian insults." An extreme case of such this occurred following the fatal shooting of Michael Brown by Darren Wilson in Ferguson, which Wingo describes as follows:

The shooting itself does not stand out from other police shootings of young unarmed black men. But perhaps the reason for the movement that grew up after it was the assault on Mr. Brown's dignity as his dead body lay unattended for hours, at first out in the open and only later partially draped with a white cloth. His body was denied that elementary privacy that he is entitled to as a member of a modern dignitarian democratic society . . . it wasn't the shooting so much as the state's indifference to the shooting that set BLM into motion.[14]

Tangible Steps

In addition to changes in attitude and affect, and using targeted rather than generalized strategies, there are some tangible steps involving changes in policies and laws that could bring us closer to a more just society.

First, murder clearance rates should be made public. Police departments and the officials who oversee them will face stronger incentives to bring killers to justice if the public can keep track of their performance on this dimension. For large departments—those that serve a population of over 200,000, say—annual publication should be the rule, while for smaller departments an aggregate of several years should be published (the number of murders has to be large enough for the variation to be meaningful). Small departments—with, say, fewer than ten murders per decade—should probably be exempt, but they are also probably too small to have specialized homicide detectives in any case. Defining clearance rates precisely is not easy—for example, is a murder with multiple offenders cleared when only one of them is arrested? how do you treat murders committed in one year and solved in another? Nonetheless, it can be done. Making sure that this publicity does not incentivize police to arrest innocent people is harder, though perhaps publishing data on arrests that don't lead to convictions will help.

These rates should also be broken out by race and ethnicity of the victim. As we observed in Chapter 4, murders with black victims are cleared at significantly lower rates than those with white victims. This contributes to a climate of fear in neighborhoods where people can be killed with impunity, and creates incentives for preemptive killing in response. High rates of criminal homicide go hand in hand with low clearance rates.

Second, more police should be hired in some locations. Several studies have found that an increase of 1 percent in the number of police in a city leads on average to a decrease in murders of around 0.5 to 1 percent. Based on standard measures of the value of reducing mortality risk, the benefits of adding police are almost certainly greater than the cost whenever the ratio of police to murders per year is less than around twenty-five.[15] This calculation ignores any other benefits that might come from the employment of a police officer, such as maintaining order, or reducing other index crimes.

Many cities in the United States, especially those with high murder rates, appear to have ratios of police to murders well under twenty-five. For instance, in the four cities with the highest homicide rates—St. Louis, Baltimore, Detroit, and New Orleans—the ratio of officers per murder is between six and eight.[16] More police for such cities would probably be a good investment.

Of course, hiring more police won't automatically reduce murder rates; a great deal depends on how they are selected and trained. But even if the added police officers are used the average way that new officers have been used in the past, the ratio of twenty-five officers to one murder provides a good guide for when to expand a police department.

Since detectives assigned to homicides probably have more effect on the murder rate than, say, patrol officers or traffic officers, assigning a significant fraction of additional officers to this function would probably be the best way for these departments to expand. Even without additional officers, many departments could probably reduce murders by assigning more detectives. Simple reassignment would not cost taxpayers much more money, but it might reduce other services.

Third, experienced and effective detectives should face incentives for longer careers. As with professional sports, a good deal of police work is a young person's job because of its physical demands. After twenty or twenty-five years, many police officers are past their prime, and pension systems that encourage them to leave at that point keep the force in good physical shape. But detectives may be different: experience can more than offset the physical deterioration that comes from aging. Many detectives retire when they are still in their prime, and take other security-related jobs, leaving behind the quotidian murders that take so many lives in tough urban neighborhoods. You can't blame them: police pension systems are designed to make staying beyond twenty or twenty-five years extremely unattractive financially. But the premature exodus of expertise may hurt the ability of police departments to solve murders.

Is there a way to slow the exodus? Keeping experienced detectives working when they are close to retirement is likely to be expensive. The pension system is designed to make retiring more attractive than regular working at this point in an officer's life, and so to prevent retirement the inducement would have to make staying on much more attractive than regular working.

Thus the more attractive alternative would have to operate early in officers' careers. Detectives who wanted to keep working would need an option to enter a different pension system, one where pension benefits accrued more slowly and for a longer time, or salaries rose faster relative to pension benefits. Designing such a compensation scheme would not be too difficult, but whether early-career detectives would be willing to opt for it, pass up retirement after twenty years, and differentiate themselves from other officers is unclear.

Fourth, policies resulting in less residential segregation are likely to also reduce crime; some research finds that murder rates are higher in more segregated cities.[17] We don't know whether this correlation arises because segregation causes higher murder rates or because of some other reason. However, segregation gives rise to neighborhoods that have a heavy-handed police presence, limited witness cooperation, low clearance rates, strong incentives for preemptive killing, and a reputation for danger, so a causal effect of segregation on homicide rates is not implausible.

Are there policies that reduce segregation? Quite a few policies may work, although rigorous studies are scarce. School desegregation has been shown to cause direct reductions in murder among young black men (and possibly young white men too).[18] Placing subsidized low-income housing in higher-income, mainly white neighborhoods may also reduce segregation. So, too, can matching Housing Choice Voucher subsidies with neighborhood rents, rather than metropolitan area rents, to enable voucher holders to live in more affluent neighborhoods. Vigorous enforcement of fair housing laws may also help.

Of course, there are many other good reasons to promote integration, aside from reducing murder (and improving the quality of eyewitness testimony). Hence the cost of reducing murder through integration is low.

Fifth, greater care needs to be taken with publicity. Some police departments and community leaders have promoted signs that either exhort people not to kill ("Stop the Shooting") or threaten dire consequences for people who carry or use guns. The police have even purchased billboards with these messages. We suspect that these signs are a bad idea. They reinforce the perception that a particular neighborhood is dangerous, and location stereotypes like that can be self-confirming.

Finally, stand-your-ground laws do not make people safer. The states that have these laws, which make it easier to claim that a homicide is justified, should repeal them. They encourage violence and increase murder, for reasons we discussed in Chapter 4.

Allegation Escrows

Witnesses who are reluctant to come forward alone are sometimes willing to do so if they know that others will corroborate their accounts. Alone, they may face retaliation and their testimony could well be futile; united with other witnesses they are more likely to prevail and to escape retaliation. But when everyone is willing to come forward as the second witness and no one is willing to be the first, none will come forward at all. There is a "first-mover disadvantage."[19]

To relieve a similar problem involving victims of sexual harassment, Ian Ayres and Cait Unkovic have proposed using an "allegation escrow."[20] This is a trusted intermediary that can be as simple as the host of a website. Harassment victims who are unwilling to act alone send their allegations, along with details, to the intermediary, who holds them in confidence. They are released to the authorities only when two or three allegations against the same harasser have accumulated. The allegation escrow gives victims a way to coordinate their reports among themselves without knowing or talking to each other, and since all moves are effectively simultaneous, it allows them to escape the first-mover disadvantage. Ayres and Unkovic have developed this scheme and many variants in detail, and have explored the legal complications. To our knowledge, allegation escrows are not used anywhere yet, but universities and academic societies are seriously considering establishing them.

Could information escrows like this help witnesses to violent crimes overcome the first-mover disadvantage? Violent crime escrows would handle only single events (a particular shooting, for instance), rather than a string of harassment events that might extend over years, and so their information-gathering task might be simpler. But fear of retaliation might be greater (losing your life is worse than losing your job), motivation might be less intense (witnesses might have suffered no direct harm), and the problem of trust would be larger.

Trust is probably the thorniest issue. Witnesses have to trust the escrow agency to hold their accounts in absolute confidence, even though the information they have provided would be very helpful to police and may even prevent future acts of violence. So the escrow agency cannot be the police or connected with the police—both because of the general distrust of the police and because the police have the greatest incentive to use the information without the potential witnesses' approval.

Other private agencies—churches, community organizations, labor unions—are possible repositories of this information, but all of them would have to contend with the threat of a subpoena, and especially in high-profile cases, the police would have reason to seek such a subpoena. The escrow process would work only if the escrow agency were somehow granted the equivalent of lawyer-client privilege. This is not impossible (perhaps the escrow agency could be a law firm that treated potential witnesses as clients), but assessing the legal and political hurdles is beyond our expertise.

Even if a trusted escrow agency could be established, the rate at which witnesses would come forward would not necessarily increase. The reason is that some witnesses who would have gritted their teeth and gone to the police in the absence of an escrow option will use that option when it becomes available. Some testimony, then, will be diverted from the police to the escrow agency, and if no one else comes forward, it will be "orphaned," to use Ayres and Unkovic's term.

Whether the escrow system increases convictions, then, depends on the relative size of the diversion of testimony from the police to the escrow agency, the likelihood that testimony is orphaned, and the amount of new testimony that the escrow option generates. These magnitudes almost certainly vary from crime to crime. For gangland slayings in public places where many people observe but traditionally no one comes forward, some experiments with information escrows seem worthwhile.

Drugs

If violence is the default mechanism for the resolution of disputes arising from illicit transactions, then perhaps violence can be lowered by reducing the range of activities deemed criminal. Many states have taken steps toward legalizing the recreational use of marijuana, and some analysts have argued for bolder action, including the decriminalization of drug possession more generally, following the example of Portugal in 2001.[21]

Here three forces are at work, pushing in different directions: illegality, toxicity, and pretextualism. The illegality of drugs promotes violence, so decriminalization should diminish it. But the physiological effects of some drugs, and the symptoms of withdrawal, also promote violence. Decriminalization has the potential to increase drug consumption, and could therefore also increase violence.

In addition, some arrests for drug possession are pretextual— police and prosecutors use drug possession to incarcerate people whom they think are likely to commit violent crimes, but don't have solid evidence against. That is probably why, for instance, 93 percent of the people the NYPD arrested on marijuana charges were men, although men and women use marijuana at roughly the same rate.[22] If small-scale possession is decriminalized but not production and sale—as in the case of Portugal—the illegality effect could be small, and the overall effect on violence through intoxication and pretextualism would be ambiguous.

James Forman's discussion of the crack epidemic of the 1980s in Washington, DC, and the concomitant spike in homicide rates, illustrates the effects of both illegality and intoxication: "Not all these deaths were related to the crack trade, but many were—either directly, as a result of turf wars or deals gone south, or indirectly, catalyzed by violent highs, destructive lows, or the sheer desperation of securing the next fix. . . . The crack markets also brought a rush of guns into the city. . . . People had begun using guns to resolve more than drug disputes: even the pettiest of arguments—over a girl, clothes, or just a hard look at the wrong person—could lead to guns being drawn."[23]

On the one hand, the fact that violence was the conflict resolution mechanism of first resort fueled killing; on the other hand, decriminalization could have led to more "violent highs, destructive lows, or the sheer desperation of securing the next fix." And decriminalization would do little to stem violence from "petty disputes." It would also take away a tool that police departments use with some frequency. Even so, decriminalization can play an important role in reducing the presence of nonviolent offenders in prison, and did so in the case of Portugal.[24]

There is reason, moreover, to doubt some of the arguments against decriminalization. Not all illicit drugs induce violent behavior. Marijuana and heroin do not—indeed, heroin is a strong depressant that induces torpor. While craving for a fix in the current drug regime may lead heroin addicts to commit crimes—both nonviolent and violent—this behavior may be induced primarily by illegality. Illegality makes heroin expensive, and it makes storing precautionary stocks dangerous. Many people are dependent on substances in their daily lives—diabetics need insulin, asthmatics need nebulizers, smokers keep cartons handy, coffee drinkers have machines nearby at work, and people with glaucoma need their eyedrops—but they can easily and legally keep and access reserves. They do not generally engage in violence.

Following the lead of California in 1996, many U.S. states have passed medical marijuana laws that decriminalize not just the consumption (for medical purposes) but also the production of marijuana. Recent evidence suggests that such laws have caused a reduction in violent crime in states adjacent to Mexico, and especially the border counties in these states, as the role of drug trafficking organizations in marijuana delivery has diminished.[25]

On pretextual arrests, Ilyana Kuziemko and Steven Levitt have found that cocaine arrests caused modest reductions in violent crimes, a finding that supports the idea that locking up drug users also locks up some people who would commit violent felonies.[26] But the reduction was modest, and their cost-benefit analysis found that these crime reductions were worth very little compared with the monetary cost of incarceration. Of course, since pretextual incarceration is not justified on retributive grounds, the cost is really much greater than the monetary estimate, which does not account for the hardships borne by prisoners and their families.

Another alternative would be to keep illegal the drugs that are now illegal, but to specify clearly what the acceptable standards are for recreational and occupational drugs. Currently only two of these are completely legal, caffeine and nicotine, and ethanol (the drug contained in alcoholic beverages) is heavily regulated. The introduction of new legal recreational or occupational drugs could reduce demand for illicit drugs (as well as for caffeine, nicotine, and ethanol). Since all of the existing drugs, legal as well as illegal, have serious shortcomings (even caffeine is quite addictive) having safer alternatives available would improve life and probably reduce crime.

Guns

Guns are like drugs in that they have legitimate uses and they can be abused. Many other things with legitimate uses can also be abused—cars, box cutters, and ammonia, for instance—but they do not stir emotion and controversy the same way drugs and guns do. Many people who are drug libertarians are gun prohibitionists, and many gun libertarians are drug prohibitionists. A lot seems to depend on whether you think of yourself as a Democrat or a Republican. But we can try to develop a consistent approach to these two issues.

Most serious studies indicate that restrictions on gun availability usually reduce index crime, with black victims gaining more consistently.[27] The gains are not huge, and a few papers even show no gains. The crime reduction benefits of gun restrictions, however, are much more certain than the crime reduction benefits of drug restrictions, where a considerable body of rigorous work (by Howard Bodenhorn on South Carolina and Melissa Dell on Mexico, as we described in Chapter 4) shows drug restrictions increasing crime.

Guns are durable capital goods, while drugs are nondurable consumer goods. A gun that you use today will still be a gun many decades from now, while drugs that you use today are gone forever. In 2013, there was probably one gun for every person in the United States (only around a quarter to a third of Americans own guns—a proportion that has been declining since the 1970s—but many of these individuals own more than one gun). Nobody knows exactly where those hundreds of millions of guns are. If the country were to prohibit guns tomorrow—manufacture, importation, sale, and possession—and spend heavily to enforce the prohibition, tens of millions of guns would still be around for decades to come (not counting the guns that would be stolen from the military and police or smuggled in).[28]

Guns are like cars (though much easier to hide): they are durable, there are hundreds of millions of them in the United States, and they can be abused. Car regulation depends on licensing, liability, and mandatory insurance, and that may be the right model for gun regulation. Licensing restricts the set of people who can drive cars to those who don't pose an unusually high risk (excluding, for instance, children and people with serious vision impairments), liability establishes who pays when something goes wrong and so provides incentives for safe operation, and mandatory insurance covers the problem of "judgment-proofness" (sometimes a car causes more damage than its owner can pay for).

A modified version of this approach might work with guns. Licensing criteria could be more restrictive because more activities in our society require operating cars than operating guns. Thus, licenses might be denied to people with certain mental health conditions, for instance, or domestic violence restraining orders.

The liability criteria might also be different. Cars in most states operate under a comparative negligence standard: you are responsible only if the level of care you were exercising as a driver was less than the normal standard, and less than the level of care the other driver was exercising. That would probably be a good standard for encounters between armed parties. But strict liability—you are responsible for the damage no matter what—is probably the appropriate standard for encounters with unarmed parties. This would be like the Chinese car insurance system, where strict liability applies in accidents involving cars and pedestrians or bicyclists.

Why strict liability? Generally strict liability is a better principle than negligence when an activity can cause great harm even though the normal standard of care is met, and when the amount of possibly dangerous activity can be varied. As an example, crane operation is governed by strict liability. Even cranes that are operated according to code can topple or drop heavy loads, with disastrous consequences; therefore, crane operators should always look for innovations beyond code that make their operations safer, and should try to reduce the number of lifts they do on windy days. Strict liability gives them an incentive to do these things, but negligence does not. With guns, accidental or mistaken shootings can occur even if someone follows basic gun etiquette, and are more likely if the owner carries loaded guns to more occasions or spends more time hunting.

Gun owners should also be responsible for damage caused by their lost or stolen guns. They need incentives to protect their guns. If Amy steals Bernard's gun and uses it to kill Carlos, Amy would be imprisoned for murder and gun theft, but Carlos's estate could sue Bernard for damages. If Bernard had been more careful, or had not purchased a gun at all, Carlos would still be alive today. (Bernard may object that if Amy had not stolen his gun she would have stolen Donald's, but this sort of argument is almost never accepted. For instance, Amy would never get away with arguing that if she had not killed Carlos, Emily would have done so instead.)

The Second Amendment

After a mass shooting with thirty-five fatalities in Port Arthur in 1996, Australia implemented a significant reform to its gun laws. The National Firearms Agreement "prohibited automatic and semiautomatic assault rifles and pump shotguns in all but unusual cases . . . tightened licensing rules, established a 28-day waiting period for gun purchases, created a national gun registry and instituted a temporary buyback program that removed more than 20 percent of firearms from public circulation."[29]

Homicide and suicide rates fell substantially after the law was implemented, but they were on a downward trajectory even before the reform, which makes it difficult to make inferences about the effects of the policy. One approach to causal identification is to look at variations across regions—the law affected some regions more than others because state-level rules and gun ownership patterns were quite heterogeneous before the introduction of uniform and stricter standards.

That is, one could uncover the effects of the law by looking at differences across states in the degree to which homicide and suicide rates fell, in relation to the rates of prior gun ownership. Using this approach, Andrew Leigh and Christine Neill found very large effects, with the firearm suicide rate falling by about 75 percent, and somewhat smaller but still substantial reductions in the firearm homicide rate.[30] Importantly, they also found no significant impact on non-firearm deaths, so people were not simply finding alternative means of taking (their own and other) lives. And there have been no mass killings—defined in Australia as involving five or more victims—since the law went into effect.

At the time of passage, the population of Australia was a little over eighteen million, smaller than that of the New York metropolitan area today, and only slightly larger than the cities of Sao Paolo and Seoul. This alone makes any international comparison difficult. But even if one were convinced that such a law would dramatically reduce homicides in the United States, it would face a significant constitutional hurdle.

The Second Amendment to the Constitution states: "A well regulated militia being necessary to the security of a free State, the right of the People to keep and bear arms shall not be infringed." This peculiar wording has given rise to endless debates about interpretation and the scope of laws that can pass constitutional muster. To some, the preamble suggests that the amendment does not speak to the private ownership of firearms at all, but only restricts federal interference with the right of states to establish well-regulated militias. But to others, the amendment guarantees to individuals an essentially unrestricted right to possess weapons.

An influential article by Sanford Levinson in 1989 shifted the terms of this debate. While recognizing that the amendment is the "worst drafted" of all constitutional provisions, Levinson made a strong case that it is part of an "American political tradition that is fundamentally mistrustful of state power" and grounded in a belief in "the ability of an armed populace, presumptively motivated by a shared commitment to the common good, to resist governmental tyranny."

Under a reasonable reading of the amendment, he argued, "the individual citizen has a right to keep and bear bazookas, rocket launchers, and other armaments that are clearly relevant to modern warfare, including, of course, assault weapons."[31]

One might argue that with the powers available to the government today—armored vehicles, nerve agents, drones, robots, and cyberweapons among them—even a citizenry armed with bazookas and hand grenades cannot hope to check tyrannical power. But as Levinson points out, an armed citizenry changes the cost-benefit calculations faced by the government: "A state facing a totally disarmed population is in a far better position, for good or for ill, to suppress popular demonstrations and uprisings than one that must calculate the possibilities of its soldiers and officials being injured or killed."[32]

This interpretation, which is close to the prevailing opinion in the courts, places the Australian reform path out of reach and is enough to cripple much more modest efforts at gun control. Rather than a strained insistence on alternative interpretation, advocates of robust gun control will probably have to press for repeal.[33]

Police Homicides

We documented in Chapter 8 that officers of the law in the United States use lethal force at a rate that far exceeds levels recorded in other industrialized democracies, with about 1,000 civilians killed each year. While this phenomenon is not new, the availability and easy distribution of video evidence has made the issue more salient than ever.

The immediate response to viral videos of police killings is to demand prosecution. This reaction is normal and expected: outrageous behavior calls for punishment. Police who commit unjustified homicides should be prosecuted; otherwise, rule of law means nothing. But prosecutions of individual officers are not likely to be an effective policy for reducing police killings, for a variety of reasons.

The most obvious one is that few police killings result in prosecutions, and few prosecutions result in convictions. Before 2015, about five police officers a year were charged in such cases, and about one a year was convicted.[34] With about 1,000 police killings a year, these are very low rates.

The reasons for low conviction rates are easy to identify. In all criminal matters, the standard of proof is very high: the charges have to be proved beyond a reasonable doubt. Thus the prosecution in these cases has to convince twelve jurors that the police officer did not believe that his life or someone else's was in jeopardy, even though he will usually say it was. Police are respected members of the community in the eyes of most jurors, and they are experts in observing crime scenes and writing reports that juries find compelling. Officers who are accused are usually supported by their colleagues, and often work on a daily basis with prosecutors and assistant prosecutors. Department procedures are often ambiguous, and officers who can show that they followed department procedures are unlikely to be convicted, no matter how unconstitutional, unscientific, or bizarre those procedures happen to be. Witnesses against the police are usually not trained observers, and sometimes they have prior run-ins with the law, which can call their credibility into question. So the rarity of prosecutions and convictions is not surprising.

Video evidence and the new attention that police killings began to receive after Ferguson in August 2014 resulted in more prosecutions, but convictions are not the norm, even in high-profile cases (which suggests that in the near future prosecutors will bring these cases less often). Criminal law and procedures can be tweaked, but because of the credibility of the police and the requirement of proof beyond a reasonable doubt, prosecution and conviction will probably never be a serious prospect except in egregious cases, not in the many incidents where the circumstances leave some room for doubt.[35] Punishing police officers in egregious cases is important for legitimacy, but by itself will not have much impact on the incidence of lethal force.

Concentrating on individual officers also indicates that the problem is a few bad apples. The vast disparities across (and within) states in the rates at which police kill civilians suggest, instead, that the problem is bad orchards. How might this problem be addressed?

Technology could play a role. Smartphone cameras created the public outcry over police killings, and one governmental response has been to proliferate cameras, both on police cars (dashcams) and on officers themselves (body cams). These cameras are in addition to the many private cameras that already may pick up policing activity— security cameras in stores and parking lots, and smartphones held by pedestrians and vehicle passengers.

Official photography, even though it may be designed to capture lethal force incidents, will capture everything, and so its greatest impact will be on the majority of police incidents that do not involve lethal force. Preliminary studies indicate that official cameras make both police and civilians more polite and make police use nonlethal force less often.[36]

Official photography will probably change the employment relationship for police. A decade ago, nobody could see how cops actually worked—neither their supervisors nor potential future employers. Official cameras let supervisors monitor officers more closely, and so constricts their autonomy on a day-to-day basis. But it may also let officers put together clips of their best work, impress future employers, and change jobs more easily, which could increase their autonomy. Police work may change from a hidden job like chimney repair or radiology to a public job like acting or professional sports. The consequences go far beyond police killing.

Cameras may allow more evidence to be introduced in cases of egregious killings, but the conviction record even in egregious killings that were filmed has not been impressive. Policies that rely on prosecution become more attractive if cameras are everywhere, but the effect does not appear to be large.

The big potential gains from cameras come from producing an archive that includes a wide range of dangerous situations, including those where nobody gets killed or injured. Current training and procedures are not based on these sorts of data. Voluminous video records will let researchers discover which situations are truly dangerous for police and which are not. They can provide material for evidence-based training for police, and guides for civilians. This progress depends on access and research funding, neither of which is guaranteed. These efforts are not likely to bear fruit for a decade or more, but the eventual gains in safety for both civilians and police could be large.

What about less lethal forms of force? Perhaps police would not kill as often if they could stop civilians in their tracks without fatal consequences. Tasers are a technology that might be able to serve that function.

Tasers are "electro-shock weapons." They fire two small dart-like electrodes that stay connected to the weapon by wires. The electrodes slice through clothing, stick in the victim's skin, and deliver electric current. The electric current causes pain and neuromuscular incapacitation; the victim loses muscle control and is effectively incapacitated. "Taser" stands for "Thomas A. Swift's electronic rifle," after Tom Swift, the inventor's fictional childhood hero. The first Tasers were made in the 1970s, but widespread dissemination probably started in the 1990s after a number of technical advances were made.

As weapons, Tasers can be nonlethal substitutes for guns (hence their appeal as a way to reduce police killings), but they can also be more powerful substitutes for traditional nonlethal tools such as batons, pepper spray, and hands. They have less range (about thirty-five feet) than guns but more than traditional police tools.

How Tasers affect the number of police killings depends on whether they are used mainly as a substitute for guns or as a substitute for traditional nonlethal tools. Some civilians die from Tasers (about fifty a year in the *Guardian* data), so if Tasers primarily replace traditional nonlethal tools, their introduction could actually increase police killings rather than reduce them. Substituting Tasers for traditional nonlethal tools has some advantages—fewer injuries to police, for instance, and possibly fewer injuries to civilians—but it's unlikely to reduce civilian deaths.

We don't know how Tasers were mainly used when they became more popular in the late twentieth and early twenty-first centuries. Several studies have shown that introducing Tasers in a department tended to reduce police injuries, and so they are likely to have been used, at least sometimes, as a substitute for traditional nonlethal tools. On the other hand, the spread of Tasers did not coincide with a decrease in killings of civilians, but as we have noted, the data for this period are very poor.

The most sophisticated study yet of Tasers follows the changes in the Chicago Police Department's use of force after Tasers were authorized for patrol officers in 2010. Tasers did not reduce the use of firearms or the extent of police injuries. They may have reduced the use of other kinds of nonlethal force, but the effect, if any, is small.[37]

By itself then, a push for greater Taser use is unlikely to reduce civilian deaths appreciably. As Franklin Zimring points out: "A Taser is an instrument, not a policy. Adding an instrument to the belts of uniformed officers will invite officers to use those instruments where they think it is appropriate and where the police department tells them that use of the instrument is appropriate. . . . If the Taser is intended to be a convenient way of physically coercing persons with whom police are struggling in nonlethal force encounters, it will be used extensively. But it will not replace the gunfire the police will use if they feel at risk of more serious injury."[38]

Next consider drones, or "unmanned aerial vehicles." These have not been used much in police work yet, but their presence is likely to be felt over the next decade. The military has used drones to gather intelligence and to deliver munitions, and civilian applications like inspecting pipelines and high-tension wires, and photographing disasters are becoming more common. Drones are good at going to places that are too dangerous or difficult for a human, and performing relatively simple tasks there.

Police are likely to use drones mainly to gather information (and possibly in hostage situations, but these are rare). For instance, drones would be useful for high-speed car chases, because they can pursue an escaping vehicle more safely than a police car can.

Drones may allow police to reduce the number of dangerous encounters they engage in. At a traffic stop, both officer and civilian could remain in their vehicles while the officer dispatched a drone to the stopped car. The drone could check identification and even conduct a preliminary search. In a domestic violence call, a drone could enter the residence first, and show the officer what was inside. Drones could search stairwells and bushes for suspects, and spare officers from exposure in those dangerous situations.

Unlike Kevlar and Tasers, drones may actually reduce civilian fatalities. Those two technologies allowed police to be safer in dangerous encounters, but did nothing to change the number of dangerous encounters between police and civilians. Drones may reduce the number of dangerous encounters and so might make both police and civilians safer simply by reducing close contact.

One possible offset, though, is that some post-drone encounters are likely to become more dangerous—police may conclude that civilians who shoot down a drone are extremely dangerous and respond accordingly, for instance. Another possible offset is that fewer police will patrol in pairs, since drones can serve as substitutes for partners for many purposes. Some evidence indicates that civilians are more likely to be killed when they confront an officer who is alone than when they confront a pair of officers working together.[39]

Aside from technology, changes in police training and procedures could result in a lower incidence of lethal force. During the 1970s, many cities that improved their training and procedures saw civilian deaths decrease, as intended.[40] Like civilian training, police training is decentralized, heterogeneous, and uncoordinated, but we know much more about it. There are about 18,000 law enforcement agencies in the United States—a lot more than you can easily make generalizations about, but a lot fewer than the 320 million civilians.

Almost everywhere, police spend a great deal of time learning how to shoot a gun accurately. In 2013, the average recruit worked on marksmanship for seventy-one hours, the biggest single investment of time in any area.[41] For many departments, however, most of this training occurs at a shooting range, not under the conditions likely to be encountered on the job.

This training on how to use a firearm is often not integrated with training on when to use it. Chuck Wexler describes a typical sequence: "Recruit training may begin with a week of training on how to use a firearm. Perhaps a month later, the recruits receive training on the legal issues governing use of lethal force. A month after that, they might receive a couple of days of training on strategies for avoiding the use of force."[42]

Many departments could probably improve their training by integrating these topics, using simulators, and teaching more problem-solving methods. Some do all of these things already. We know that departments differ greatly in how well they keep civilians and officers safe, and so it should not be at all surprising that they differ greatly in how they train. But we don't know much yet about how training correlates with outcomes.

Another area where training may matter is implicit bias and its possible connection with disparate treatment in police killings. Recall that in Chapter 1 we discussed a finding that among Spokane police implicit bias in laboratory settings did not translate into a greater propensity to shoot black suspects in simulated encounters. This suggests that in places where implicit biases are a problem, currently known training methods could overcome them. Whether this holds true more generally, across multiple locations, remains an open question.

For reducing police homicides, the sole focus should not be on what an officer should do when she finds herself in a position of extreme danger. That may be too late. Training should teach officers how to avoid such situations in the first place, when they think they have to choose between their lives and someone else's. There are many techniques for doing this—calling for backup, assessing conditions from a distance, and speaking in ways that defuse a situation, for instance. Reducing drama can save both police and civilian lives.

The criminologist Lawrence Sherman has suggested that officers also be trained in how to handle the aftermath of a shooting.[43] They should be equipped with battlefield-grade hemostatic bandages, such as those used by the military, and be taught to apply them to victims whom they shoot. Procedures should also require officers to transport their shooting victims to emergency rooms immediately. Clearly Sherman's suggestion is appropriate: police are authorized to use force to stop perpetrators from harming others; they are not authorized to punish them. If these procedures do not cause officers to shoot more often, then they are likely to save lives. But one must also consider the possibility that officers will shoot more often when they can shoot less lethally. The lesson of Tasers appears to be that giving police additional tools does not necessarily make them less likely to shoot to kill, and hemostatic bandages may be the equivalent of Tasers in this respect. Ongoing experiments designed to assess these effects should provide some answers in due course.

In addition to the questions about how to train police officers, there are questions about what the content of training should be—what police should be trained to do. Here both science and values matter. We consider three issues as examples.

The first issue is training officers on when to call for backup. The scientific questions are, how many crimes will go unpunished if officers often wait to call for backup, and how many more police-related killings are likely to occur if lone officers generally act quickly and don't wait for backup. The value question is, how much enforcement of other laws should be sacrificed to reduce police-related killings? Ultimately, officers in the field will make these decisions themselves, but they will make them quickly and perhaps poorly in the absence of explicit guidance.

The second example is how officers should react when knives are brandished. Many police are now trained according to the 21-foot rule: "Police confronted by persons lunging toward them with knives and other cutting instruments must start shooting their attackers when the attacking distance closes to 21 feet."[44] This rule is not supported by any experimental evidence, and the empirical record makes it look dubious. In the most recent periods for which we have evidence (2008–2012 for Germany and 2010–2014 for the United Kingdom), no police officers were killed by knives in either Germany or the United Kingdom. Neither country teaches the 21-foot rule. In the United States, over the period 2008–2013, only two officers were killed by knives, but the 21-foot rule was irrelevant: in both cases the attacker hid a small knife on his person and used it at exceptionally close range. During this period no American police officer was killed by someone with a visible knife.[45]

But while visible knives are not a lethal threat to police officers, the 21-foot rule is a lethal threat to civilians. According to the *Guardian* database, 152 civilians who were armed with knives were killed by police in 2015, and 158 were killed in 2016. It seems likely that many of these civilians could have been disarmed without the use of lethal force.[46]

These data are hardly definitive. For instance, we have not compared areas in the United States where police are taught the 21-foot rule with areas where they are not taught this rule. Knives cause injuries to police, and the 21-foot rule may reduce injuries. But the 21-foot rule may result in over one hundred civilian deaths a year, and so both the science and the values that lie behind it deserve serious study.

The final example is the number of shots that police fire. Police are currently trained to fire multiple shots. A victim who is hit by multiple shots is more likely to die than one who has been hit by only one shot, and because of the multiple shot practice, victims whom police shoot are considerably more likely to die than victims whom civilians shoot.[47] If police were trained instead to fire only one or two shots and then quickly evaluate whether the victim still posed a threat, fewer civilians might die. Perhaps firing fewer shots and pausing might expose police to more risk, but at the moment there is no evidence on whether the multiple shooting practice protects police. The science is missing—how many civilian lives would pausing save at what cost in police lives? Clearly this involves a value judgment.

As one police use-of-force instructor writes, "Law enforcement is more inclined to be archaic and married to non-forensic speculative dogma that often goes unchallenged and becomes widely accepted as fact."[48] Police training in backup calls, the 21-foot rule, and multiple shots is static and archaic, and civilian deaths are probably greater than they would be if training were more responsive to current conditions and information.

The unchanging nature of police training may explain one of the mysteries we've seen—why Kevlar and Tasers did not reduce civilian deaths. In Chapter 4, we talked about agents who continually assessed the world around them and adjusted their behavior to improve their situation in changing circumstances. Because shooting had harmful consequences for the shooter, when one party to a dispute became safer, she also became less likely to shoot the other party. This requires parties to be alert to changes in their circumstances and to adjust to these changes.

But we see now that police threatened by civilians differ from private parties to a dispute in two important respects, and so the reasoning in Chapter 4 does not quite apply. The first respect is that police officers do not freely choose their responses to circumstances in many cases. Instead, they tend to respond in the way that they were taught, and this way is not responsive to a changing world. Police tend to respond this way in part because they have to act quickly and their brains follow the circuits that have been implanted by repetition (much like a tennis player returning a serve). They also tend to respond in the way they were taught because the rewards and punishments that are most pertinent and immediate to them come from the police department, and those depend on what was taught.

The second respect in which the police differ is that they gain less from being more cautious than the standards they were taught. When a party to a dispute becomes more cautious about preemptively killing the other party, he is rewarded by a lessened probability of being charged with murder. But when a police officer becomes more cautious, his probability of being charged with murder falls very little, since there was almost no chance that he would have been charged in the first place, provided he met the training standard. As long as the training standard does not change in response, there is no reason to expect innovations like Kevlar to make much difference.

We are not arguing that police officers are indifferent about killing civilians. For many, it is a horrible and traumatic experience. But the same is true for many civilians who engage in preemptive killing also. The point is that the legal system does not provide the same extra disincentive to police officers that it provides to private parties.

The effect here may be asymmetric. Changes in the external world that make police safer, like Kevlar, don't change the rate at which civilians are killed, while changes that make people less safe, like high-powered weapons in the hands of civilians, might. But the predominant story of the last forty years (and perhaps last eighty years) has been that police have become safer, as seen in the statistics of officers killed in action.

Why don't police training standards change when circumstances change or when science progresses? The easiest and most compelling explanation is that for most mayors and police chiefs, minimizing the number of civilian casualties has not been a high priority. Many of the civilians killed were not respected citizens, and few people, if any, knew whether their killings were necessary to protect life. Even the egregious cases where killings appeared to be unjustified could be dismissed as the actions of bad apples, not the products of poor training or department procedures. Mayors and police chiefs did not demand research on these training methods and department procedures, and so it was not done, and could not be implemented.

After Ferguson, the public has paid much more attention to police killings, and mayors and police chiefs have too. But most of that attention has still been focused on individual police officers, and very little on training and department procedures. Police officers may have seen themselves as getting most of the blame, and in some cases (Baltimore,

Chicago, and St. Louis in particular), this perception may have caused work slowdowns, with predictably dire consequences for public safety. Unless mayors and police chiefs assign some priority to preserving civilian lives, long-run outcomes are not likely to change much.

What could be done to make the public, mayors, and police chiefs pay attention to training and procedures and care about how many civilians the police are killing? To begin with, they have to know how many civilians the police are killing. One of the most appalling facts to come out of the post-Ferguson discussion of police killings is that the federal government does not keep reliable statistics on police homicides. This task is neither impossible nor prohibitively expensive; Zimring, for instance, proposes an inexpensive and workable system.[49] But heretofore the desire to know these numbers has not been strong enough to get them collected.

Having these data would make a difference, and not just to statisticians. Californians could ask why their police were so much more deadly than New York's. Mayors who wanted to claim progress in reducing civilian deaths could have credible data on which to do so, and mayors who had made little progress would have to worry about opponents who could credibly say that that progress was not enough and point to cities that were doing better. Police chiefs could burnish their résumés by recording progress in reducing civilian deaths, or worry about what the city council or the media would say when civilian deaths went up by 20 percent from one year to the next. These events would not happen every month everywhere, but they would happen sometimes if the data were available. Without the data they could never happen.

Absent these data, when an officer who is following training and department procedures kills a civilian, only the victim's family (and possibly the officer's) feels the pain, no matter how unfounded or counterproductive the department procedures are. When data are present, the people who can change the training and the department procedures may feel some of the pain too. Numbers matter.

Another mechanism to improve police procedures and training would be for police departments to respond to police killings the same way airplane regulators respond to crashes. When an airplane crashes, the National Transportation Safety Board sends in a team of experts to comb through the wreckage and interview witnesses and survivors. The team has two questions to answer: What went wrong? How can we fix it? Forensic teams in the military respond to accidents in much the same way, and hospitals engage in root cause analysis and hold M & M (mortality and morbidity) rounds to understand incidents that they do not want to repeat.

In most states, police have nothing comparable. When a police officer kills a civilian, or when a civilian kills a police officer, there are many reactions (outrage, cover-up, vindictiveness, lawyering up); but an expert analysis of what went wrong and how a recurrence could be prevented is usually not one of them. The exception is Wisconsin, which has recently adopted legislation to mandate such reviews. A national program like that of the National Transportation Safety Board might be a good thing, since knowledge can cross state boundaries.

Lawrence Sherman has argued, building on prior work by Charles Perrow, that policing should be viewed as a system characterized by interactive complexity and tight coupling, much like a power grid or air traffic control system, and that "historical evidence from other complex systems suggests that their collateral death rates decline more substantially by re-engineering their social and technical systems than by increasing the certainty, speed, or severity of punishment."[50] He notes that the fatal shooting of Tamir Rice involved seven errors, the avoidance of any one of which could have saved the boy's life, and laments that "fatal police shootings shine the spotlight on the shooter rather than on the complex organizational processes that recruited, hired, trained, supervised, disciplined, assigned, and dispatched the shooter before anyone faced a split-second decision to shoot."

We showed in Chapter 8 that there are staggering geographic variations in the use of lethal force in America. Understanding the reasons for these variations is of paramount importance. The political scientist Elisabeth Wood has documented similarly large variations among military and paramilitary forces in the incidence of wartime rape.[51] She argues that even when it serves strategic goals, wartime rape is often more usefully viewed as a practice that is tolerated rather than an explicit organizational policy. When it is not an explicit policy, variation across fighting units arises in her theory because of differences in institutions, particularly those for discipline and socialization. Her emphasis on the role of field commanders who tolerate rape and on socialization processes among peers in the emergence of rape as a practice may hold lessons for understanding why some law enforcement agencies appear to use force—including lethal force—at significantly higher rates than others.[52]

Finally, consider the precautions that civilians could take to avoid becoming victims of lethal force at the hands of police officers.

To some people it may seem strange or even immoral to consider this question. Listing actions that civilians could take to reduce the probability of being killed by police seems to place the blame on the wrong party. But taking preventive measures need have no direct connection with blame. Burglars are morally culpable for burglaries, but homeowners still lock their doors and carry keys. Morally blameless noncriminals pay for police departments, even though police departments would be much smaller and cheaper if no one did anything blameworthy. People buy and carry umbrellas even though they do not cause rain.

Parents, schools, churches, and some voluntary associations teach people, especially young black men, how to act in encounters with police. If civilians can signal to the police that they are not dangerous, their probability of survival may be higher. Since most of this training is informal, we don't know how extensive it is and whether it is effective. But we do know that it exists, as our discussion of "the talk" in Chapter 7 demonstrated.

Training that is shown to be effective should be expanded. Police departments are an obvious agency to take responsibility for expanding training. Police know what scares them, and young people know that police know.

Videos of police encounters may also be good training tools, since many of them are vivid and realistic. But to be effective, training needs to show successful encounters, where everyone survives unscathed, as well as unsuccessful ones. People who see only the currently viral videos that end tragically might conclude that once a cop stops you, you have no options and thus nothing to lose. Generating videos of successful encounters is one benefit of widespread police recording through dashcams and body cams.

Training civilians in how to deal with a police officer in a calm and nonthreatening manner could save lives, but it is not likely to be popular where aggressive policies like undirected and rough street stops have created ill will. In addition, such behavioral adjustments are akin to "whistling Vivaldi," or what Glenn Loury calls "strategies of social identity manipulation used by racially marked people to inhibit their being stereotyped—their methods of 'partial passing.'"[53] And such partial passing puts those who are unwilling or unable to practice it in even greater danger.

Incarceration

Some people should be in prison or jail, but probably far fewer than are there now. Simple solutions with broad appeal like freeing nonviolent drug offenders cannot get us back to incarceration levels in line with historical and international norms; there just aren't that many of them relative to the overall population behind bars.[54] On the other hand, some states have engineered large drops in prison population without noticeable increases in crime. Between 1999 and 2016, the New Jersey state prison population fell 37 percent and the New York State prison population fell 30 percent. The California state prison population fell 26 percent between 2006 and 2016. The experience of these states suggests that sizable reductions in prison population are possible without major crime impacts.

The great prison population declines in New Jersey and New York were not the result of a single public change in policy. In contrast, the decline in California was deliberately engineered and well documented. It was spurred by court orders that found the state prisons to be so overcrowded that the constitutional ban on "cruel and unusual punishment" was being violated. But a large fraction of the public also supported it. Two major changes in law (and several smaller ones) were involved.

In 2011, the legislature passed Assembly Bill 109, known as Public Safety Realignment, or simply Realignment. Under Realignment, offenders convicted of nonserious, nonviolent, and nonsexual felonies (the "triple-non" offenses), with no prior convictions for triple-non offenses, serve their time in county jails or on probation. In addition, parole violators who were not convicted of new prison-eligible felonies also serve their remaining sentences in county jails. Realignment reduced the state prison population and increased the county jail population (the state subsidized the counties), but the total incarcerated population declined.

In 2014, California voters adopted Proposition 47. This initiative reclassified a number of drug and property offenses as misdemeanors, resulting in reduced penalties for future convictions and allowing inmates already serving time for these offenses to petition for reduced sentences. Proposition 47 cut the populations of both prisons and jails, and so by 2016 the jail population was also below its pre-Realignment level. In all, the incarceration rate (including both jails and prisons) fell from 701.7 per 100,000 residents in 2006 to 514.5 per 100,000 residents in December 2015.

Violent crime continued its decline in California, parallel with the rest of the country. Thus, the reduction in incarceration probably did not affect violent crime. Property crime increased a little, however, particularly motor vehicle theft.

Expenditures for corrections went up despite the fall in incarcerated population. Court-mandated increases in spending for inmate health care are part of the reason, but the most salient fact is that California has not closed any prisons. Neither have New York and New Jersey, despite their even larger prison declines. That may be the political price for more free people.

Is it politically possible to close a prison once it's open? From the three states with big prison population drops, we see no affirmative evidence. John Pfaff suggests that states with mainly empty prisons follow the example of the federal government when it confronted the issue of obsolete and unneeded military bases.[55] Everyone in Congress may have agreed that there were too many bases, but no one would let his be the one to close. Congresspeople with endangered bases cared a lot more about the immediate issue of keeping their bases open than they cared about the abstract issue of too many bases.

To solve this problem, the federal government set up the Base Realignment and Closure (BRAC) process. Under BRAC, the Pentagon performs a study and recommends a comprehensive plan of base closures and realignments. The plan is treated as a package. Either the president or Congress may disapprove it, but neither can amend it. If either disapproves, the whole package dies. Congresspeople with bases in their districts still have reason to oppose the package, but they are a minority, and those whose districts do not include a threatened base have many reasons to support the package. BRAC has allowed the federal government to close and consolidate military bases, and a similar process for state governments may allow them to close prisons.

The issue is more than one of fiscal responsibility (although fiscal responsibility is an important concern). As long as a lot of prisons are half-empty, the cost to state governments of putting more people in prison will be small, and reversing progress against mass incarceration will be a cheap and inviting "solution" to any future rise in crime.

Under the current system (in most states), county officials—prosecutors and judges—send people to state prisons, but counties don't pay for these prisons. However much imprisonment counties decide they want, the state provides for free. The counties call the tune, but the states pay the piper.

If crimes were uniquely linked to times, as in the *Baretta* world, this misalignment of incentives would pose no problem. County officials would just uncover the truth about what crimes were committed and by whom, and this would automatically lead to the appropriate use of prisons. But as we have seen, we do not live in such a world, and prosecutors and judges have a lot of discretion in determining how much time is assigned to each crime. They do a lot more than simply uncover the truth.

One of the indirect goals of Realignment in California was to make counties bear a part of the costs for the decisions their officials made—in this case, the costs for the triple-non offenses. Parts of the state subsidy package later blunted this incentive, but the initial fall in combined prison and jail population suggests that the incentives made a difference: some triple-non offenders who would have been incarcerated when the state paid the whole tab were placed on probation or their cases were dropped when the counties had to pay a share. Incentives matter, even for prosecutors and judges.

John Pfaff considers several ways that incentives could be aligned better. The simplest would be to charge a county a modest per diem fee for each prisoner sent to a state prison. More sophisticated mechanisms are possible too: for instance, a "cap-and-trade" scheme, as is used for some pollutants, where each county is entitled to use a certain quota of cell years for free, but if it isn't using them all, can sell some to another county that feels the need to exceed its quota.

Pfaff also emphasizes the enormous discretion that prosecutors have. In many ways, the change in how prosecutors used that discretion is what made the United States a "nation of jailers."[56] Channeling that discretion in the right direction moves the whole criminal justice system in the right direction.

In most states under the current system, voters are supposed to be the force that channels the prosecutor's discretion: if voters don't like the job the prosecutor is doing, they can vote her out at the next election. But voters are a weak and somnolent force when it comes to prosecutors. Pfaff writes: "Prosecutors running for reelection win about 95 percent of their primary and general election campaigns, owing in no small part to the fact that 85 percent of the races are unopposed in both the primary and general elections. When incumbents face challengers . . . they come out ahead in 64 percent of their contested primaries and 69 percent of their contested general elections. . . . Even in contested elections, turnout is often low."[57]

To the extent that voters pay attention, they often pay attention to the wrong things. In counties with affluent, relatively crime-free neighborhoods and towns, voters turn out more heavily than those in poorer and more crime-prone neighborhoods. Hence prosecutors are more likely to be concerned about issues that affluent voters can imagine affecting them and their families, like drugs, rather than issues poor people might care more about, like murder. These political facts contribute to Jill Leovy's assessment of policing in America as "at once oppressive and inadequate."[58]

Voters may also pay more attention to anecdotes than data. In particular, a prosecutor's career can be wrecked by one story about giving some truly heinous criminal a slap on the wrist, or dismissing a charge against someone who then goes out and bombs a subway train. Voters' attention to anecdotes makes being too lenient a much more dangerous mistake for a prosecutor than being too harsh.

What can be done? The obvious response is for concerned and wise citizens to get involved in prosecutorial politics. Long-entrenched prosecutors have recently been defeated in several major cities. This trend could mark an end to the somnolence of prosecutorial elections. Whether a revived electorate can give productive direction remains to be seen, but some of the latest signs are hopeful.

The alternative to electoral discipline is bureaucratic discipline. In some states, such as New Jersey, prosecutors are appointed rather than elected. The administration of criminal justice is not conspicuously worse in those states than in the states with elected prosecutors. Appointed prosecutors don't have to devote time to fund-raising and campaigning, they don't have to try to make people think that they have pleasant personalities, and they are a little more insulated from death by anecdote (because ambitious opponents don't have the same incentive to defeat them). On the other hand, appointed prosecutors may face rewards and penalties much weaker than those of elected prosecutors, and so may not work as hard to advance the public good. But sometimes what you are doing matters more than how hard you work at it. Sometimes weak incentives are better than strong incentives to do the wrong thing.

The argument for weak incentives is probably strongest for judges. The ideal judge does not strive for anything other than justice. Since the pursuit of justice has no immediate material rewards, the ideal judge does not look like she is responding to any external incentives whatsoever. Better an indolent judge than one who is ambitious, greedy, or ideological.

Giving judges an incentive to seek reelection or election to a higher office therefore conflicts in many ways with the goal of inducing real judges to act as ideal judges. This is especially the case in fractured communities where biases against a minority group are rampant. Writing in 1944, Gunnar Myrdal was emphatic on this point:

> The dependence of the judge on local prejudices strikes at the very root of orderly government. It results in the danger of breaking down the law in its primary function of protecting the minority against the majority, the individual against society, indeed democracy itself against the danger of its nullifying in practice the settled principles of law and impartiality of justice.[59]

Although "local prejudices" are probably less acute now than when these words were written, some incentive problems have grown in recent years as improvements in campaign technology have made money more efficacious in producing votes, and social media and rapid news cycles have made the dangers of a single slip in the direction of leniency greater. In the federal system and in many states, judges are appointed rather than elected. For criminal matters especially, the other states should start moving in that direction.

Punishing an innocent person is worse than letting a guilty person go free, even though the incentives of prosecutors and judges clearly point in the opposite direction. Both retributivists and consequentialists believe this—retributivists because it violates the innocent person's right to freedom, and consequentialists because it feeds fatalism and disrespect for the law. Trials have some safeguards against wrongful convictions, such as the requirement of jury unanimity and the standard of "beyond a reasonable doubt," but hardly any criminal cases go to trial. Plea bargaining doesn't have these safeguards, especially if a defendant doesn't have the means to go to trial or does not receive good advice on how to negotiate with the prosecutor and what his prospects at trial are.

That's why public defenders should be plentiful, skilled, and well compensated. Public defenders are also another way to hold prosecutors and judges accountable, as Pfaff emphasizes. Perhaps state constitutions should require that a fixed proportion of prosecutor appropriations go to fund public defenders.

While judges and prosecutors may have too much of the wrong type of accountability, prisons may have too little accountability of any kind. Like public schools, prisons have many and imprecise goals, and so strong incentive schemes would probably be counterproductive. But public schools have made some modest progress by publishing test scores and adopting publicized goals, and prisons might learn something from them.[60]

On retributivist accounts, prisons should keep their inmates healthy and safe. Offenders are sentenced to confinement, not to hell. Prisons should set goals for age-adjusted mortality and morbidity rates (disinterested third parties should measure morbidity rates so that a prison cannot make itself look better by denying treatment to sick prisoners and claiming that they are well) and publish them.

For most consequentialist accounts of imprisonment, low recidivism rates are desirable, but simply rewarding prisons for achieving this would give them an incentive to keep prisoners as long as possible. One alternative might be to measure excess recidivism. Prisons would have goal recidivism rates that would decline by number of years in prison and age at release. "Excess recidivism" would be any recidivism over the goal.[61]

Many former prisoners have a hard time getting jobs. These difficulties may encourage recidivism and are costly to prisoners, their families, and the rest of the economy. (Employers' beliefs that former prisoners are highly likely to commit crimes may be self-fulfilling.)

One popular policy for improving former prisoners' job prospects is to reduce the amount of information that employers get. This policy is called ban-the-box. It forbids employers from asking applicants about criminal records until late in the hiring process. The hope is that introducing this information later in the process will give former prisoners an opportunity to showcase their abilities and strengths and be hired more often.

Evaluations of ban-the-box have not been entirely positive. Ban-the-box may or may not improve the employment prospects of former prisoners, but it reduces the employment of young, low-skilled black and Hispanic men.[62] Taking away the box prevents the law-abiding majority of young, low-skilled minority men from showing prospective employers that they follow the law; some employers, in turn, think all young, low-skilled minority men are likely to be criminals. As we discussed in Chapter 1, such beliefs can have strong incentive effects. People facing discrimination in labor markets have less to gain from investing in productivity enhancing skills.

Young-Chul Kim and Glenn Loury have proposed an alternative approach.[63] Instead of suppressing information, they want to generate and distribute information more freely. Instead of making it harder for law-abiding nonincarcerated men to prove that they follow the law, they want to make it easier for former prisoners who are intent on going straight to demonstrate this commitment.

The way to do this is simple: set up a voluntary program for former prisoners that is challenging and requires sacrifices to complete. It would be especially beneficial if the program increased productivity in the legitimate sector, but it doesn't have to. This program will not be helpful to former prisoners who think they are likely to recidivate, and so they are not likely to volunteer. But former prisoners who plan to go straight will volunteer if legitimate employers pay higher wages to those who complete the program (or are more likely to hire them).

And legitimate employers will pay them higher wages. Why? Because they can infer that those who complete the program intend to go straight. The program lets former prisoners who intend to go straight identify themselves to employers.

The Center for Employment Opportunities (CEO) operates a program like this in sixteen cities. According to Kim and Loury: "Each ex-convict who joins the program is assigned to a five-to-seven person crew that cleans public facilities . . . and maintains public housing properties. A crew generally operates from 9 am to 5 pm under line-of-sight supervision of a supervisor to enforce the rules (e.g., punctuality, dress codes, and phone usage). Depending on the severity and frequency of a violation, participants may receive a verbal repri- mand, lose a day's pay, be asked to attend a disciplinary meeting, or be terminated. Participants also receive daily feedback from their super- visors on job performance through a small booklet called *Passport to Success*. After the period of working for CEO, participants are encour- aged to present graded passports during job interviews with employers as evidence of their work and performance."[64]

Perhaps better information can solve problems that pervasive doubt creates.

CONCLUSION
Hope

In her book *Cuz*, Danielle Allen tells the moving story of her cousin Michael, who was arrested for an attempted carjacking at the age of fifteen. It was a botched effort, with Michael being shot through the neck with his own weapon. It was also his first arrest. While in the ambulance, without a family member or a lawyer present, he confessed to two prior robberies during the previous week, which had netted him a total of twenty-two dollars. He was to be tried as an adult, and the confession left him facing twenty-five years to life under California's three-strikes law. He accepted a twelve-year sentence in a plea deal and was transferred from a juvenile facility to an adult prison when he turned seventeen.

Here is how Allen describes the punitive environment at the time:

> By the time Michael, as a teenager, was punished in 1995, California legislators had given up on rehabilitation in prison. They had given up on rehabilitation even for juveniles. . . . Legislators had also given up on retribution, the idea that the punishment should fit the crime. Retribution actually puts a limit on how much punishment you can impose. The California Assembly members who voted unanimously to try as adults sixteen-year-olds, and then fourteen-year-olds, for carjacking had all become deterrence theorists. They were designing sentences not for people but for a thing: the aggregate level of crime. They wanted to reduce the totality of crime; they didn't have any interest in justice for any individual person, whether victim or

perpetrator. The target of Michael's sentence was not Michael, a fifteen-year-old boy with a bright mind and a mild proclivity, as we shall see, for theft, but the 2,663 carjackings that occurred in Los Angeles between January and August of 1993. . . . Michael stood in, in essence, for all of those jackings, just as did every other defendant who passed before the bench. Deterrence dehumanizes. It directs at the individual the full hate that society understandably bears toward an aggregate phenomenon. But no individual can or should bear that kind of responsibility. Such an approach to punishment is unconscionable. The concept of "just deserts" is meant to protect people from excess.

Since antiquity, mankind has known that anger drives retribution, the desire to make someone pay. When punishment fits the crime, anger sates itself; it modulates; it softens. This is what makes it anger, not hatred, a distinction recognized by philosophers all the way back in antiquity. Hatred is distinguished by its unending quality, its rigid fixity and imperviousness to softening. A proposed punishment for a fifteen-year-old of twenty-five years to life for a first arrest after a freely confessed week's crime spree and failed carjacking in all of which that fifteen-year-old was the only person physically injured is one of the purest expressions of hatred I can imagine.[1]

While in prison, Michael fell in love with a fellow inmate, a trans woman who went by the name of Bree. The relationship continued after the two were released, but it was intense and volatile, and eventually led to his death: Bree shot him in her kitchen and left his bullet-ridden body wrapped in a blanket in the passenger seat of his car. Michael did not live to see his thirtieth birthday.

What Allen does in *Cuz* is to paint a picture of a good-hearted and enormously talented young man who was also deeply vulnerable, and—despite the best efforts of a loving family—who was destroyed by his environment and a criminal justice system that had become unspeakably harsh and indiscriminately punitive. According to his records, Michael had entered a guilty plea for a violent felony. But what these records miss, and what Allen's portrait shows us, is that he was also a courageous firefighter (while still in prison) and a gifted writer who could have achieved professional success and personal happiness had he been given the opportunity.

Every individual incarcerated for a violent offense has a story, but few of these are ever told. Allen's portrait in *Cuz* manages to humanize Michael in ways that the imprisoned are seldom humanized.

What Allen does for Michael in *Cuz*, Bryan Stevenson does for numerous condemned men, women, and children in *Just Mercy*. These individuals include not just the wrongly convicted, for whom sympathy comes naturally, but also those who have "committed terrible crimes but nonetheless struggle to recover and to find redemption." Of these he writes: "I have discovered, deep in the hearts of many condemned and incarcerated people, the scattered traces of hope and humanity—seeds of restoration that come to astonishing life when nurtured by very simple interventions."[2]

John Pfaff has argued, correctly, that limiting decarceration efforts to nonviolent offenses will do little to move our incarceration rates back in the range of historical and international norms. But less punitive approaches toward individuals who commit violent felonies—especially when young and vulnerable—will not be possible unless they are humanized in this way. Such humanization is necessary if we are to have hope.

Hope is a virtue. It is "a movement of the appetite towards a future good, which though hard to attain is possible of attainment." As Václav Havel describes it, hope "is an orientation of the spirit, an orientation of the heart; it transcends the world that is immediately experienced, and is anchored somewhere beyond its horizons."[3] It is the opposite of despair. And it can thwart the fulfillment of negative self-fulfilling beliefs.

On an individual level, hope is the source of forgiveness. This relationship has been confirmed in social psychology experiments, and is recognized in ancient wisdom.[4] Most people's lives are mixtures of good and bad, and remembering only the bad about someone is to despair of their capacity to be other than their worst. Forgiveness allows someone who has done something bad (possibly after atoning for it) not to be judged entirely by the bad; it reflects hope that their life will rise above whatever they may have previously done.

Recently, revelations that rich and famous men have harassed women have left the accused and their friends wishing that they be remembered for the best things they have done, not the worst. Perhaps this is a worthy aspiration, but it should not be reserved for the rich and famous. Millions of men and women, most of them poor and powerless, have had their lives blighted by being branded by the worst things they ever did, and many observers could say no more than "they deserved it."

Technology may be responsible, in part, for this hopelessness. In past generations, a young man who made a big mistake could migrate, join the Marines, or wander off to a place where no one knew him and could start fresh, just another stranger with a blank slate. The web has eviscerated this option. The online world is not symmetrical: it records that a young man robbed a liquor store but not that he was kind to his neighbor or nurtured puppies or stood up for his friends against bullies. It remembers forever the worst about ordinary people but hardly ever records the best. Human minds have not adjusted to this asymmetry yet.

Despair about people and the lack of forgiveness that accompanies it can give rise to self-fulfilling beliefs in two ways. The obvious effect is on the person who has not been forgiven. His opportunities in licit markets are severely constrained, and he has no reputation for law-abiding left to conserve. Labeling someone a criminal can induce him to become a criminal.

The second effect occurs earlier in life. Sometimes young men who try to live law-abiding lives commit crimes by mistake or in moments of weakness or uncontrollable emotion. And sometimes police and prosecutors make mistakes and punish innocents (and even if innocents are arrested and released, the arrest record can survive). Realizing this, if you are a young man contemplating a future with many opportunities for something to go wrong, either because of your weakness and mistakes or because of a criminal justice error, then you may realize that whether or not you abide by the law today, sooner or later you are very likely to get in trouble at least once. If getting in trouble just once will ruin your life forever, there is no real advantage to abiding by the law now.

The possibility of forgiveness, however, defeats fatalism. If you pay a price for every crime but then are forgiven, your lifetime punishment depends on the number of crimes you commit. Your life prospects, in the end, depend on your average day, not your worst day.

Fatalism can operate on the other side of the criminal justice system, too. If police and prosecutors believe that some young men are bad apples who will always commit crimes, then they believe that they are reducing crime by arresting these men on any pretext and incarcerating them on any charge. In a world without forgiveness, young men who see that the authorities believe they are bad apples will become fatalistic—they will figure out that they are highly likely to go to prison and be stigmatized no matter what they try to do, and so they will have little incentive to abide by the law. Because police and prosecutors believe these young men are bad apples, they will be bad apples, and the police and prosecutors will feel justified. Without forgiveness and hope, police and prosecutor fatalism can be self-fulfilling too.

Even in the realm of public policy, hope is needed to defeat self-fulfilling beliefs. If people believe that crime is ineradicable or that it can be contained only by massive incarceration, then crime will be rampant (since mass incarceration cannot contain it, as we saw in Chapter 11). If the public believes that the price of safety is police killing 1,000 people a year, police will kill 1,000 people a year. Despair, as a motivation for public policy, is self-fulfilling. But we have seen throughout this book that despair is not warranted. Between 1991 and 2015, index crime fell by half, and in New York City it fell by 80 percent. We are asking for hope, not faith. Hope is what makes justice and security compatible.

Finally, there is doubt, which creates the space that stereotypes rush in to fill. Doubt cannot be extinguished, but it can be recognized, reflected on, and managed.

The acclaimed writer J. Edgar Wideman published an opinion piece in the *New York Times* in which he reported on the following informal experiment. For four years, while commuting twice a week between New York and Providence on the Acela train, he would go to the station early and secure a vacant double seat. With rare exceptions, the space next to him would remain empty for the entire trip. He concluded that "color will determine, even if it doesn't exactly clarify, why 9 times out of 10 people will shun a free seat if it means sitting beside me."[5]

Wideman was right on both counts: color was implicated, but for reasons that aren't entirely clear. One possibility is racial animus; perhaps other passengers simply found the prospect of sitting next to him distasteful. But there is also the possibility that they believed that he would find sitting next to them distasteful, and were willing to accommodate what they perceived to be his preference. Reasons may vary for different passengers, even if they act in indistinguishable ways.

In his book *Chokehold*, Paul Butler recounts a similar experience while commuting between New York and Washington, DC, but adds that for a month or so after the publication of Wideman's piece, "white folks on the train made a beeline to sit next to me."[6] At least for some passengers, any reluctance to sit next to a black man on a train is swamped by the desire to demonstrate a lack of such reluctance.

Interactions that cross racial boundaries in America are shrouded in doubts—both reasonable and unreasonable. People navigate in these shadows guided by stereotypes about which they are only dimly aware. Their stereotypes appear resistant to change at any point in time, but over generations they can evolve in sometimes surprising ways.

In the late nineteenth century, the state of Mississippi sought to disenfranchise black citizens but was restricted from doing so by the requirement that explicitly discriminatory exclusions were impermissible under the Constitution. As a result, the state tried to find proxies that would exclude blacks from the polling booth without significant impact on whites. It did so by carefully selecting a set of crimes to which the former (but not the latter) were believed to be prone: "Burglary, theft, arson, and obtaining money under false pretenses were declared to be disqualifications, while robbery and murder and other crimes in which violence was the principal ingredient were not."[7]

Why were robbers and murderers allowed to vote in Mississippi while burglars, thieves, arsonists, and fraudsters were denied? Because the state viewed blacks as "a patient, docile people, but careless, landless, and migratory within narrow limits, without forethought . . . its criminal members given rather to furtive offenses than to the robust crimes of the whites." It is safe to say that this is no longer the prevailing view.

But while the content of stereotypes evolves over time, the existence of stereotypes cannot be avoided. Psychologists have long recognized that "*erroneous generalization* and *hostility* . . . are natural and common capacities of the human mind."[8] There is little we can do to alter our own psychological limitations, but we can become more self-aware and recognize the effects that our beliefs have on others. We can acknowledge our stereotypes, and—as Walter Lippmann urged almost a century ago—we can choose to "hold them lightly, to modify them gladly."[9] For each of us in our daily lives, we can think of no better advice.

Notes

PREFACE

1 Anderson (2010, p. 53).

INTRODUCTION

1 Taylor (2013, pp. 93–94). He points out that money is "epistemically objective. I can't just decide, unilaterally, that my green pieces of paper will be worth a thousand dollars each."

2 Many of the data sources we reference in this book use the terms black and African American interchangeably, or allow people to self-identify using either term. The same is true of the terms Hispanic and Latino. According to a survey by the Pew Research Center, about half of those identifying as Hispanic or Latino have no preference among these terms, but Hispanic is preferred by a two-to-one margin among those who do declare a preference (Lopez, 2013). A significant proportion of those identifying as Hispanic or Latino (by ethnicity) on the Census also identify as white (by race). We will generally use the term white to refer to non-Hispanic whites.

3 Loury (in press).

4 Taylor (2013, pp. 142–143).

1. STEREOTYPES

1 Hawkins (2016).

2 Wible (2016).

3 Banaji and Greenwald (2013). The riddle is also posed by Kevin Costner's character in the 1996 film *Tin Cup*.

4 "I have a dream that my four little children will one day live in a nation where they will not be judged by the color of their skin but by the content of their character." Martin Luther King Jr., "I Have a Dream" (speech, Lincoln Memorial, Washington, DC, August 28, 1963).

5 Bruner (1957, p. 43).

6 Lippmann (1922, p. 90).

7 Allport (1954, pp. 9–27).

8 Lippmann (1922, pp. 119–120).

9 Katz and Braly (1933).

10 See Gilbert (1951), Karlins, Coffman, and Walters (1969), and Madon et al. (2001).

11 By the time of the Madon et al. (2001) study, not only had the demographic composition of Princeton undergraduates changed dramatically, but the original list of adjectives was no longer adequate. The authors therefore conducted a second study with a significantly larger list of descriptors to choose from. This substantially reduced the frequency with which words on the original list were chosen, replaced by new descriptors for African Americans such as noisy and athletic (among white respondents) and tough, humorous, and rebellious (among nonwhites).

12 Katz and Braly (1933, p. 288).

13 See Goffman (1959) on impression management, and Loury (1994) on how this can result in self-censorship.

14 See Schuman et al. (1997).

15 Banaji and Greenwald (2013, p. 46).

16 Banaji and Greenwald (2013, chapter 3).

17 Some psychologists have questioned the predictive validity of the Race IAT, arguing, based on a meta-analysis of empirical studies, that it "provides little insight into who will discriminate against whom, and provides no more insight than explicit measures of bias" (Oswald et al., 2013, p. 188). Others have defended the superior predictive performance of the test (Greenwald, Banaji, and Nosek, 2015). While the test has good internal reliability (a person's score on odd-numbered trials tends to be close to the score on the even-numbered trials), it does not show acceptable test-retest reliability (a person's score can differ greatly if the test is retaken in a few days). The classic Race IAT, however, is not the only test of implicit racial attitudes, as we show in the next section, and there is a consensus that these measures predict behavior under some conditions, although the precise specification of those conditions remains hotly

debated among psychologists (National Academies of Sciences, Engineering, and Medicine, 2017, pp. 7–22).

18 Banaji and Greenwald (2013, p. 105).

19 Correll et al. (2002).

20 See Payne (2006) for an overview and interpretation.

21 Payne (2001).

22 Greenwald, Oakes, and Hoffman (2003).

23 James, James, and Vila (2016).

24 Richeson and Shelton (2007, p. 316).

25 Richeson and Shelton (2007, p. 317).

26 Richeson et al. (2003).

27 The pioneering contributions here are by Phelps (1972) and Arrow (1973). Behavioral economists have developed models that are more in tune with the work of psychologists; see, for instance, Rabin and Schrag (1999) and Bordalo et al. (2016).

28 See Coate and Loury (1993) for a formal model of this process and an exploration of the consequences of affirmative action policies. Such policies can have either positive or negative effects in their model: eliminating stereotypes altogether under some conditions, and lowering investment levels even further under other conditions.

29 Sherman, Gartin, and Buerger (1989).

30 Ebony Photo-Editorial (1966, p. 92).

31 This "place effect" is the main channel through which police use of force places a disproportionate burden on African Americans (Terrill and Reisig, 2003).

32 Haslam et al. (2006). This is the sense in which we use the term here, while recognizing that it has many other uses.

33 Bloom (2010).

34 James (2017).

35 See O'Flaherty (2015, chapter 3) for a more detailed discussion of race and racial essentialism.

36 Muhammad (2010, pp. 20–21). An undiluted expression of the essentialist perspective may be found in Hinton Rowan Helper's references in 1868 to the "crime-stained blackness" and "base and beastlike savagery" of emancipated slaves (Muhammad, 2010, p. 16).

37 Muhammad (2010, pp. 5, 10, 96–98). In *The Philadelphia Negro*, Du Bois examined data from a penitentiary on the causes of criminal involvement for a set of 541 prisoners and concluded that most of them had suffered adverse environmental conditions, including "the influence of homes badly situated and badly managed, with parents untrained for their responsibilities; the influence of social surroundings which by poor laws and inefficient administration leave the bad to be made worse; the influence of economic exclusion which admits Negroes only to those parts of the economic world where it is hardest to retain ambition and self-respect; and finally that indefinable but real and mighty moral influence that causes men to have a real sense of manhood or leads them to lose aspiration and self-respect" (Du Bois, 1899, pp. 285–286).

38 See Rogers (in press), who is referring here to the writings of David Walker, Maria Stewart, Hosea Easton, Martin Delany, and Frederick Douglass.

39 Kitcher (2007, p. 299).

40 Haslam et al. (2006).

41 Du Bois (1897).

42 Quine (1961, p. 41).

43 Loury (2002, p.70).

44 Loury (2002, pp. 70–71). See also Goffman (1963) and Patterson (1982).

45 Myrdal (1944, vol. 1, p. 42).

46 Corey (2012).

47 "Sen. Tim Scott (R-SC) on Race Relations—Full Speech (C-SPAN)," YouTube, July 13, 2016, https://www.youtube.com/watch?v=OKgYgq GfeIE. For a complete transcript, see "Read Senator Tim Scott's Candid Account of Getting Stopped by Police," *Time,* July 14, 2016, http://time .com/4406540/senator-tim-scott-speech-transcript/.

48 Butler (2017, p. 24).

49 Kahneman and Tversky (1972, p. 431).

50 Tversky and Kahneman (1983). Bordalo et al. (2016) have expanded on this idea, arguing that a characteristic is considered to be typical or representative in a group if the group possesses this trait with high relative frequency in comparison with a reference group, even if the absolute frequency of the trait is low in all groups. According to the theory, Flo-

ridians are stereotyped as being elderly, even though less than a fifth of Florida residents are senior citizens, because the retiree population in Florida is quite a bit higher than that in other states, even if it is low everywhere.

51 Anderson (2010, p. 53). See also the discussion in the preface.
52 Butler (2017, p. 42).
53 Union (2017, pp. 218–219).
54 Staples (1994, pp. 202–203). This episode inspired the title of Claude Steele's book *Whistling Vivaldi*.

2. CRIME

1 FBI: UCR (2018).
2 See National Research Council (2014) for a similar approach to visualizing the data.
3 Lauritsen, Rezey, and Heimer (2016).
4 See Figure 11.2 for incarceration rates and trends.
5 For similar reasons, whites are less likely to be robbery victims than blacks, even though many robbery offenders selectively target whites (O'Flaherty and Sethi, 2007).
6 See Robinson and Rand (2011, Table 16) for 2008 data. Per 1,000 households, the motor vehicle theft rates were 12.6 for blacks and 5.4 for whites; the burglary rates were 42.0 and 23.6, respectively.
7 Only 42 percent of black households had such access in 2015, as opposed to two-thirds of white households, according to the American Housing Survey.

3. ROBBERY

1 Staples (1994, p. 204).
2 National Research Council (2014); see Figure 2.1 in Chapter 2.
3 We are grateful to Rachel Morgan, a statistician with the Bureau of Justice Statistics, for providing us with the data for this period.
4 This is an approximation, because injury can also occur in the absence of resistance, as in the case of "strike-first" robberies. For a detailed discussion of the method described here, see O'Flaherty and Sethi (2009).

5　This has long been the case; see O'Flaherty and Sethi (2008). The ratio appears to be fourteen in the table because of rounding.

6　O'Flaherty and Sethi (2007).

7　See FBI: UCR (2016) and Figure 2.3 in Chapter 2.

8　O'Flaherty and Sethi (2009).

9　Many other factors are implicated in the overall decline in crime, including reduced exposure to lead in childhood and greater availability of psycho-pharmaceuticals; see O'Flaherty and Sethi (2015) for a discussion of these and other explanations.

10　O'Flaherty and Sethi (2009).

11　Wright and Decker (1997).

12　These estimates are based on data from the Bureau of Justice Statistics. See O'Flaherty and Sethi (2008) for similar patterns in data from earlier periods.

13　Our hypothesis also suggests that white victims will face a greater likelihood of violence when resisting white offenders than when resisting black offenders, and again this is confirmed in the data: the likelihood of violence conditional on resistance was 64 percent for white-on-white robberies.

14　Wright and Decker (1997, p. 84).

15　Wright and Decker (1997, p. 84).

16　Wright and Decker (1997, pp. 77–82).

17　Wright and Decker (1997, pp. 84–85).

18　See table 2.2 in Raphael and Stoll (2013) for data on the incidence of various index crimes, as well as arrests per crime and prison admissions per arrest for the years 1984, 2004, and 2009.

19　Harcourt (2007) has argued that racial profiling in police stops will create a divergence between the racial composition of the arrest pool and that of the offender pool. We consider this argument, and police stops more generally, in Chapter 6.

20　Hacker (2003, p. 218).

21　Wright and Decker (1997, p. 7).

4. MURDER

1　See Adler (2006, p. 101) for discussion of this and a number of similar cases.

2 Reliable estimates of the relationship between offender and victim, the motivation of offenders, and the circumstances of the killing can be obtained only for cases that are solved. Since cases involving strangers are less likely to be solved, data from closed cases can provide us with a lower bound for stranger homicides. Using a random sample of 200 killings from each of four cities in 1994 and 1995 (with status evaluated in late 1997 and early 1998), Wellford and Cronin (1999) find that about three-fourths of cases are solved, and among these 30 percent involve strangers. Since the proportion of strangers among unsolved cases is considerably higher, and some others involve acquaintances, this is likely to be an underestimate. Using national data, Riedel (1998) estimates that stranger homicides are in the 18–25 percent range. There is also a large category of homicides for which the victim and the offender are believed to be friends or acquaintances, and among these are some in which they are only superficially acquainted with each other.

3 Schelling (1960, p. 207). See Baliga and Sjöström (2004) for a formal model of this process, and the role of communication in averting the tragedy.

4 O'Flaherty and Sethi (2010b).

5 Kennedy (1998, p. 30).

6 Litwack (1979, p. 286).

7 Powdermaker (1939, pp. 173–174).

8 In fact, Powdermaker's four-way ranking of punishments for homicide mirrors a principle subsequently articulated by Donald Black in *The Behavior of Law,* but with wealth rather than race signifying social position: "In cases of homicide . . . the most severe punishment befalls a poor man who kills a wealthy man, followed by a wealthy man who kills another equally wealthy, then a poor man whose victim is equally poor, while the least severe punishment is given to a wealthy man who kills a poor man" (1976, p. 28).

9 Forman (2017, p. 83). The report also discusses abusive behavior by white police officers toward innocent black citizens, a topic to which we return below.

10 National Advisory Commission on Civil Disorders (1968, p. 161). Along similar lines, Anderson (1999, p. 321) notes: "In the inner-city community

there is a generalized belief that the police simply do not care about black people. . . . If a black man shoots another black man the incident will not be thoroughly investigated."

11 Furman v. Georgia (1972).

12 United States Government Accountability Office (1990).

13 Baldus et al. (1998).

14 Rohrlich and Tulsky (1996). The analysis excluded homicides classified as accidental, vehicular, or justifiable.

15 See Lee (2005) for a detailed discussion of the methodology and results, as well as estimates of the time to clearance, which also revealed similar effects of victim race.

16 Rohrlich and Tulsky (1996).

17 Lowery et al. (2018).

18 Puckett and Lundman (2003).

19 Puckett and Lundman (2003, pp. 176, 185). Note that it is the racial composition rather than the average income or wealth in a neighborhood that is the critical factor here, in contrast with the response of law enforcement officials to the *Los Angeles Times* study.

20 See O'Flaherty and Sethi (2010a) for a model of this process with application to racial disparities in rates of homicide victimization and offending.

21 See Cheng and Hoekstra (2013) and McClellan and Tekin (2017).

22 Powdermaker (1939, p. 171).

23 Coates (2015, pp. 14–15).

24 Miron (2004, p. 3).

25 Okrent (2010, p. 276).

26 Owens (2014, p. 466). See also Owens (2011), which documents an increase in market-based violence and a decrease in intoxication-related violence resulting from temperance laws.

27 Bodenhorn (2016).

28 Dell (2015).

29 Lindo and Padilla-Romo (2018).

30 Chimeli and Soares (2017).

31 United States Kerner Commission (1968, p. 161).

32 Myrdal (1944, vol. 2, p. 977).

33 Washington (1915). The concentration of street vice in black neighborhoods of cities is due to both the entry of vice and the exit of whites (Sethi and O'Flaherty, 2010c).

34 O'Flaherty and Sethi (2015). We are referring here to the portion of the Newark Metropolitan Division that lies in New Jersey; a small portion of this division also lies in Pennsylvania.

35 Papachristos, Hureau, and Braga (2012) show this to be the case using data from Boston, and Papachristos et al. (2015) do the same for Chicago. Networks are constructed using police records in both cases: individuals who are recorded as being together at any given time and place are classified as associates in the Boston study, and those who are arrested together for the same crime are associates in the Chicago study.

36 Papachristos (2009, p. 74); the author is here referring specifically to gang murders.

37 Puckett and Lundman (2003, p. 176).

5. PUBLIC ACTION

1 John Pfaff (2017) has observed that the decentralized nature of law enforcement actions in the country was a key factor in allowing for the massive growth in incarceration. By the same token, however, decentralization can allow for local experimentation with less punitive policies, as Heather Gerken (in press) has argued.

2 Moody-Adams (2003, p. 97).

3 Cooper (1999).

4 Greenblatt (2013).

5 Loury (2002, p. 86).

6 Loury (2002, p. 79).

7 Hart (2017).

8 See Tonry (2011) for a detailed discussion of differences in offending and incarceration rates for various crimes.

6. POLICE STOPS

1 The Supreme Court affirmed the constitutionality of this more permissive standard in *Terry v. Ohio* (1968). Such stops are sometimes referred to as Terry stops.

2 See Langton and Durose (2013), who describe results from the most recent wave of the Police-Public Contact Survey.

3 See New York City Commission on Human Rights (2017) for the laws pertaining to public spaces, including taxi cabs.

4 See, for instance, Mueller (2015).

5 New York City Commission on Human Rights (2017).

6 Moreau (2010, p. 147).

7 Becker (1957, p. 14).

8 Becker (1993, p. 389). These remarks do not appear in the original lecture posted on www.nobelprize.org.

9 Ayres (2002, pp. 133–134). See also Ayres (2001) and Knowles, Persico, and Todd (2001).

10 See Kennedy (1998, p. 227) for a discussion of the differences between the two forms of discrimination, as well as the difficulty of distinguishing between them in practice.

11 Refusal of service in violation of the law is an extremely common occurrence; many celebrities and public figures have published firsthand accounts. See Glanville (2015) for a representative case. Ge et al. (2016) argue that such discrimination persists on ride-sharing apps such as Uber and Lyft, despite the absence of face-to-face interaction at the time of the service request. By assigning fictitious names to otherwise similar profiles, they found that riders with black-sounding names face longer wait times and more frequent cancellations than those with white-sounding names; this approach to testing for discrimination was introduced in an influential paper by Bertrand and Mullainathan (2004).

12 See Ayres (2002), Anwar and Fang (2006), and Bjerk (2007) for further discussion of this issue, which is called the problem of infra-marginality.

13 Pierson et al. (2017). The reported rates of contraband recovery were 28 percent for black and white drivers, and 22 percent for Hispanics.

14 Knowles, Persico, and Todd (2001) examined Maryland traffic stops and found contraband recovery rates of about one-third for whites and blacks, but just 11 percent for Hispanics.

15 They do this by adopting a parametric specification for the probability distributions and estimating the parameters while allowing for these to

vary by driver race and stop location. Specifically, they assume a (two-parameter) beta distribution for the likelihood of contraband possession; see Figure 6.1 for two distributions from this family.

16 See Kennedy (1998, chapter 4) for a detailed discussion of the extent to which racial profiling is permissible under the Constitution.

17 This particular program, as well as similar initiatives adopted in other cities, are usually referred to simply as "stop-and-frisk" strategies, and we will also generally use the latter term.

18 Goel, Rao, and Shroff (2017).

19 Goel, Rao, and Shroff (2017, p. 367). Coviello and Persico (2015) also make this point and claim that the evidence does not support bias against black citizens within precincts, though it is consistent with bias in the allocation of police resources across precincts.

20 Specifically, the authors estimate a logistic regression for weapon recovery, using this large set of explanatory variables as well as pairwise interactions among them. They estimate the model using the 2009–2010 data and then show that it provides a good out-of-sample fit for the 2010–2011 data.

21 Goel, Rao, and Shroff (2017, p. 367). These findings are broadly consistent with those of Gelman, Fagan, and Kiss (2007), who looked at similar data from an earlier period (a fifteen-month window starting in January 1998) and also considered the question of whether precinct-level variations in stops could account for racial disparities. This study found that for stops involving suspicion of a violent crime or weapons offense, blacks and Hispanics were stopped at higher rates than whites across all precinct types. Furthermore, disparities in stops exceeded disparities in prior-year arrest rates, suggesting a level of bias that could not be accounted for by perceived differences in offending. The authors concluded that "differences in stop rates among ethnic groups are real, substantial, and not explained by previous arrest rates or precincts" (Gelman, Fagan, and Kiss, 2007, p. 822).

22 Knowles, Persico, and Todd (2001).

23 As noted by Bjerk (2007), random searches of this kind would be unlawful, since they are not based on "reasonable suspicion" arising from "specific and articulable facts" specific to the individual searched.

24 Antonovics and Knight (2009). The authors accounted for information other than race in predicting the likelihood of a stop, including motorist age and gender, vehicle attributes, time and location, and the infraction that allegedly led to the stop.

25 Anwar and Fang (2006). The authors do not infer from this that white troopers exhibit racial bias, since their behavior is consistent with a more aggressive search posture applied to motorists of all groups, including fellow whites.

26 Phelps (1972) and Arrow (1973) independently developed theories of statistical discrimination in the 1970s to examine the incentive effects of stereotypes in labor markets. The two approaches are different in some important respects: Arrow looked at ex ante identical groups who end up with different behavior through the operation of self-fulfilling negative stereotypes, while Phelps was concerned with a situation in which employers are able to assess more precisely the productivity levels of applicants belonging to their own group. Both approaches are relevant to police stops.

27 According to the first-person observations of Chambliss (1994, p. 179), quoted in Forman (2017, p. 170): "The RDU patrols the ghetto continuously looking for cars with young black men in them. They are especially attentive to newer-model cars . . . based on the belief that they are the favorite cars of drug dealers. During our observations, however, the RDU officers came to the conclusion that drug dealers were leaving their fancy cars at home to avoid vehicular stops. It thus became commonplace for RDU officers to stop any car with young black men in it."

28 See Bjerk (2007) for a precise statement of the conditions under which this happens, and Harcourt (2007) for a broader discussion of the phenomenon and its implications.

29 Harcourt (2007).

30 We discuss the sources and extent of harm at the end of this chapter.

31 Dell (2015).

32 Risse and Zeckhauser (2004, p. 150) support this a priori conclusion: "For instance, our utilitarian argument might support searches for contraband in certain neighborhoods with the aid of profiling. It seems less plausible that drug searches on the New Jersey Turnpike will be supported. The

prospects of diminishing drug traffic by intercepting cars on major highways seems slim—too slim to outweigh the incremental effects on minority sentiments."

33 Sherman, Gartin, and Buerger (1989); see the discussion of location in Chapter 1.

34 National Research Council, Committee to Review Research on Police Policy and Practices(2004, p. 250).

35 National Research Council, Committee to Review Research on Police Policy and Practices (2004, pp. 239–240).

36 Groff et al. (2015) and Ratcliffe et al. (2011).

37 Rosenfeld, Deckard, and Blackburn (2014). We are not aware of any studies that have explicitly tested the effects of police being directed to adopt stop-and-frisk tactics.

38 Weisburd et al. (2016).

39 Weisburd et al. (2016).

40 MacDonald, Fagan, and Geller (2016). The authors don't have a true experiment or even a natural experiment, so they derive this result by comparing changes and trends in impact zones with changes and trends in nearby neighborhoods. These methods are usually not as persuasive at establishing causality through randomized control trials or natural experiments, but we can be reasonably confident about their finding because it confirms many other studies on hot spots policing that used stronger tests of causality.

41 See Di Tella and Schargrodsky (2004) on the Argentine mobilization, Klick and Tabarrok (2005) on the effects of terror alert levels, Poutvaara and Priks (2006) on the 9 / 11 attacks and the South Asian tsunami, Draca, Machin, and Witt (2011) on the London attacks, and Evans and Owens (2007) and Chalfin and McCrary (2013) on evidence from U.S. cities.

42 Weisburd et al. (2016). The New York Police Department patrol division had about 18,000 members in the early 2000s, including supervisors (Zimring, 2012, pp. 114–116). Officers worked five shifts a week, each was eight hours and thirty-five minutes, but that included setup and preparation time. Officers received on average twenty vacation days, depending on seniority, and unlimited sick time (NY Police Department, 2012). Other

time may have been required for training and court appearances. Thus, the average officer probably patrolled for well less than a fifth of the hours worked in a year.

43 The number of stops has fallen precipitously since its peak, and in 2016 there were around 12,000 stops. See New York Civil Liberties Union (2018) for an overview and data.

44 Steele (2010, p. 2). The title of Steele's memoir is a reference to the stereotype-deflecting tactic used by Brent Staples that we discussed in Chapter 2. For another example of the harm that is imposed on innocents by profiling, see Elijah Anderson's account of an interview with an anonymous law school graduate in *The Cosmopolitan Canopy* (2011, pp. 249–253).

45 Blow (2013).

46 Risse and Zeckhauser (2004, p. 146).

47 Risse and Zeckhauser (2004, p. 147).

48 Durlauf (2006, p. F409).

49 Consider a slight modification of Durlauf's fairness principle: among innocent people with the same visible nonracial indicia of guilt, the probability of being stopped should not depend on race. A black man walking down a New York City street brandishing a machete should be as likely to be stopped as a white man walking down the street doing the same. But both of them should be more likely to be stopped than a man of any race walking down the street brandishing a book of ancient philosophy. At present we cannot tell whether this augmented fairness principle is being violated, because no study so far looks at fine descriptions of people who were not stopped.

7. USE OF FORCE

1 Bittner (1970, p. 40).

2 Bittner (1970, pp. 37–46).

3 See Hortense Powdermaker's discussion of this point in Chapter 4.

4 Myrdal (1944, vol. 2, p. 541).

5 Myrdal (1944, vol. 2, p. 1342).

6 Myrdal (1944, vol. 2, pp. 540–541).

7 King (2000, p. 66).

8 King (2000, p. 82).

9 Reprinted in King (1992).

10 Forman (2017, p. 154). Butler (2017, p. 97) likens even routine frisks to sexual assaults: "The *Terry* opinion characterized stop and frisk as a 'serious intrusion on the sanctity of the person, which may inflict great indignity and arouse strong resentment.' I would go further and say that the invasive aspect of the frisk—the 'feel with sensitive fingers every portion of the prisoner's body [including] the groin and areas about the testicles,' in the words of the police manual referenced in *Terry*—makes the injury analogous to sexual assault. Frisks are frequently experienced as offensive sexual touchings."

11 Fryer (2016).

12 Forman (2017, p. 83).

13 Forman (2017, p. 154).

14 United States Department of Justice (2013).

15 McFarland (2017).

16 This issue is especially important when making inferences about bias in the use of lethal force, as we discuss in Chapter 8.

17 Kennedy (1998, p. 157).

18 See Lai et al. (2015). Footage (with audio) of the traffic stop may be viewed at Texas Department of Public Safety (2015).

19 Fernandez and Montgomery (2017).

20 Hauser (2016).

21 See Nathan (2016) for evidence of this and the claims to follow. The practice of using fines and fees arising from traffic violations as a major source of funding for public expenditures is widespread in many jurisdictions; on Ferguson, Missouri, see United States Department of Justice (2015a).

22 See the report by the Cambridge Review Committee (2010) for separate accounts of the incident by Gates and Crowley, and Ogletree (2010) for further analysis.

23 The photograph may be seen at Boston Globe (2009), which also contains links to a number of news reports related to the incident.

24 See Anderson Cooper 360 Degrees (2009) for a transcript of the conversation.

25 International Association of Chiefs of Police (2016).

26 However, immigration enforcement often bears some resemblance to enforcement of the Fugitive Slave Act.

27 U.S. Department of Justice (2015a, pp. 2–5).

28 U.S. Department of Justice (2015a, pp. 2–6, 18–19). We examine the consequences of such practices for witness cooperation and the clearance rates for violent offenses in Chapter 9.

29 United States Department of Justice (2015b). In particular, several witnesses "recanted large portions of their accounts, admitting that they did not in fact witness the shooting as they initially claimed" (p. 27).

30 Fryer (2016).

8. LETHAL FORCE

1 *Tennessee v. Gardner* (1985).

2 United States Bureau of Labor Statistics (2010, 2013).

3 FBI: UCR (2016). An additional twenty-three officers were killed in Puerto Rico, and one in the U.S. Virgin Islands. Unless otherwise stated, we use "state" to include the District of Columbia.

4 Davis and Lowery (2015).

5 Butler (2017, p. 53). See Kets and Sethi (2016) for a discussion of information that is needed but currently unavailable.

6 Zimring (2017) argues that the *Guardian* provides the most reliable data, and so we rely on this source throughout the chapter.

7 National Consortium for the Study of Terrorism and Responses to Terrorism (2015).

8 Zimring (2017, pp. 78–84).

9 Zimring (2017, pp. 84, 94–97).

10 Kirk and Quandt (2015).

11 For these calculations, we used the 2010 census for civilian populations, the *Guardian* data for civilian victims of lethal force in 2015–2016, and LEOKA for police victims during the 2006–2015 period, per million 2010 officer population. The general murder rate per 100,000 population is from FBI: UCR 2015.

12 Zimring (2017, pp. 99–100).

13 McMullen and Williams (2008).

14 Zimring (2017, pp. 106–107).

15 Zimring (2017, pp. 107–108)

16 Raper (1940, p. 274 and Appendix III, table A-2). Lynchings (not all of them of blacks) occurred about thirteen times per year on average in the 1930s, and in the 228 cities for which Raper had data (far from the majority of the U.S. population), police killed fifty-five blacks per year on average.

17 According to the FBI Supplemental Homicide Reports, whites murdered about 207 blacks per year on average in single victim–single offender homicides between 2010 and 2016. Since almost all homicides by police are ruled justifiable, almost all these white offenders were civilians. Roman (2013) found that between 2005 and 2010 whites killed blacks in about 235 justifiable homicides, or about 39 per year. Adding this to murders yields 246 blacks killed by white civilians a year. The *Guardian* data set lists an average of 286.5 blacks killed by police per year for 2015 and 2016. Not all of these killings involved white officers, and we do not know how many civilians killed blacks in murders involving multiple offenders, multiple victims, or unknown offenders. If the sum of these unknown murders averages more than 40 a year, the majority of whites who killed blacks were civilians. That is probably the case. We have not included here the executions of inmates, which number about 10 a year.

18 Raper (1940, pp. 42–43) and Simpson (2013).

19 In addition, it is likely that Rice was viewed as being substantially older than he was. Goff et al. (2014, p. 540) demonstrate experimentally that black boys tend to be "misperceived as older than they actually are and prematurely perceived as responsible for their actions during a developmental period where their peers receive the beneficial assumption of childlike innocence."

20 State of Missouri v. Darren Wilson (2014).

21 Bouie (2014). The research referenced here is Waytz et al. (2015). The language used by Darren Wilson brings to mind similar statements by Sergeant Stacey Koon, one of four officers charged with assault in the 1991 beating of Rodney King. Koon claimed that he was "flabbergasted" at King's ability to withstand repeated baton blows and felt that he "could, in a moment, turn into the 'Hulk.'"

22 South Carolina Department of Public Safety (2014).

23 Choi (2016).

24 *State of Minnesota v. Jeronimo Yanez* (2016).

25 See Chan (2016) and Smith, Capecchi, and Furber (2016).

26 Moskos (2016a).

27 Butler (2017, p. 126)

28 The Kerner Commission report, discussed in detail below, documented 164 civil disorders in 128 cities. Eight of these were deemed major and a further thirty-three serious.

29 National Advisory Commission on Civil Disorders (1968, pp. 32, 47).

30 National Advisory Commission on Civil Disorders (1968, p. 37).

31 National Advisory Commission on Civil Disorders (1968, pp. 180, 37). The quote is from Newark director of police Dominick Spina.

32 National Advisory Commission on Civil Disorders (1968, p. 56).

33 "Any use of force produces many effects, not all of which can be foreseen. The more force applied, the greater the chance of collateral damage and mistakes. Using substantial force also increases the opportunity for insurgent propaganda to portray lethal military activities as brutal. In contrast, using force precisely and discriminately strengthens the rule of law that needs to be established" (United States Army, 2006, p. 1–27).

34 Forman (2017) provides a vivid example to make this point.

35 See Dias, Eligon, and Oppel Jr. (2018) for an account of this and several related incidents.

36 As Andrew Gelman (2015) puts it, "This is an argument over the denominator," which in this case is the arrest rate.

37 Fryer (2016).

38 Fatalities occur in about 10–30 percent of weapon discharges. See Geller and Scott (1992, pp. 97–106). This compounds fatality rates (fatality contingent on hit) and incident hit rates.

39 Quoted in Bui and Cox (2016).

40 Houston is unusual in other respects. As we show later in this chapter, according to the *Guardian* data, white civilians face a greater likelihood of lethal force in Houston than black civilians do in New York City.

41 United States Federal Bureau of Investigation (2015, table 19).

42 *Washington Post* (2017).

43 For this reason, studies based on 2015 data, such as Nix et al. (2017), need to be interpreted with caution.

44 Hutson et al. (1998) and Mohandie, Meloy, and Collins (2009).

45 Mullainathan (2015).

46 Our work with the *Guardian* data in this book is preliminary. With José Montiel Olea, we are expanding our analysis with more data sets, more data, more years, more covariates, and more sophisticated econometric techniques.

47 In an examination of police-related homicides in the American South during the 1930s, Arthur Raper (1940, p. 53) claimed that there were substantial differences across jurisdictions in the risks faced by officers: "In 170 of the 202 Southern cities and towns studied, no policeman had been killed in the last five years, in 32 communities 51 were killed." We discuss a number of other findings from this study later in this chapter.

48 The other western states with high rates of civilian fatalities are similar to New Mexico in the racial composition of victims; Hispanics and non-Hispanic whites were generally killed at similar rates. In some states, such as Alaska, Native Americans were killed at very high rates, but the absolute numbers involved were relatively small.

49 These states are the original seven that chose to secede before the Civil War (South Carolina, Mississippi, Florida, Alabama, Georgia, Louisiana, and Texas) and the four that subsequently chose to join them (Virginia, Arkansas, Tennessee, and North Carolina). If we drop Florida and Virginia from this list (because extensive migration has changed the character of these states), the results are even more striking.

50 Bobo et al. (2012) and White (2013) show this with survey data, and Ingraham (2015) obtains similar results using Google searches.

51 Raper (1940).

52 Lum and Ball (2015) use statistical methods based on the degree to which multiple lists have common elements to estimate that the total number of fatalities from police use of force is above 1,250 per year, with a best guess of 1,500. This implies significant underreporting even in the *Guardian* data, and this underreporting is unlikely to be random across jurisdictions. See Ball (2016) for an overview of the methods and results.

53 In trying to explain differences across the South in the 1930s, Raper (1940, p. 39) wrote: "High and low rates, are accounted for, it seems, by community organization factors. Direct force is still relied upon in Mississippi, rural and urban; ritual and traditional race roles suffice in Georgia and South Carolina, except in Atlanta, where racial competition emerges more or less as in the industrial centers of Tennessee and the Middle Northern states, which also have high rates." Raper also speculated that familiarity may inhibit murders and the anonymity of big cities may encourage them: "Officers have implicit faith in some of the Negroes they know, but they also know Negroes who they are convinced will kill a white man. But policemen cannot know all the Negroes in a city, and besides newcomers are always around, and there is the possibility that almost any one of these strange faces may be the front of a 'bad nigger.' And that is why the officer killed blind Grover Davis, why Negroes are in more danger of being killed in the large cities, where impersonal relations obtain, than in the smaller communities where Negroes are personally acquainted with the policemen" (p. 53). Since it is in the South today that the proportion of blacks who live in rural areas is greatest, the familiarity effect may have something to do with the relatively low rate of recorded police killings there.

54 For these calculations we used 1940 census data and the 209 cities out of Raper's 228 for which we could find good data.

55 Raper (1940, p. 40) and Brearley (1932).

56 Raper (1940, p. 53).

57 Muhammad (2010, p. 116). In one of the most dramatic instances of pre-emptive violence, Robert Charles shot seven New Orleans police officers, killing four of them, during a sequence of clashes in 1900 that began when an officer attacked him with a baton and drew his gun. See Wells-Barnett (1900) and Hair (1976) for accounts of the incidents and the riot that followed.

58 "Stop Police Brutality! Washington's Record of Official Murder and abuse . . . ," Washington Council of the National Negro Congress, July 25, 1938, p. 1, cited by Raper (1940, p. 38).

59 The Raper data set is for five years, while the *Guardian* covers just two. Since random fluctuations are better smoothed out in the Raper data, the *Guardian* data should have a greater incidence of very high and very low

values, even if both data sets are drawn from the same universe. Hence the small proportion of very high values in the *Guardian* data actually understates the decline in black mortality from police encounters.

60 Sherman (2018) reports that in many big cities, especially New York, the rate at which police killed civilians fell considerably in the 1970s, which he attributes to reforms in procedures and training designed to preserve life. He also notes, based on Mendez (1983), that the rate for blacks fell more than the rate for whites. This may be an important decade in the fall of the black victimization rate between 1940 and 2015.

61 The correlations were −0.17 for black civilians and 0.17 for whites.

62 Moskos (2016b). Graphic video evidence in the Daniel Shaver case was released after the officer who fired the fatal shots was acquitted of all charges. It reveals an unarmed man who "sobbed and pleaded" for his life while lying flat on his stomach, attempting to follow a confusing and contradictory set of commands before being shot dead (Wang, 2017; Lowery, 2017).

63 The standard reference is to Simpson (1951), though it was familiar to earlier statisticians. In a study on gender bias in graduate admissions at Berkeley, Bickel, Hammel, and O'Connell (1975) demonstrated the empirical relevance of the phenomenon.

64 Recall that Coviello and Persico (2015) attribute racial disparities in stop-and-frisk activity to the assignment of resources across precincts in New York City rather than to bias in the use of stops within precincts. One might be able to tease out racial attitudes from a data set that had information on individual officers, where each officer was observed in a wide variety of incidents in many different kinds of neighborhoods. But with 838,000 police officers and an average police career of twenty years, just 1 officer in 38 is involved in a police killing in their entire career.

65 The ten states here are Florida, Georgia, North Carolina, Louisiana, Texas, the District of Columbia, Colorado, New Mexico, California, and Oklahoma.

9. TESTIMONY

1 Simon (1991, p. 464).

2 Cook (2009, p. 317) notes that even "victims are unlikely to benefit in any tangible way from cooperation with police, and most victims do not

bother to report the crime. . . . Citizens who become involved in a crime are invited to make a charitable contribution of their time and possibly their safety, in exchange for knowing that they have done a good deed for their community."

3 Tyler and Fagan (2008, p. 234). See Tyler (2006) for a more general discussion of compliance with the law.

4 Tyler and Fagan (2008, p. 262). The authors also note that a belief that one has been stopped "because of one's ethnicity" undermines legitimacy and "encourages resistance and antagonism" (p. 265). This suggests that profiling in police stops, even if motivated by legitimate law enforcement concerns such as contraband recovery, can lower clearance rates and increase crime because it is thought to violate procedural fairness.

5 Williams (2014).

6 United States Department of Justice (2015b).

7 Capehart (2015).

8 Schmidt and Apuzzo (2015).

9 Capehart (2017).

10 Adler (2006, pp. 185–187).

11 Adler (2006, p. 193).

12 Kocieniewski (2007).

13 Homicide and witness cooperation are characterized by what economists call "strategic complementarity": greater involvement by some raises incentives for involvement by others. This can lead otherwise identical environments to have very different levels of homicide and witness cooperation. See O'Flaherty and Sethi (2010d) for a discussion of witness cooperation along these lines.

14 Jacobs (2006).

15 Preston (2005).

16 Iyengar (2009).

17 Hobson (2018).

18 Macur (2018).

19 Hobson (2018).

20 Gross (2017). See Mayer (1995) for a detailed account and analysis of the Thomas confirmation.

21 *New York Times* (2018).

22 Haberman and Baker (2018).

23 Quinnipiac University (2018)

24 See McCrummen, Reinhard, and Crites (2017) for the initial report, and Gattis (2017) for the open letter. In January 2018, Corfman sued Moore and his campaign for defamation, demanding only an apology and legal fees (Kirby, 2018). Along similar lines, Summer Zervos—one of nineteen women who have accused Donald Trump of sexual misconduct—filed a defamation suit against Trump for claiming that her accusations were fabrications and lies (Sellers, 2017).

25 Macur (2018).

26 Kantor and Twohey (2017) and Farrow (2017).

27 McQuade (2014).

28 Steel and Schmidt (2017); the quote is from Farhi (2017).

29 Nyong'o (2017).

30 Meissner and Brigham (2001) and Golby et al. (2001).

31 See Fryer and Jackson (2008) for a formal model of this process.

32 Gross et al. (2005).

33 Anderson (2010, p. 129).

34 Scalese (2014).

35 Montaldo (2016).

36 Kennedy (1998, pp. 100–104).

37 "With the Southern white man, any mésalliance existing between a white woman and a colored man is a sufficient foundation for the charge of rape. . . . In numerous instances where colored men have been lynched on the charge of rape, it was positively known at the time of lynching, and indisputably proven after the victim's death, that the relationship sustained between the man and woman was voluntary and clandestine, and that in no court of law could even the charge of assault have been successfully maintained" (Wells-Barnett, 1894, p. 6).

38 Wells-Barnett (1894, p. 67).

39 *New York Times* (2012).

40 A complete list may be found at https://www.innocenceproject.org/.

41 Aviv (2017).

42 See, for instance, Loftus (2005), Kassin et al. (2010), and Shaw and Porter (2015).

10. JUDGMENT

1 *Peña-Rodriguez v. Colorado* (2017) and Howe (2017).

2 Kennedy (1998, pp. 193, 219).

3 Kennedy (1998, p. 218).

4 Forman (2003, p. 897). Forman documents the centrality of jury trials to the abolitionist cause.

5 Kennedy (1998, p. 230).

6 Kennedy (1998, p. 174).

7 Smallwood (1981, p. 33). Justice Kennedy referenced this example in *Peña-Rodriguez v. Colorado*, citing Forman (2003).

8 Rorlich and Tulsky (1996).

9 Mauro (1997).

10 Kennedy (1998, p. 288).

11 Pew Research Center (2016).

12 Quinnipiac University (2017) and Wolf (2014).

13 Crocker et al. (1999).

14 Brigham and Wasserman (1999). For a discussion of the implications of such public disagreement for standard models of beliefs and information in economics, and the development of an alternative approach, see Sethi and Yildiz (2012, 2016).

15 Mydans (1991) and Rosenthal (1991).

16 The Latina juror was among four who had held out for a guilty verdict on the excessive force charge, and claimed that other jurors mocked her for wanting to view the videotape again (Reinhold, 1992).

17 Eberhardt et al. (2006).

18 The statistical analysis made allowances for nonracial determinants of punishment severity, including defendant characteristics such as age and prior criminal history, victim characteristics such as socioeconomic status or employment as a police officer, and aggravating or mitigating characteristics of the crime itself. That is, physical appearance was not simply a proxy for differences across defendants in such nonracial characteristics. The defendants were drawn from a large pool of death-eligible cases from Philadelphia, all from the post-*Furman* period, originally compiled by Baldus et al. (1998).

19 Eberhardt et al. (2006, p. 385).

20 Fleury-Steiner (2004, p. 45).

21 See Stevenson (2014) for several accounts of prosecutors who seemed uninterested in examining exculpatory evidence in capital cases.

22 Arnold, Dobbie, and Yang (2017).

23 Arnold, Dobbie, and Yang (2017, p. 3). This study also demonstrates the importance of taking the inframarginality problem seriously: if one looked at all released defendants rather than just those on the margin of release, the opposite conclusion would arise, since black defendants overall are more likely to be rearrested in the pretrial period for all three crime categories relative to white defendants.

24 Gupta, Hansman, and Frenchman (2016) and Dobbie, Goldin, and Yang (2018).

25 In practice, the training phase also involves out-of-sample predictions on some items in order to tune "hyperparameters" such as the level of complexity associated with the function. This is what distinguishes machine learning from more traditional statistical model fitting. Too great a level of complexity can result in overfitting, leading to a tight fit with the items in the training set but poor predictions when confronting new items.

26 Kleinberg et al. (2017).

27 Danziger, Levav, and Avnaim-Pesso (2011, p. 6892).

28 Mocan and Eren (2018).

29 Around 85 percent of African American smokers report preferring menthol brands, as compared with around a third of white smokers (Boyles, 2016).

30 See National Research Council (2014, p. 97) and Spohn (2013).

31 Rehavi and Starr (2014).

32 Anwar, Bayer, and Hjalmarsson (2012).

33 National Research Council (2014, p. 98).

34 Rehavi and Starr (2014).

35 Reaves (2013, table 21).

36 Since the cases that actually go to trial are not randomly selected from the universe of all cases, there is a serious problem of sample selection involved when making inferences from actual trial outcomes. As a result,

even the best statistician would have difficulty making confident predictions about what would happen in a future trial if a negotiated settlement were not reached.

11. PUNISHMENT

1 Wagner (2012).
2 Loury (2009).
3 Walmsley (2011).
4 National Research Council (2014, p. 13).
5 We estimated racial incarceration rates for 1972 from the ratio of racial incarceration rates for the 1970s reported in National Research Council (2014, table 2.2) and the 1972 proportion of the black population in Centers for Disease Control and Prevention (n.d.), under the assumption of only two racial identity groups. Hispanic incarceration rates for 1972 are not available.
6 Of course, if slavery is considered incarceration, U.S. rates were much higher in 1860 than modern rates.
7 See Figures 2.1 and 2.2 in Chapter 2.
8 Civitas (2012).
9 Even in theory, it is not clear what form such a correspondence should take.
10 FindLaw (2017).
11 National Research Council (2014, table 3.2).
12 See, especially, Alexander (2010), Raphael and Stoll (2013), the National Research Council (2014), and Pfaff (2017).
13 One consequence of disparate impact arising from laws, policies, and procedures is that the population most deeply affected by these policies can change over time. That is, policies that once led to mass incarceration of blacks can end up affecting large numbers of whites as circumstances change. See, for example, Mauer (2013) for a discussion of dramatic changes in the racial composition of female incarceration.
14 Carson and Anderson (2016).
15 Kaeble and Bonczar (2016, tables 1 and 4).
16 Kaeble and Bonczar (2016, tables 4 and 6).
17 Harris, Evans, and Beckett (2010).

18 Raper (1940, pp. 155–162).

19 Lofstrom and Raphael (2016a, pp. 115–118).

20 Alexander (2010, p. 2).

21 FBI: UCR (2016, table 29).

22 Carson and Anderson (2016, table 7) and Kaeble and Bonczar (2016). About two million people entered probation overall, but about half of these individuals were convicted of misdemeanors.

23 Pfaff (2017, pp. 132–133).

24 Pfaff (2017, p. 132).

25 Bureau of Justice Statistics (1985) and Minton and Zeng (2016).

26 Murder is a partial exception: the arrest rate fell about 20 percent after 2000 (National Research Council, 2014, p. 49).

27 National Research Council (2014, pp. 50–51).

28 Carson and Golinelli (2013, table 10).

29 Raphael and Stoll (2013, table 2.4) and National Research Council (2014, pp. 52–55).

30 We use data from Raphael and Stoll (2013, tables 2.2 and 2.4), who use 1984 and 2009 as end points.

31 Raphael and Stoll (2013, pp. 58–66).

32 Kaeble and Bonczar (2016) and Bureau of Justice Statistics (1982).

33 Blumstein and Cohen (1973).

34 University at Albany (2013, table 1.76.2007).

35 The number of prosecutors grew at an annual rate of 1.5 percent between 1970 and 2007, and 2.4 percent between 1990 and 2007. The number of state judges grew at an annual rate of 0.5 percent between 1980 and 2011, and 0.6 percent between 1993 and 2011. See Pfaff (2017, pp. 129, 137) on prosecutors and public defenders, and Malega and Cohen (2013) on judges.

36 Pfaff (2017).

37 Bjerk (2005).

38 Owens (2011b).

39 Pfaff (2017) provides a detailed account of how this happened.

40 Associated Press-NORC Center for Public Affairs Research (2014). We don't know whether public attitudes were different before the 1970s, but they probably were: before 1964, crime was rarely an election issue. If voters could have been swayed by tough-on-crime rhetoric in, say, the

1950s the way they were swayed later, then the rhetoric would probably have proliferated earlier.

41 National Research Council (2014, p. 123). These assertions are consistent with survey results indicating that large numbers of blacks wanted harsher punishments for those rightly convicted of noncapital crimes.

42 Raphael and Stoll (2013, pp. 113–117).

43 Alexander (2010, p. 40).

44 Beckett (1997).

45 Blumstein and Cohen (1973).

46 The specific question was "Is there more crime in the U.S. than there was a year ago, or less?" The time series is reported in Gallup Poll (2018).

47 Forman (2017, p. 10).

48 University at Albany (2013, table 6.29.2012).

49 Carson and Golinelli (2013).

50 Fletcher (2000, p. 417).

51 Walen (2016, Section 4.3.2).

52 President Trump's admonition to police officers not to care if suspects hit their heads when being placed in patrol cars involves a similar disregard of this distinction.

53 Loury (2002, pp. 81–82).

54 Hetey and Eberhardt (2014, pp. 1950–1951).

55 Hetey and Eberhardt (2014, p. 1952).

56 Stevenson (2014, pp. 158–159).

57 Butler (2017, p. 17)

58 Mauer (2013). Sethi (2019) argues that recent decarceration initiatives are driven in part by these trends.

59 At times, criminal offenders have also been seen as "race traitors" in black communities (Forman, 2017, p. 29). Randall Kennedy (1998, p. 194) quotes a Mississippi jury commissioner who observed in 1910 that black jurors were "much more inclined to convict Negroes charged with crime than . . . [were] the white jurors."

60 See Keller and Pearce (2016) for an overview of national trends and a case study.

61 National Research Council (2014, pp. 315, 261).

62 See Dobbie et al. (2018), who use data from Sweden.

63 There were about 1.824 million sentenced prisoners in 2015, of whom we estimate that at least 75,000 were wrongly convicted. Gross et al. (2014) estimate that if all death-sentenced defendants remained under sentence of death indefinitely (so their cases could be reviewed intensively), at least 4.1 percent would be exonerated. Since no one agrees to a death sentence as a plea bargain, this is probably a lower bound on the rate of wrongful convictions for less serious offenses. On an average day in 2015 there were 350,000 jail inmates (Minton and Zeng, 2016, table 3).

64 Carson and Anderson (2016).

65 Hoppe (2017).

66 Mueller-Smith (2015).

67 Lofstrom and Raphael (2016a, p. 104).

68 Lofstrom and Raphael (2016b).

69 National Research Council (2014, p. 150).

70 Mueller-Smith (2015) and Aizer and Doyle (2015).

12. JUSTICE

1 Leovy (2015, p. 9).

2 Leovy (2015, p. 8).

3 Kennedy (1998, p. 29).

4 Kennedy (1998, p. 153).

5 See, for instance, Mac Donald (2013).

6 See the discussion of Goel, Rao, and Shroff (2016) in Chapter 6.

7 Southall (2017) and New York Civil Liberties Union (2018).

8 Johnson (2016) and Harris (2018).

9 National Academies of Sciences, Engineering, and Medicine (2017, pp. 8–18).

10 Taylor, Koper, and Woods (2011, p. 158) and National Academies of Sciences, Engineering, and Medicine (2017, pp. 4–15).

11 Papachristos, Wildeman, and Roberto (2015, p. 148)..

12 Kennedy (1998, p. 26).

13 See the discussion of trust in Chapter 7.

14 Wingo (in press).

15 The Environmental Protection Agency, for instance, uses $7.4 million in 2006 dollars, which is about $9.2 million in 2017 dollars, to estimate

the value of reducing mortality risk by an amount that saves one life (United States Environmental Protection Agency, 2017). We use this estimate, together with an estimated cost of $100,000 per year for an additional police officer.

16 See *Bismarck Tribune* (2017) for a list of cities with the highest homicide rates in 2015, and the total number of murders for each of these cities. To compute the ratio of officers per murder we used police employment from FBI: UCR (2016, 2017). The *Bismarck Tribune* article uses data from the Uniform Crime Reports and notes that "some cities including Cleveland, Ohio, and Newark, New Jersey, had higher than average murder rates in the past, but are not reported on by the 2015 FBI UCR." We estimate that the ratio of police to murders was approximately eleven for both Newark and Cleveland in 2016.

17 Shihadeh and Flynn (1996) and Bjerk (2010).

18 Weiner et al. (2009).

19 A stark illustration of the first-mover disadvantage involves the proverbial "Texas ranger" who can keep a crowd at bay with a single bullet in his gun by threatening to shoot the person who steps forward first; see Kleiman and Kilmer (2009) for the logic of the argument and why it is likely to fail when the crowd is large.

20 Ayres and Unkovic (2012).

21 See, for instance, Hart (n.d.).

22 Zimring (2012, pp. 124–125).

23 Forman (2017, pp. 160–161).

24 See Hughes and Stevens (2010), who also claim that overall increases in drug use were minor, and that problematic drug use actually declined.

25 Gavrilova, Kamada and Zoutman (in press).

26 Kuziemko and Levitt (2004).

27 Duggan (2001), Cook and Ludwig (2003, 2006), Williams (2017).

28 Pew Research Center (2013).

29 Ramzy, Innis, and Boehler (2015).

30 Leigh and Neill (2010).

31 Levinson (1989, pp. 648–655).

32 Levinson (1989, p. 657).

33 Acceptance of Levinson's interpretation, and arguments for repeal, span ideological boundaries; see, for instance, Will (1991) and Wittes (2007).

34 Zimring (2017, pp. 173–175).

35 See, for instance, Zimring (2017, chapter 9).

36 Zimring (2017, p. 216).

37 Ba and Grogger (2018).

38 Zimring (2017, p. 226).

39 Zimring (2017, pp. 59–61).

40 Sherman (2018).

41 Reaves (2016).

42 Wexler (2015, p. 10).

43 Sherman (2018).

44 Zimring (2017, p. 100).

45 Zimring (pp. 101–102).

46 See Sherman (2018) for an account of an incident in Camden, New Jersey, where a knife-wielding civilian with clear signs of mental illness was cordoned off and eventually disarmed through the use of patience and a Taser.

47 Zimring (2017, pp. 67–68).

48 Martinelli (2014).

49 Zimring (2017, chapter 8).

50 Sherman (2018, p. 422), citing Perrow (1984).

51 Wood (2018).

52 See also Dara Kay Cohen (2013), who argues that wartime rape is a socialization tool used to build coherence in fighting units composed of strangers, many of whom were compelled to join. Although there is no compulsion to join a law enforcement agency, there is some evidence of initiation involving tattoos and other rituals into cliques that "promote a hard-charging style of policing" in the Los Angeles Police Department (Lau, 2018).

53 Loury (2002, pp. 50–52).

54 Pfaff (2017).

55 Pfaff (2017).

56 Loury (2009).

57 Pfaff (2017, p. 141).

58 Leovy (2015, p. 9).

59 Myrdal (1987, p. 82).

60 Dee and Jacob (2011).

61 To illustrate, suppose that the goal recidivism rate for thirty-five-year-olds who served five years in prison was 25 percent and the goal for thirty-six-year-olds with six years in prison was 20 percent. The prison would have an incentive to keep a parole-eligible thirty-five-year-old with five years served if and only if it thought it could reduce his probability of recidivism by 5 percent over the next year.

62 Doleac and Hansen (2017) and Agan and Starr (2018).

63 Kim and Loury (2018).

64 Kim and Loury (2018, pp. 363–364).

CONCLUSION: HOPE

1 Allen (2017, pp. 150–151).

2 Stevenson (2014, p. 12).

3 Havel (1990, p. 181).

4 Wenzel et al. (2017).

5 Wideman (2010).

6 Butler (2017, p. 19).

7 See Kennedy (1998, p. 87), quoting the Mississippi Supreme Court in *Ratliff v. Beale*.

8 Allport (1954, p. 17).

9 Lippmann (1922, p. 91).

Works Cited

Adler, Jeffrey S. *First in Violence, Deepest in Dirt: Homicide in Chicago, 1875–1920*. Cambridge, MA: Harvard University Press, 2006.

Agan, Amanda, and Sonja Starr. "Ban the Box, Criminal Records, and Racial Discrimination: A Field Experiment." *Quarterly Journal of Economics* 133, no. 1 (2018): 191–235.

Aizer, Anna, and Joseph J. Doyle. "Juvenile Incarceration, Human Capital, and Future Crime: Evidence from Randomly Assigned Judges." *Quarterly Journal of Economics* 130, no. 2 (2015): 759–803.

Alexander, Michelle. *The New Jim Crow: Mass Incarceration in the Age of Colorblindness*. New York: New Press, 2010.

Allen, Danielle. *Cuz: The Life and Times of Michael A*. New York: Norton, 2017.

Allport, Gordon W. *The Nature of Prejudice*. Cambridge, MA: Perseus, 1954.

American Housing Survey. *AHS 2015 Summary Tables*. https://www.census.gov/programs-surveys/ahs/data.2015.html (accessed October 23, 2018).

Anderson Cooper 360 Degrees. "The Politics of Race; Millions Recovered for Jackson Family." July 24, 2009. http://transcripts.cnn.com/TRANSCRIPTS/0907/24/acd.01.html (accessed August 1, 2017).

Anderson, Elijah. *Code of the Street: Decency, Violence, and the Moral Life of the Inner City*. New York: Norton, 1999.

———. *The Cosmopolitan Canopy: Race and Civility in Everyday Life*. New York: Norton, 2011.

Anderson, Elizabeth. *The Imperative of Integration*. Princeton, NJ: Princeton University Press, 2010.

Antonovics, Kate, and Brian G. Knight. "A New Look at Racial Profiling: Evidence from the Boston Police Department." *Review of Economics and Statistics* 91, no. 1 (2009): 163–177.

Anwar, Shamena, Patrick Bayer, and Randi Hjalmarsson. "The Impact of Jury Race in Criminal Trials." *Quarterly Journal of Economics* 127, no. 2 (2012): 1017–1055.

Anwar, Shamena, and Hanming Fang. "An Alternative Test of Racial Prejudice in Motor Vehicle Searches: Theory and Evidence." *American Economic Review* 96, no. 1 (2006): 127–151.

Arnold, David, Will Dobbie, and Crystal S. Yang. "Racial Bias in Bail Decisions." National Bureau of Economic Research Working Paper No. w23421. 2017.

Arrow, Kenneth J. "The Theory of Discrimination." Edited by Orley Ashenfelter and Albert Rees. *Discrimination in Labor Markets.* Princeton, NJ: Princeton University Press, 1973. 3–33.

Associated Press-NORC Center for Public Affairs Research. "Crime and Law Enforcement in America: Racial and Ethnic Differences in Attitudes toward the Criminal Justice System." 2014. http://www.apnorc.org /projects/Pages/HTML%20Reports/crime-and-law-enforcement-in -america-racial-and-ethnic-differences-in-attitudes-toward-the-criminal -justice-system0402-7262.aspx (accessed January 17, 2018).

Aviv, Rachel. "Remembering the Murder You Didn't Commit." *New Yorker,* June 19, 2017.

Ayres, Ian. "Outcome Tests of Racial Disparities in Police Practices." *Justice Research and Policy* 4, nos. 1–2 (2002): 131–142.

———. *Pervasive Prejudice? Unconventional Evidence of Race and Gender Discrimination.* Chicago: University of Chicago Press, 2001.

Ayres, Ian, and Cait Unkovic. "Information Escrows." *Michigan Law Review* 111 (2012): 145–196.

Ba, Bocar, and Jeffrey Grogger. "The Introduction of Tasers and Police Use of Force: Evidence from the Chicago Police Department." National Bureau of Economic Research Working Paper No. w24202. 2018.

Baldus, David C., George Woodworth, David Zuckerman, Neil Alan Weiner, and Barbara Broffitt. "Racial Discrimination and the Death Penalty in the Post-Furman Era: An Empirical and Legal Overview with Recent Findings from Philadelphia." *Cornell Law Review* 83 (1998): 1638–1770.

Baliga, Sandeep, and Tomas Sjöström. "Arms races and negotiations." *Review of Economic Studies* 71, no. 2 (2004): 351–369.

Ball, Patrick. "Violence in Blue." *Granta.* 2016. https://granta.com/violence -in-blue/(accessed September 30, 2017).

Banaji, Mahzarin R., and Anthony G. Greenwald. *Blindspot: Hidden Biases of Good People*. New York: Delacorte Press, 2013.

Becker, Gary S. *The Economics of Discrimination*. Chicago: University of Chicago Press, 1957.

———. "Nobel Lecture: The Economic Way of Looking at Behavior." *Journal of Political Economy* 101, no. 3 (1993): 385–409.

Beckett, Katherine. *Making Crime Pay: Law and Order in Contemporary American Politics*. New York: Oxford University Press, 1997.

Bertrand, Marianne, and Sendhil Mullainathan. "Are Emily and Greg More Employable Than Lakisha and Jamal? A Field Experiment on Labor Market Discrimination." *American Economic Review* 94, no. 4 (2004): 991–1013.

Bickel, Peter J., Eugene A. Hammel, and J. William O'Connell. "Sex Bias in Graduate Admissions: Data from Berkeley." *Science* 187 (February 1975): 398–404.

Bismarck Tribune. "The 30 Cities with the Highest Murder Rates in the US." November 13, 2017. http://bismarcktribune.com/news/national/the -cities-with-the-highest-murder-rates-in-the-us/collection_5a789407 -4d43-5403-ad56-7c47880bda8e.html#1 (accessed January 30, 2018).

Bittner, Egon. *The Functions of the Police in Modern Society: A Review of Background Factors, Current Practices, and Possible Role Models*. Cambridge, MA: Oelgeschlager, Gunn & Hain, 1970.

Bjerk, David. "Making the Crime Fit the Penalty: The Role of Prosecutorial Discretion under Mandatory Minimum Sentencing." *Journal of Law and Economics* 48, no. 2 (2005): 591–625.

———. "Racial Profiling, Statistical Discrimination, and the Effect of a Colorblind Policy on the Crime Rate." *Journal of Public Economic Theory* 9, no. 3 (2007): 521–545.

———. "Thieves, Thugs, and Neighborhood Poverty." *Journal of Urban Economics* 68, no. 3 (2010): 231–246.

Black, Donald J. *The Behavior of Law*. New York: Academic Press, 1976.

Bloom, Paul. *How Pleasure Works: The New Science of Why We Like What We Like*. New York: Norton, 2010.

Blow, Charles. "The Whole System Failed Trayvon Martin." *New York Times*, July 15, 2013.

Blumstein, Alfred, and Jacqueline Cohen. "A Theory of the Stability of Punishment." *Journal of Criminal Law and Criminology* 64, no. 2 (1973): 198–207.

Bobo, Lawrence, Camille Z. Charles, Maria Krysan, and Alicia D. Simmons. "The Real Record on Racial Attitudes." Edited by Peter V. Marsden. *Social Trends in American Life: Findings from the General Social Survey Since 1972*. Princeton, NJ: Princeton University Press, 2012. 38–61.

Bodenhorn, Howard. "Blind Tigers and Red-Tape Cocktails: Liquor Control and Homicide in Late-Nineteenth-Century South Carolina." National Bureau of Economic Research Working Paper 22980. 2016.

Bordalo, Pedro, Katherine Coffman, Nicola Gennaioli, and Andrei Shleifer. "Stereotypes." *Quarterly Journal of Economics* 131, no. 4 (2016): 1753–1794.

Boston Globe. "The Arrest of Henry Louis Gates Jr." August 4, 2009. http://archive.boston.com/news/local/massachusetts/specials/072409_henry_louis_gates_arrest/ (accessed August 1, 2017).

Bouie, Jamelle. "Michael Brown Wasn't a Superhuman Demon." *Slate.* November 26, 2014. http://www.slate.com/articles/news_and_politics/politics/2014/11/darren_wilson_s_racial_portrayal_of_michael_brown_as_a_superhuman_demon.html (accessed September 22, 2017).

Boyles, Salynn. "Menthol Cig Use Reported Rising in US, Especially among Young." *Medpage Today.* October 17, 2016. https://www.medpagetoday.com/pulmonology/smoking/60826 (accessed July 16, 2018).

Brearley, Harrington Cooper. *Homicide in the United States.* Chapel Hill: University of North Carolina Press, 1932.

Brigham, John C., and Adina W. Wasserman. "The Impact of Race, Racial Attitude, and Gender on Reactions to the Criminal Trial of OJ Simpson." *Journal of Applied Social Psychology* 29, no. 7 (1999): 1333–1370.

Bruner, Jerome S. "Going beyond the Information Given." *Contemporary Approaches to Cognition.* Cambridge, MA: Harvard University Press, 1957. 41–70.

Bui, Quoctrung, and Amanda Cox. "Surprising New Evidence Shows Bias in Police Use of Force but Not in Shootings." *New York Times,* July 11, 2016.

Bureau of Justice Statistics. *Jail Inmates, 1983.* Office of Justice Programs, U.S. Department of Justice, 1985.

———. *Probation and Parole 1981.* U.S. Department of Justice, 1982.

Butler, Paul. *Chokehold: Policing Black Men*. New York: New Press, 2017.

Cambridge Review Committee. *Missed Opportunities, Shared Responsibilities*. Final Report, 2010.

Capehart, Jonathan. "'Hands Up, Don't Shoot' Was Built on a Lie." *Washington Post*, March 16, 2015.

———. "Standing by My Opinion That 'Hands Up, Don't Shoot' Was Built on a Lie." *Washington Post*, March 16, 2017.

Carson, E. Ann, and Elizabeth Anderson. *Prisoners in 2015*. Office of Justice Programs, U.S. Department of Justice, Bureau of Justice Statistics, 2016.

Carson, E. Ann, and Daniela Golinelli. *Prisoners in 2012: Trends in Admissions and Releases, 1991–2012*. Office of Justice Programs, U.S. Department of Justice, Bureau of Justice Statistics, 2013.

Centers for Disease Prevention and Control. *Population by Age Groups, Race, and Sex for 1960–97*. No date. https://www.cdc.gov/nchs/data/statab/pop6097.pdf (accessed October 21, 2018).

Chalfin, Aaron, and Justin McCrary. "The Effect of Police on Crime: New Evidence from US Cities, 1960–2010." National Bureau of Economic Research Working Paper No. w18815. 2013.

Chambliss, William J. "Policing the Ghetto Underclass: The Politics of Law and Law Enforcement." *Social Problems* 41, no. 2 (1994): 177–194.

Chan, Melissa. "Minnesota Governor Does Not Think Philando Castile Would Have Been Killed If He Were White." *Time*, July 7, 2016. http://time.com/4397248/minnesota-gov-mark-dayton-philando-castile-shooting/(accessed July 5, 2017).

Cheng, Cheng, and Mark Hoekstra. "Does Strengthening Self-Defense Law Deter Crime or Escalate Violence? Evidence from Expansions to Castle Doctrine." *Journal of Human Resources* 48, no. 3 (2013): 821–854.

Chimeli, Ariaster B., and Rodrigo R. Soares. "The Use of Violence in Illegal Markets: Evidence from Mahogany Trade in the Brazilian Amazon." *American Economic Journal: Applied Economics*, 9, no. 4 (2017): 30–57.

Choi, John J. "State v. Jeronimo Yanez: Press Conference Remarks as Prepared for Delivery." November 16, 2016.

Civitas. *Comparisons of Crime in OECD Countries*. 2012. http://www.civitas.org.uk/content/files/crime_stats_oecdjan2012.pdf (accessed October 22, 2018).

Coate, Stephen, and Glenn C. Loury. "Will Affirmative-Action Policies Eliminate Negative Stereotypes?" *American Economic Review* 83, no. 5 (1993): 1220–1240.

Coates, Ta-Nehisi. *Between the World and Me*. New York: Spiegel & Grau, 2015.

Cohen, Dara Kay. "Explaining Rape during Civil War: Cross-National Evidence (1980–2009)." *American Political Science Review* 107, no. 3 (2013): 461–477.

Cook, Philip J. "Crime in the City." Edited by Robert P. Inman. *Making Cities Work: Prospects and Policies for Urban America*. Princeton, NJ: Princeton University Press, 2009. 297–327.

Cook, Philip J., and Jens Ludwig. "The Effects of Gun Prevalence on Burglary: Deterrence versus Inducement." Edited by Philip J. Cook and Jens Ludwig. *Evaluating Gun Policy: Effects on Crime and Violence*. Washington, DC: Brookings Institution Press, 2003. 74–118.

———. "The Social Costs of Gun Ownership." *Journal of Public Economics* 90, nos. 1–2 (2006): 379–391.

Cooper, Michael. "Officers in Bronx Fire 41 Shots, and an Unarmed Man Is Killed." *New York Times*, February 5, 1999.

Corey, Angela B. "State of Florida vs. George Zimmerman: Affidavit of Probable Cause—Second-Degree Murder." Jacksonville, FL, April 11, 2012.

Correll, Joshua, Bernadette Park, Charles M. Judd, and Bernd Wittenbrink. "The Police Officer's Dilemma: Using Ethnicity to Disambiguate Potentially Threatening Individuals." *Journal of Personality and Social Psychology* 83, no. 6 (2002): 1314–1329.

Coviello, Decio, and Nicola Persico. "An Economic Analysis of Black-White Disparities in the New York Police Department's Stop-and-Frisk Program." *Journal of Legal Studies* 44, no. 2 (2015): 315–360.

Crocker, Jennifer, Riia Luhtanen, Stephanie Broadnax, and Bruce Evan Blaine. "Belief in US Government Conspiracies against Blacks among Black and White College Students: Powerlessness or System Blame?" *Personality and Social Psychology Bulletin* 25, no. 8 (1999): 941–953.

Danziger, Shai, Jonathan Levav, and Liora Avnaim-Pesso. "Extraneous Factors in Judicial Decisions." *Proceedings of the National Academy of Sciences* 108, no. 17 (2011): 6889–6892.

Davis, Aaron C., and Wesley Lowery. "FBI Director Calls Lack of Data on Police Shootings 'Ridiculous,' 'Embarrassing.'" *Washington Post*, October 7, 2015.

Dee, Thomas S., and Brian Jacob. "The Impact of No-Child-Left-Behind on Student Achievement." *Journal of Policy Analysis and Management* 30, no. 3 (2011): 418–446.

Dell, Melissa. "Trafficking Networks and the Mexican Drug War." *American Economic Review* 105, no. 6 (2015): 1738–1779.

Di Tella, Rafael, and Ernesto Schargrodsky. "Do Police Reduce Crime? Estimates Using the Allocation of Police Forces after a Terrorist Attack." *American Economic Review* 94, no. 1 (2004): 115–133.

Dias, Elizabeth, John Eligon, and Richard A. Oppel Jr. "Philadelphia Starbucks Arrests, Outrageous to Some, Are Everyday Life for Others." *New York Times*, April 17, 2018.

Dobbie, Will, Jacob Goldin, and Crystal Yang. "The Effects of Pre-trial Detention on Conviction, Future Crime, and Employment: Evidence from Randomly Assigned Judges." *American Economic Review* 108, no. 2 (2018): 201–240.

Dobbie, Will, Hans Grönqvist, Susan Niknami, Mårten Palme, and Mikael Priks. "The Intergenerational Effects of Parental Incarceration." National Bureau of Economic Research Working Paper No. 24186. 2018.

Doleac, Jennifer L., and Benjamin Hansen. "The Unintended Consequences of 'Ban the Box': Statistical Discrimination and Employment Outcomes When Criminal Histories Are Hidden." Working paper, University of Virginia Department of Economics. 2017.

Draca, Mirko, Stephen Machin, and Robert Witt. "Panic on the Streets of London: Police, Crime, and the July 2005 Terror Attacks." *American Economic Review* 101, no. 5 (2011): 2157–2181.

Du Bois, William Edward Burghardt. *The Conservation of Races*. Washington, DC: American Negro Academy, 1897.

———. *The Philadelphia Negro: A Social Study*. Philadelphia: Publications of the University of Pennsylvania, 1899.

Duggan, Mark. "More Guns, More Crime." *Journal of Political Economy* 109, no. 5 (2001): 1086–1114.

Durlauf, Steven N. "Assessing Racial Profiling." *Economic Journal* 116, no. 515 (2006): F402–F426.

Eberhardt, Jennifer L., Paul G. Davies, Valerie J. Purdie-Vaughns, and Sheri Lynn Johnson. "Looking Deathworthy: Perceived Stereotypicality of Black Defendants Predicts Capital-Sentencing Outcomes." *Psychological Science* 17, no. 5 (2006): 383–386.

Ebony Photo-Editorial. "A Man around the House." *Ebony,* January 1966.

Evans, William N., and Emily G. Owens. "COPS and Crime." *Journal of Public Economics* 91, no. 1 (2007): 181–201.

Farhi, Paul. "Bill O'Reilly's Fox News Career Comes to a Swift End amid Growing Sexual Harassment Claims." *Washington Post,* April 19, 2017.

Farrow, Ronan. "From Aggressive Overtures to Sexual Assault: Harvey Weinstein's Accusers Tell Their Stories." *New Yorker,* October 10, 2017. https://www.newyorker.com/news/news-desk/from-aggressive -overtures-to-sexual-assault-harvey-weinsteins-accusers-tell-their -stories (accessed October 14, 2018).

FBI: UCR. *2015 Crime in the United States.* 2016. https://ucr.fbi.gov/crime -in-the-u.s/2015/crime-in-the-u.s.-2015 (accessed January 11, 2018).

———. *2016 Law Enforcement Officers Killed and Assaulted.* 2017. https://ucr .fbi.gov/leoka/2016/home (accessed July 28, 2018).

———. *Offense Definitions.* 2018. https://ucr.fbi.gov/crime-in-the-u.s/2017 /crime-in-the-u.s.-2017/topic-pages/offense-definitions (accessed October 12, 2018).

Fernandez, Manny, and David Montgomery. "Perjury Charge Dropped against Ex-trooper in Sandra Bland Case." *New York Times,* June 18, 2017.

FindLaw. *"Three Strikes" Sentencing Laws.* 2017. https://criminal.findlaw .com/criminal-procedure/three-strikes-sentencing-laws.html (accessed October 22, 2018).

Fletcher, George. *Rethinking Criminal Law.* New York: Oxford University Press, 2000.

Fleury-Steiner, Benjamin. *Jurors' Stories of Death: How America's Death Penalty Invests in Inequality.* Ann Arbor: University of Michigan Press, 2004.

Forman, James, Jr. "Juries and Race in the Nineteenth Century." *Yale Law Journal* 113 (2003): 895–938.

————. *Locking Up Our Own: Crime and Punishment in Black America*. New York: Farrar, Straus and Giroux, 2017.

Fryer, Roland, Jr. "An Empirical Analysis of Racial Differences in the Police Use of Force." NBER Working Paper 22399. 2016.

Fryer, Roland, Jr., and Matthew O. Jackson. "A Categorical Model of Cognition and Biased Decision Making." *BE Journal of Theoretical Economics* 8, no. 1 (2008): Article 6.

Furman v. Georgia. 408 (U.S. 238, 1972).

Gallup Poll. *Social and Policy Issues: Crime*. https://news.gallup.com/poll /1603/crime.aspx (accessed October 22, 2018).

Gattis, Paul. "Exclusive: Accuser to Roy Moore, 'Where Does Your Immorality End?'" *AL.com*. November 28, 2017. http://www.al.com/news /index.ssf/2017/11/roy_moore_leigh_corfman_accuse.html (accessed February 3, 2018).

Gavrilova, Evelina, Takuma Kamada, and Floris Zoutman. "Is Legal Pot Crippling Mexican Drug Trafficking Organisations? The Effect of Medical Marijuana Laws on US Crime." *Economic Journal* (in press).

Ge, Yanbo, Christopher R. Knittel, Don MacKenzie, and Stephen Zoepf. "Racial and Gender Discrimination in Transportation Network Companies." National Bureau of Economic Research Working Paper w22776, 2016.

Geller, William A., and Michael S. Scott. *Deadly Force: What We Know: A Practitioner's Desk Reference on Police-Involved Shootings*. Washington, DC: Police Executive Research Foundation, 1992.

Gelman, Andrew. "It's All about the Denominator: Rajiv Sethi and Sendhil Mullainathan in a Statistical Debate on Racial Bias in Police Killings." *Statistical Modeling, Causal Inference, and Social Science*. October 21, 2015. http://andrewgelman.com/2015/10/21/its-all-about-the-denomi nator-and-rajiv-sethi-and-sendhil-mullainathan-in-a-statistical-debate -on-racial-bias-in-police-killings/(accessed September 25, 2017).

Gelman, Andrew, Jeffrey Fagan, and Alex Kiss. "An Analysis of the New York City Police Department's 'Stop-and-Frisk' Policy in the Context of Claims of Racial Bias." *Journal of the American Statistical Association* 102, no. 479 (2007): 813–823.

Gerken, Heather. "Second-Order Diversity: An Exploration of Decentralization's Egalitarian Possibilities." Edited by Danielle Allen and Rohini Somanathan. *Difference without Domination: Pursuing Justice in Diverse Democracies.* Chicago: University of Chicago Press, in press.

Gilbert, Gustave Mark. "Stereotype Persistence and Change among College Students." *Journal of Abnormal and Social Psychology* 46, no. 2 (1951): 245–254.

Glanville, Doug. "Why I Still Get Shunned by Taxi Drivers." *The Atlantic,* October 24, 2015. https://www.theatlantic.com/politics/archive/2015/10/why-i-still-get-shunned-by-taxi-drivers/411583/(accessed January 6, 2018).

Goel, Sharad, Justin M. Rao, and Ravi Shroff. "Precinct or Prejudice? Understanding Racial Disparities in New York City's Stop-and-Frisk Policy." *Annals of Applied Statistics* 10, no. 1 (2016): 365–394.

Goff, Phillip Atiba, Matthew Christian Jackson, Brooke Allison, Lewis Di Leone, Carmen Marie Culotta, and Natalie Ann DiTomasso. "The Essence of Innocence: Consequences of Dehumanizing Black Children." *Journal of Personality and Social Psychology* 106, no. 4 (2014): 526–545.

Goffman, Erving. *The Presentation of Self in Everyday Life.* New York: Doubleday Anchor, 1959.

———. *Stigma: Notes on the Management of Spoiled Identity.* New York: Simon and Schuster, 1963.

Golby, Alexandra, John Gabrieli, Joan Chiao, and Jennifer Eberhardt. "Differential Responses in the Fusiform Region to Same-Race and Other-Race Faces." *Nature Neuroscience* 4, no. 8 (2001): 845–850.

Greenblatt, Alan. "The Racial History of the 'Grandfather Clause.'" *NPR Code Switch.* October 22, 2013. https://www.npr.org/sections/codeswitch/2013/10/21/239081586/the-racial-history-of-the-grandfather-clause (accessed January 8, 2018).

Greenwald, Anthony G., Mahzarin R. Banaji, and Brian A. Nosek. "Statistically Small Effects of the Implicit Association Test Can Have Societally Large Effects." *Journal of Personality and Social Psychology* 108, no. 4 (2015): 553–561.

Greenwald, Anthony G., Mark A. Oakes, and Hunter G. Hoffman. "Targets of Discrimination: Effects of Race on Responses to Weapons Holders." *Journal of Experimental Social Psychology* 39, no. 4 (2003): 399–405.

Griggs v. Duke Power Co. 401 U.S. 424 (United States Supreme Court, 1971).

Groff, Elizabeth R., Jerry H. Ratcliffe, Cory P. Haberman, Evan T. Sorg, Nola M. Joyce, and Ralph B. Taylor. "Does What Police Do at Hot Spots Matter? The Philadelphia Policing Tactics Experiment." *Criminology* 53, no. 1 (2015): 23–53.

Gross, Samuel R., Kristen Jacoby, Daniel J. Matheson, Nicholas Montgomery, and Sujata Patil. "Exonerations in the United States 1989 through 2003." *Journal of Criminal Law and Criminology* 95, no. 2 (2005): 523–560.

Gross, Samuel R., Barbara O'Brien, Chen Hu, and Edward H. Kennedy. "Rate of False Conviction of Criminal Defendants Who Are Sentenced to Death." *Proceedings of the National Academy of Sciences* 111, no. 20 (2014): 7230–7235.

Gross, Terry. "For Years, Anita Hill Was a 'Canary in the Coal Mine' for Women Speaking Out." *NPR.* November 30, 2017. https://www.npr.org /2017/11/30/567430106/for-years-anita-hill-was-a-canary-in-the-coal -mine-for-women-speaking-out (accessed January 28, 2018).

Gupta, Arpit, Christopher Hansman, and Ethan Frenchman. "The Heavy Costs of High Bail: Evidence from Judge Randomization." *Journal of Legal Studies* 45, no. 2 (2016): 471–505.

Haberman, Maggie, and Peter Baker. "Trump Taunts Christine Blasey Ford at Rally." *New York Times.* October 2, 2018. https://www.nytimes.com/2018 /10/02/us/politics/trump-me-too.html (accessed October 14, 2018).

Hacker, Andrew. *Two Nations: Black and White, Separate, Hostile, Unequal.* New York: Scribner, 2003.

Hair, William Ivy. *Carnival of Fury: Robert Charles and the New Orleans Race Riot of 1900.* Baton Rouge: Louisiana State University Press, 1976.

Harcourt, Bernard E. *Against Prediction: Profiling, Policing, and Punishing in an Actuarial Age.* Chicago: University of Chicago Press, 2007.

Harris, Alexes, Heather Evans, and Katherine Beckett. "Drawing Blood from Stones: Legal Debt and Social Inequality in the Contemporary United States." *American Journal of Sociology* 115, no. 6 (2010): 1753–1799.

Harris, Harry. "Violent Crime in Oakland Down 23 Percent Since 2012." *East Bay Times,* January 9, 2018. https://www.eastbaytimes.com/2018 /01/09/decline-in-oakland-violent-crime-sparks-hope/(accessed January 18, 2018).

Hart, Carl. "Congress Needs to Decriminalize All Drugs." *dr.carlhart*. http://
drcarlhart.com/congress-needs-decriminalize-all-drugs/(accessed January 18, 2018).

———. "The Real Opioid Emergency." *New York Times*, August 18, 2017.

Haslam, Nick, Brock Bastian, Paul Bain, and Yoshihisa Kashima. "Psychological Essentialism, Implicit Theories, and Intergroup Relations." *Group
Processes & Intergroup Relations* 9, no. 1 (2006): 63–76.

Hauser, Christine. "Sandra Bland's Family Settles $1.9 Million Civil Suit,
Lawyer Says." *New York Times*, September 15, 2016.

Havel, Václav. *Disturbing the Peace: A Conversation with Karel Hvížd'ala*. New
York: Vintage, 1990.

Hawkins, Derek. "Flight Attendant to Black Female Doctor: 'We're Looking
for Actual Physicians.'" *Washington Post*, October 14, 2016.

Hetey, Rebecca C., and Jennifer L. Eberhardt. "Racial Disparities in Incarceration Increase Acceptance of Punitive Policies." *Psychological Science*
25, no. 10 (2014): 1949–1954.

Hobson, Will. "Twenty Years of Failure: Many Groups Missed Chances to
Stop Larry Nassar." *Washington Post*, January 26, 2018.

Hoppe, Trevor. "Are Sex Offender Registries Reinforcing Inequality?" *The
Conversation*. August 8, 2017. http://theconversation.com/are-sex-offender
-registries-reinforcing-inequality-79818 (accessed January 18, 2018).

Howe, Amy. "Opinion Analysis: Divided Court Rules for Defendant in
Juror-Bias Case." *SCOTUSblog*. March 6, 2017. http://www.scotusblog
.com/2017/03/opinion-analysis-divided-court-rules-defendant-juror
-bias-case/(accessed January 20, 2018).

Hughes, Caitlin Elizabeth, and Alex Stevens. "What Can We Learn from the
Portuguese Decriminalization of Illicit Drugs?" *British Journal of Criminology* 50, no. 6 (2010): 999–1022.

Hutson, H. Range, Deirdre Anglin, John Yarbrough, Kimberly Hardaway,
Marie Russell, Jared Strote, Michael Canter, and Bennett Blum. "Suicide
by Cop." *Annals of Emergency Medicine* 32, no. 6 (1998): 665–669.

Ingraham, Christopher. "The Most Racist Places in America." *Washington
Post*, April 28, 2015.

International Association of Chiefs of Police. "Statement by IACP President
Terrence M. Cunningham on the Law Enforcement Profession and

Historical Injustices." October 17, 2016. http://www.theiacp.org/View Result?SearchID=2690 (accessed July 23, 2017).

Iyengar, Radha. "Does the Certainty of Arrest Reduce Domestic Violence? Evidence from Mandatory and Recommended Arrest Laws." *Journal of Public Economics* 93, nos. 1–2 (2009): 85–98.

Jacobs, Andrew. "When Rappers Keep Their Mouths Shut Tight." *New York Times*, February 19, 2006.

James, Lois, Stephen M. James, and Bryan J. Vila. "The Reverse Racism Effect: Are Cops More Hesitant to Shoot Black Than White Suspects?" *Criminology & Public Policy* 15, no. 2 (2016): 457–479.

James, Michael. "Race." Edited by Edward N. Zalta. *The Stanford Encyclopedia of Philosophy (Spring 2017 Edition)*. 2017. https://plato.stanford .edu/archives/spr2017/entries/race/ (accessed October 11, 2018).

Johnson, Chip. "Oakland's Unspoken Good News: Homicide Rate Is Way Down." *San Francisco Chronicle*, March 17, 2016. http://www.sfchronicle .com/bayarea/johnson/article/Oakland-s-unspoken-good-news -homicide-rate-6913876.php (accessed January 18, 2018).

Kaeble, Danielle, and Thomas P. Bonczar. *Probation and Parole in the United States, 2015*. Office of Justice Programs, U.S. Department of Justice, Bureau of Justice Statistics, 2016.

Kahneman, Daniel, and Amos Tversky. "Subjective Probability: A Judgment of Representativeness." *Cognitive Psychology* 3, no. 3 (1972): 430–454.

Kantor, Jodi, and Megan Twohey. "Harvey Weinstein Paid Off Sexual Harassment Accusers for Decades." *New York Times*, October 5, 2017.

Karlins, Marvin, Thomas L. Coffman, and Gary Walters. "On the Fading of Social Stereotypes: Studies in Three Generations of College Students." *Journal of Personality and Social Psychology* 13, no. 1 (1969): 1–16.

Kassin, Saul M., Steven A. Drizin, Thomas Grisso, Gisli H. Gudjonsson, Richard A. Leo, and Allison D. Redlich. "Police-Induced Confessions: Risk Factors and Recommendations." *Law and Human Behavior* 34, no. 1 (2010): 3–38.

Katz, Daniel, and Kenneth Braly. "Racial Stereotypes of One Hundred College Students." *Journal of Abnormal and Social Psychology* 28, no. 3 (1933): 280–290.

Keller, Josh, and Adam Pearce. "This Small Indiana County Sends More People to Prison Than San Francisco and Durham, N.C., Combined. Why?" *New York Times*, September 2, 2016.

Kennedy, Randall. *Race, Crime, and the Law*. New York: Vintage, 1998.

Kets, Willemien, and Rajiv Sethi. "Police Brutality Drivers Impossible to Uncover without Accurate Stats." *The Hill*, July 19, 2016. http:// thehill.com/blogs/congress-blog/judicial/288204-police-brutality -drivers-impossible-to-uncover-without-accurate (accessed September 17, 2017).

Kim, Young-Chul, and Glenn C. Loury. "Rebranding Ex-convicts." *Journal of Public Economic Theory* 20, no. 3 (2018) 356–366.

King, Martin Luther, Jr. *I Have a Dream: Writings and Speeches That Changed the World*. Edited by James Melvin Washington. New York: Harper Collins, 1992.

———. "Letter from a Birmingham Jail." In *Why We Can't Wait*. London: Penguin, 2000. 64–84.

Kirby, Jen. "Leigh Corfman, Who Accused Roy Moore of Sexual Misconduct, Is Suing Him for Defamation." *Vox*. January 4, 2018. https://www .vox.com/2018/1/4/16851512/leigh-corfman-roy-moore-defamation -lawsuit (accessed February 3, 2018).

Kirk, Chris, and Katie Rose Quandt. "Gun Control Laws by State." *Slate*, October 7, 2015. http://www.slate.com/blogs/the_slatest/2015/10/07 /gun_control_laws_by_state_oregon_new_york_texas_california.html (accessed July 5, 2017).

Kitcher, Philip. "Does 'Race' Have a Future?" *Philosophy & Public Affairs* 35, no. 4 (2007): 293–317.

Kleiman, Mark, and Beau Kilmer. "The Dynamics of Deterrence." *Proceedings of the National Academy of Sciences* 106, no. 34 (2009): 14230–14235.

Kleinberg, Jon, Himabindu Lakkaraju, Jure Leskovec, Jens Ludwig, and Sendhil Mullainathan. "Human Decisions and Machine Predictions." National Bureau of Economic Research Working Paper No. w23180. 2017.

Klick, Jonathan, and Alexander Tabarrok. "Using Terror Alert Levels to Estimate the Effect of Police on Crime." *Journal of Law and Economics* 48, no. 1 (2005): 267–279.

Knowles, John, Nicola Persico, and Petra Todd. "Racial Bias in Motor Vehicle Searches: Theory and Evidence." *Journal of Political Economy* 109, no. 1 (2001): 203–229.

Kocieniewski, David. "A Little Girl Shot, and a Crowd That Didn't See." *New York Times,* July 9, 2007.

Kuziemko, Ilyana, and Steven D. Levitt. "An Empirical Analysis of Imprisoning Drug Offenders." *Journal of Public Economics* 88, no. 9 (2004): 2043–2066.

Lai, K. K. Rebecca, Haeyoun Park, Larry Buchanan, and Wilson Andrews. "Assessing the Legality of Sandra Bland's Arrest." *New York Times,* July 22, 2015.

Langton, Lynn, and Matthew Durose. *Police Behavior during Traffic and Street Stops, 2011.* Special Report, Office of Justice Programs, U.S. Department of Justice, Washington, DC: Bureau of Justice Statistics, 2013.

Lau, Maya. "Inked with a Skull in a Cowboy Hat, L.A. County Sheriff's Deputy Describes Exclusive Society of Lawmen at California Station." *Los Angeles Times,* August 4, 2018.

Lauritsen, Janet L., Maribeth L. Rezey, and Karen Heimer. "When Choice of Data Matters: Analyses of US Crime Trends, 1973–2012." *Journal of Quantitative Criminology* 32, no. 3 (2016): 335–355.

Lee, Catherine. "The Value of Life in Death: Multiple Regression and Event History Analyses of Homicide Clearance in Los Angeles County." *Journal of Criminal Justice* 336 (2005): 527–534.

Leigh, Andrew, and Christine Neill. "Do Gun Buybacks Save Lives? Evidence from Panel Data." *American Law and Economics Review* 12, no. 2 (2010): 505–557.

Leovy, Jill. *Ghettoside.* New York: Spiegel and Grau, 2015.

Levinson, Sanford. "The Embarrassing Second Amendment." *Yale Law Journal* 99, no. 3 (1989): 637–659.

Lindo, Jason M., and María Padilla-Romo. "Kingpin Approaches to Fighting Crime and Community Violence: Evidence from Mexico's Drug War." *Journal of Health Economics* 58, 2018: 253–268.

Lippmann, Walter. *Public Opinion.* New York: Harcourt, Brace, 1922.

Litwack, Leon F. *Been in the Storm So Long: The Aftermath of Slavery.* New York: Vintage, 1979.

Lofstrom, Magnus, and Steven Raphael. "Crime, the Criminal Justice System, and Socioeconomic Inequality." *Journal of Economic Perspectives* 30, no. 2 (2016a): 103–126.

———. "Incarceration and Crime: Evidence from California's Public Safety Realignment Reform." *Annals of the American Academy of Political and Social Science* 664, no. 1 (2016b): 196–220.

———. *Public Safety Realignment and Crime Rates in California.* San Francisco: Public Policy Institute of California, 2013.

Loftus, Elizabeth F. "Planting Misinformation in the Human Mind: A 30-Year Investigation of the Malleability of Memory." *Learning & Memory* 12, no. 4 (2005): 361–366.

Lopez, Mark Hugo. "Three-Fourths of Hispanics Say Their Community Needs a Leader." *Pew Research Center Hispanic Trends.* October 22, 2013. http://www.pewhispanic.org/2013/10/22/three-fourths-of-hispanics-say-their-community-needs-a-leader/(accessed October 11, 2018).

Loury, Glenn C. *The Anatomy of Racial Inequality.* Cambridge, MA: Harvard University Press, 2002.

———. "A Nation of Jailers." *Cato Unbound.* May 11, 2009. https://www.cato-unbound.org/2009/03/11/glenn-loury/nation-jailers (accessed August 12, 2017).

———. "Relations before Transactions: Forty Years of Thinking about Persisting Racial Inequality in the United States." Edited by Danielle Allen and Rohini Somanathan. *Difference without Domination: Pursuing Justice in Diverse Democracies.* Chicago: University of Chicago Press, in press.

———. "Self-Censorship in Public Discourse: A Theory of 'Political Correctness' and Related Phenomena." *Rationality and Society* 6, no. 4 (1994): 428–461.

Lowery, Wesley. "Graphic Video Shows Daniel Shaver Sobbing and Begging Officer for His Life before 2016 Shooting." *Washington Post*, December 8, 2017.

Lowery, Wesley, Kimbriell Kelly, Ted Mellnik, and Steven Rich. "Murder with Impunity: Where Killings Go Unsolved." *Washington Post*, June 6, 2018.

Lum, Kristian, and Patrick Ball. "Estimating Undocumented Homicides with Two Lists and List Dependence." Human Rights Data Analysis Group, 2015.

Mac Donald, Heather. "How to Increase the Crime Rate Nationwide." *Wall Street Journal*, June 11, 2013.

MacDonald, John, Jeffrey Fagan, and Amanda Geller. "The Effects of Local Police Surges on Crime and Arrests in New York City." *PLoS One* 11, no. 6 (2016): e0157223.

Macur, Juliet. "In Larry Nassar's Case, a Single Voice Eventually Raised an Army." *New York Times*, January 24, 2018.

Madon, Stephanie, Max Guyll, Kathy Aboufadel, Eulices Montiel, Alison Smith, Polly Palumbo, and Lee Jussim. "Ethnic and National Stereotypes: The Princeton Trilogy Revisited and Revised." *Personality and Social Psychology Bulletin* 27, no. 8 (2001): 996–1010.

Malega, Ron, and Thomas H. Cohen. "State Court Organization, 2011." Bureau of Justice Statistics, U.S. Department of Justice, 2013.

Martinelli, Ron. "Revisiting the '21-Foot Rule.'" *Police Magazine*, September 18, 2014.

Mauer, Marc. *The Changing Racial Dynamics of Women's Incarceration.* Sentencing Project Briefing Paper, February 2013.

Mauro, Tony. "Race Factor Tilts the Scales of Public Opinion." *USA Today*, February 5, 1997. https://usatoday30.usatoday.com/news/index/nns212.htm (accessed January 20, 2018).

Mayer, Jane. *Strange Justice: The Selling of Clarence Thomas.* New York: Plume Books, 1995.

McClellan, Chandler, and Erdal Tekin. "Stand Your Ground Laws, Homicides, and Injuries." *Journal of Human Resources* 52, no. 3 (2017): 621–653.

McCrummen, Stephanie, Beth Reinhard, and Alice Crites. "Woman Says Roy Moore Initiated Sexual Encounter When She Was 14, He Was 32." *Washington Post*, November 9, 2017.

McFarland, Melanie. "A Matter of Survival: 'The Talk' Is a Conversation about Parents, Kids and Police." *Salon*. February 20, 2017. http://www.salon.com/2017/02/20/a-matter-of-survival-the-talk-is-a-conversation-about-parents-kids-and-police/ (accessed July 23, 2017).

McMullen, Mary Jo, and C. J. Williams. "Injuries to Law Enforcement Officers Shot Wearing Personal Body Armor: A 30-Year Review." *Police Chief* 75, no. 8 (2008): 20–22.

McQuade, Dan. "Hannibal Buress on Bill Cosby: 'You're a Rapist.'" *Philadelphia Magazine*, October 17, 2014. http://www.phillymag.com/ticket/2014/10/17/hannibal-buress-bill-cosby-rapist/(accessed October 22, 2017).

Meissner, Christian, and John Brigham. "Thirty Years of Investigating the Own-Race Bias in Memory for Faces: A Meta-Analytic Review." *Psychology, Public Policy, and Law* 7, no. 1 (2001): 3–35.

Mendez, Garry A. *The Role of Race and Ethnicity in the Incidence of Police Use of Deadly Force.* Rockville, MD: National Institute for Justice, 1983.

Minton, Todd D., and Zhen Zeng. *Jail Inmates in 2015.* Office of Justice Programs, U.S. Department of Justice, Bureau of Justice Statistics, 2016.

Miron, Jeffrey A. *Drug War Crimes: The Consequences of Prohibition.* Oakland, CA: Independent Institute, 2004.

Mocan, Naci, and Ozkan Eren. "Emotional Judges and Unlucky Juveniles." *American Economic Journal: Applied Economics* 31, no. 1 (2018): 1–44.

Mohandie, Kris, J. Reid Meloy, and Peter I. Collins. "Suicide by Cop among Officer-Involved Shooting Cases." *Journal of Forensic Sciences* 54, no. 2 (2009): 456–462.

Montaldo, Charles. "Susan Smith—Profile of a Child Killer." *ThoughtCo.com.* December 31, 2016. https://www.thoughtco.com/susan-smith-profile-of-child-killer-972686 (accessed October 21, 2017).

Moody-Adams, Michele. "Racism." Edited by R. G. Frey and Christopher Heath Wellman. *A Companion to Applied Ethics.* Malden, MA: Blackwell, 2003. 89–101.

Moreau, Sophia. "What Is Discrimination?" *Philosophy & Public Affairs* 38, no. 2 (2010): 143–179.

Moskos, Peter. "Philando Castile." *Cop in the Hood.* July 7, 2016a. http://www.copinthehood.com/2016/07/philando-castile.html (accessed September 21, 2017).

———. "Reducing Police-Involved Shooting & 'The List.'" *Cop in the Hood.* July 14, 2016b. http://www.copinthehood.com/2016/07/reducing-police-involved-shooting.html (accessed September 23, 2017).

Mueller, Benjamin. "$25,000 Fine Proposed in Taxi Driver's Snub of Black Family." *New York Times,* August 6, 2015.

Mueller-Smith, Michael. "The Criminal and Labor Market Impacts of Incarceration." Unpublished manuscript, University of Michigan. 2015.

Muhammad, Khalil Gibran. *The Condemnation of Blackness.* Cambridge, MA: Harvard University Press, 2010.

Mullainathan, Sendhil. "Police Killings of Blacks: Here Is What the Data Say." *New York Times,* October 16, 2015.

Mydans, Seth. "4 White Policemen Indicted in Beating of Black Motorist." *New York Times,* March 16, 1991.

Myrdal, Gunnar. *An American Dilemma: The Negro Problem and Modern Democracy.* 2 vols. New Brunswick, NJ: Harper and Row, 1944.

Myrdal, Gunnar. "Inequality of Justice." *The Review of Black Political Economy* 16, no. 1–2 (1987): 81–98.

Nathan, Debbie. "What Happened to Sandra Bland?" *The Nation,* April 21, 2016.

National Academies of Sciences, Engineering, and Medicine. *Proactive Policing: Effects on Crime and Communities.* Edited by David Weisburd and Malay K. Majimundar. Washington, DC: National Academies Press, 2017.

National Advisory Commission on Civil Disorders. *Report of the National Advisory Commission on Civil Disorders.* Washington, DC: United States Government Printing Office, 1968.

National Consortium for the Study of Terrorism and Responses to Terrorism. "Fact Sheet: American Deaths in Terrorist Attacks." October 2015. https://www.start.umd.edu/pubs/START_AmericanTerrorismDeaths_FactSheet_Oct2015.pdf (accessed June 17, 2017).

National Research Council. *The Growth of Incarceration in the United States: Exploring Causes and Consequences.* Edited by Jeremy Travis, Bruce Western, and Steve Redburn. Washington, DC: National Academies Press, 2014.

National Research Council, Committee to Review Research on Police Policy and Practices. *Fairness and Effectiveness in Policing: The Evidence.* Edited by Wesley Kogan and Kathleen Frydl. Washington, DC: National Academies Press, 2004.

New York City Commision on Human Rights. "In Public Spaces." 2017. https://www1.nyc.gov/site/cchr/law/in-public-spaces.page (accessed January 6, 2018).

New York Civil Liberties Union. "Stop-and-Frisk Data." 2018. https://www.nyclu.org/en/stop-and-frisk-data (accessed January 17, 2018).

New York Times. "Central Park Jogger Case." October 3, 2012. https://www.nytimes.com/topic/subject/central-park-jogger-case-1989 (accessed October 21, 2017).

———. "Read Christine Blasey Ford's Prepared Statement." September 26, 2018. https://www.nytimes.com/2018/09/26/us/politics/christine-blasey-ford-prepared-statement.html (accessed October 15, 2018).

Nix, Justin, Bradley A. Campbell, Edward H. Byers, and Geoffrey P. Alpert. "A Bird's Eye View of Civilians Killed by Police in 2015." *Criminology & Public Policy* 1, no. 16 (2017): 309–340.

New York Job Source. "NY Police Department." December 6, 2012. http://www.nyjobsource.com/nypd.html (accessed January 7, 2018).

Nyong'o, Lupita. "Speaking Out about Harvey Weinstein." *New York Times,* October 19, 2017.

O'Flaherty, Brendan. *The Economics of Race in the United States.* Cambridge, MA: Harvard University Press, 2015.

O'Flaherty, Brendan, and Rajiv Sethi. "Crime and Segregation." *Journal of Economic Behavior & Organization* 64, no. 3 (2007): 391–405.

———. "Homicide in Black and White." *Journal of Urban Economics* 68, no. 3 (2010a): 215–230.

———. "Peaceable Kingdoms and War Zones: Preemption, Ballistics and Murder in Newark." Edited by Rafael Di Tella, Sebastian Edwards, and Ernesto Schargrodsky. *The Economics of Crime: Lessons for and from Latin America.* Chicago: University of Chicago Press, 2010b. 305–353.

———. "The Racial Geography of Street Vice." *Journal of Urban Economics* 67, no. 3 (2010c): 270–286.

———. "Racial Stereotypes and Robbery." *Journal of Economic Behavior & Organization* 68, no. 3 (2008): 511–524.

———. "Urban Crime." Edited by Gilles Duranton, J. Vernon Henderson, and William C. Strange. *Handbook of Regional and Urban Economics.* Amsterdam: Elsevier, 2015. 1519–1621.

———. "Why Have Robberies Become Less Frequent but More Violent?" *Journal of Law, Economics, and Organization* 25, no. 2 (2009): 518–534.

———. "Witness Intimidation." *Journal of Legal Studies* 39, no. 2 (2010d): 399–432.

Ogletree, Charles. *The Presumption of Guilt: The Arrest of Henry Louis Gates, Jr. and Race, Class and Crime in America*. New York: St. Martin's Press, 2010.

Okrent, Daniel. *Last Call: The Rise and Fall of Prohibition*. New York: Simon and Schuster, 2010.

Oswald, Frederick L., Gregory Mitchell, Hart Blanton, James Jaccard, and Philip E. Tetlock. "Predicting Ethnic and Racial Discrimination: A Meta-analysis of IAT Criterion Studies." *Journal of Personality and Social Psychology* 105, no. 2 (2013): 171–192.

Owens, Emily G. "The American Temperance Movement and Market-Based Violence." *American Law and Economics Review* 16, no. 2 (2014): 433–472.

———. "Are Underground Markets Really More Violent? Evidence from Early 20th Century America." *American Law and Economics Review* 13, no. 1 (2011a): 1–44.

———. "Truthiness in Punishment: The Far Reach of Truth-in-Sentencing Laws in State Courts." *Journal of Empirical Legal Studies* 8, no. S1 (2011b): 239–261.

Papachristos, Andrew V. "Murder by Structure: Dominance Relations and the Social Structure of Gang Homicide." *American Journal of Sociology* 115, no. 1 (2009): 74–128.

Papachristos, Andrew V., Anthony A. Hureau, and David M. Braga. "Social Networks and the Risk of Gunshot Injury." *Journal of Urban Health* 89, no. 6 (2012): 992–1003.

Papachristos, Andrew V., Christopher Wildeman, and Elizabeth Roberto. "Tragic, but Not Random: The Social Contagion of Nonfatal Gunshot Injuries." *Social Science & Medicine* 125 (2015): 139–150.

Patterson, Orlando. *Slavery and Social Death: A Comparative Study*. Cambridge, MA: Harvard University Press, 1982.

Payne, B. Keith. "Prejudice and Perception: The Role of Automatic and Controlled Processes in Misperceiving a Weapon." *Journal of Personality and Social Psychology* 81, no. 2 (2001): 181–192.

———. "Weapon Bias: Split-Second Decisions and Unintended Stereo-typing." *Current Directions in Psychological Science* 15, no. 6 (2006): 287–291.

Peña-Rodrigue₇ *v. Colorado*. 15–606 (Supreme Court of the United States, March 6, 2017).

Perrow, Charles. *Normal Accidents: Living with High Risk Technologies*. New York: Basic Books, 1984.

Pew Research Center. "A Minority of Americans Own Guns, but Just How Many Is Unclear." *FACTTANK*. June 4, 2013. http://www.pewresearch.org/fact-tank/2013/06/04/a-minority-of-americans-own-guns-but-just-how-many-is-unclear/ (accessed February 10, 2018).

———. "On Views of Race and Inequality, Blacks and Whites Are Worlds Apart." *Social and Demographic Trends*. June 27, 2016. http://www.pewsocialtrends.org/2016/06/27/on-views-of-race-and-inequality-blacks-and-whites-are-worlds-apart/ (accessed January 22, 2018).

Pfaff, John. *Locked In: The True Causes of Mass Incarceration—and How to Achieve Real Reform*. New York: Basic Books, 2017.

Phelps, Edmund S. "The Statistical Theory of Racism and Sexism." *American Economic Review* 62, no. 4 (1972): 659–661.

Pierson, Emma, Camelia Simoiu, Jan Overgoor, Sam Corbett-Davis, Vignesh Ramachandran, Cheryl Phillips, and Sharad Goel. "A Large-Scale Analysis of Racial Disparities in Police Stops across the United States." *arXiv preprint arXiv:1706.05678*, 2017.

Poutvaara, Panu, and Mikael Priks. "Hooliganism in the Shadow of the 9 / 11 Terrorist Attack and the Tsunami: Do Police Reduce Group Violence?" CESifo Working Paper Series No. 1882. 2006.

Powdermaker, Hortense. *After Freedom: A Cultural Study in the Deep South*. New York: Viking Press, 1939.

Preston, Julia. "Lil' Kim Gets One Year in Prison." *New York Times*, July 7, 2005.

Puckett, Janice L., and Richard J. Lundman. "Factors Affecting Homicide Clearances: Multivariate Analysis of a More Complete Conceptual Framework." *Journal of Research in Crime and Delinquency* 40, no. 2 (2003): 171–193.

Quine, Willard Van Orman. *From a Logical Point of View: Nine Logico-Philosophical Essays*. 2nd ed. Cambridge, MA: Harvard University Press, 1961.

Quinnipiac University. "Hatred on the Rise, American Voters Say, Quinnipiac University National Poll Finds; Concern about Anti-Semitism Jumps in One Month." March 9, 2017. https://poll.qu.edu/national/release-detail?ReleaseID=2438 (accessed January 22, 2018).

Quinnipiac University. "More U.S. Voters Say Don't Confirm Kavanaugh, Quinnipiac University National Poll Finds; More Voters Believe Ford Than Kavanaugh." October 1, 2018. https://poll.qu.edu/national/release-detail?ReleaseID=2574 (accessed October 14, 2018).

Rabin, Matthew, and Joel L. Schrag. "First Impressions Matter: A Model of Confirmatory Bias." *Quarterly Journal of Economics* 114, no. 1 (1999): 37–82.

Ramzy, Austin, Michelle Innis, and Patrick Boehler. "How a Conservative-Led Australia Ended Mass Killings." *New York Times*, December 4, 2015.

Raper, Arthur F. "Race and Class Pressures." The Carnegie-Myrdal Study, 1940.

Raphael, Steven, and Michael A. Stoll. *Why Are So Many Americans in Prison?* New York: Russell Sage Foundation, 2013.

Ratcliffe, Jerry H., Travis Taniguchi, Elizabeth R. Groff, and Jennifer D. Wood. "The Philadelphia Foot Patrol Experiment: A Randomized Controlled Trial of Police Patrol Effectiveness in Violent Crime Hotspots." *Criminology* 49, no. 3 (2011): 795–831.

Reaves, Brian A. "Felony Defendants in Large Urban Counties, 2009—Statistical Tables." Office of Justice Programs, U.S. Department of Justice, 2013.

———. *State and Local Law Enforcement Training Academies, 2013*. Office of Justice Programs, U.S. Department of Justice, Bureau of Justice Statistics, 2016.

Rehavi, M. Marit, and Sonja B. Starr. "Racial Disparity in Federal Criminal Sentences." *Journal of Political Economy* 122, no. 6 (2014): 1320–1354.

Reinhold, Robert. "After Police-Beating Verdict, Another Trial for the Jurors." *New York Times*, May 9, 1992.

Richeson, Jennifer A., and J. Nicole Shelton. "Negotiating Interracial Interactions: Costs, Consequences, and Possibilities." *Current Directions in Psychological Science* 16, no. 6 (2007): 316–320.

Richeson, Jennifer A., Abigail A. Baird, Heather L. Gordon, Todd F. Heatherton, Carrie L. Wyland, Sophie Trawalter, and J. Nicole Shelton. "An fMRI Investigation of the Impact of Interracial Contact on Executive Function." *Nature Neuroscience* 6, no. 12 (2003): 1323–1328.

Riedel, Marc. "Counting Stranger Homicides: A Case Study of Statistical Prestidigitation." *Homicide Studies* 2, no. 2 (1998): 206–219.

Risse, Mathias, and Richard Zeckhauser. "Racial Profiling." *Philosophy & Public Affairs* 32, no. 2 (2004): 131–170.

Robinson, Jayne E., and Michael R. Rand. "Criminal Victimization in the United States, 2008—Statistical Tables." *Bureau of Justice Statistics.* May 12, 2011. https://www.bjs.gov/index.cfm?ty=pbdetail&iid=2218 (accessed September 7, 2017).

Rogers, Melvin L. "Race, Domination, and Republicanism." Edited by Danielle Allen and Rohini Somanathan. *Difference without Domination: Pursuing Justice in Diverse Democracies.* Chicago: University of Chicago Press, in press.

Roman, John K. *Race, Justifiable Homicide, and Stand Your Ground Laws: Analysis of FBI Supplementary Homicide Reports Data.* Washington, DC: Urban Institute, 2013.

Rohrlich, Ted, and Fredric N. Tulsky. "Not All L.A. Murder Cases Are Equal." *Los Angeles Times,* December 3, 1996. http://articles.latimes.com/1996-12-03/news/mn-6131_1_murder-case (accessed October 12, 2018).

Rosenfeld, Richard, Michael J. Deckard, and Emily Blackburn. "The Effects of Directed Patrol and Self-Initiated Enforcement on Firearm Violence: A Randomized Controlled Study of Hot Spot Policing." *Criminology* 52, no. 3 (2014): 428–449.

Rosenthal, Andrew. "Bush Calls Police Beating 'Sickening.'" *New York Times,* March 22, 1991.

Saperstein, Aliya, and Andrew M. Penner. "The Race of a Criminal Record: How Incarceration Colors Racial Perception." *Social Problems* 57, no. 1 (2010): 92–113.

Scalese, Roberto. "The Charles Stuart Murders and the Racist Branding Boston Just Can't Seem to Shake." *boston.com*, October 22, 2014. https://www.boston.com/news/local-news/2014/10/22/the-charles -stuart-murders-and-the-racist-branding-boston-just-cant-seem-to -shake (accessed October 20, 2017).

Schelling, Thomas C. *The Strategy of Conflict*. Cambridge, MA: Harvard University Press, 1960.

Schmidt, Michael, and Matt Apuzzo. "South Carolina Officer Is Charged with Murder of Walter Scott." *New York Times*, April 7, 2015.

Schuman, Howard, Charlotte Steeh, Lawrence Bobo, and Maria Krysan. *Racial Attitudes in America: Trends and Interpretations*. Cambridge, MA: Harvard University Press, 1997.

Sellers, Frances Stead. "Trump May Face a Reckoning in Case Brought by Female Accuser." *Washington Post*, December 4, 2017.

Sethi, Rajiv. "Crime and Punishment in a Divided Society." Edited by Danielle Allen and Rohini Somanathan. *Difference without Domination: Pursuing Justice in Diverse Democracies*. Chicago: University of Chicago Press, in press.

Sethi, Rajiv, and Muhamet Yildiz. "Communication with Unknown Perspectives." *Econometrica* 84, no. 6 (2016): 2029–2069.

———. "Public Disagreement." *American Economic Journal: Microeconomics* 4, no. 3 (2012): 57–95.

Shaw, Julia, and Stephen Porter. "Constructing Rich False Memories of Committing Crime." *Psychological Science* 26, no. 3 (2015): 291–301.

Sherman, Lawrence W. "Reducing Fatal Police Shootings as System Crashes: Research, Theory, and Practice." *Annual Review of Criminology* 1 (2018): 421–449.

Sherman, Lawrence W., Patrick R. Gartin, and Michael E. Buerger. "Hot Spots of Predatory Crime: Routine Activities and the Criminology of Place." *Criminology* 27, no. 1 (1989): 27–56.

Shihadeh, Edward S., and Nicole Flynn. "Segregation and Crime: The Effect of Black Isolation on the Rates of Urban Violence." *Social Forces* 74, no. 4 (1996): 1325–1352.

Simon, David. *Homicide: A Year on the Killing Streets*. Boston: Houghton Mifflin, 1991.

Simpson, Craig. "Shootings by DC Police Spark Fight against Brutality 1936–41." *Washington Area Spark*. April 21, 2013. https://washingtonspark.wordpress.com/tag/national-negro-congress/ (accessed February 11, 2018).

Simpson, Edward H. "The Interpretation of Interaction in Contingency Tables." *Journal of the Royal Statistical Society. Series B (Methodological)*, 1951: 238–241.

Smallwood, James M. *Time of Hope, Time of Despair: Black Texans during Reconstruction*. Port Washington, NY: Kennikat Press, 1981.

Smith, Mitch, Christina Capecchi, and Matt Furber. "Peaceful Protests Follow Minnesota Governor's Call for Calm." *New York Times*, July 8, 2016.

South Carolina Department of Public Safety. "Second Follow Up: Trooper Involved Shooting in Richland County on September 4, 2014." September 19, 2014. http://www.scdps.gov/comm/nr2014/091914.html (accessed September 21, 2017).

Southall, Ashley. "Crime in New York City Plunges to a Level Not Seen since the 1950s." *New York Times*, December 27, 2017.

Spohn, Cassia. "The Effects of Offender's Race, Ethnicity and Sex on Federal Sentencing in the Guidelines Era." *Law and Contemporary Problems* 76, no. 1 (2013): 75–104.

Staples, Brent. *Parallel Time*. New York: Pantheon, 1994.

State of Minnesota v. Jeronimo Yanez. File number 0620373879 (District Court, Second Judicial District, November 15, 2016).

State of Missouri v. Darren Wilson. Grand Jury (Circuit Court of St. Louis County, August 20, 2014).

Steel, Emily, and Michael S. Schmidt. "Bill O'Reilly Thrives at Fox News, Even as Harassment Settlements Add Up." *New York Times*, April 1, 2017.

Steele, Claude M. *Whistling Vivaldi: And Other Clues to How Stereotypes Affect Us*. New York: Norton, 2010.

Stevenson, Bryan. *Just Mercy: A Story of Justice and Redemption*. New York: Spiegel & Grau, 2014.

Taylor, Bruce, Christopher S. Koper, and Daniel J. Woods. "A Randomized Controlled Trial of Different Policing Strategies at Hot Spots of Violent Crime." *Journal of Experimental Criminology* 7, no. 2 (2011): 149–181.

Taylor, Paul C. *Race: A Philosophical Introduction.* 2nd ed. Malden, MA: Polity Press, 2013.

Tennessee v. Gardner. 1471 (US 1, 1985).

Terrill, William, and Michael D. Reisig. "Neighborhood Context and Police Use of Force." *Journal of Research in Crime and Delinquency* 40, no. 3 (2003): 291–321.

Terry v. Ohio. 392 U.S. 1 (U.S. Supreme Court, 1968).

Texas Department of Public Safety. "Sandra Bland Traffic Stop." July 22, 2015. https://www.youtube.com/watch?v=CaWo9Ymr2BA (accessed July 23, 2017).

Tonry, Michael. *Punishing Race: A Continuing American Dilemma.* Oxford: Oxford University Press, 2011.

Tversky, Amos, and Daniel Kahneman. "Extensional versus Intuitive Reasoning: The Conjunction Fallacy in Probability Judgment." *Psychological Review* 90, no. 4 (1983): 293–315.

Tyler, Tom R. *Why People Obey the Law.* Princeton, NJ: Princeton University Press, 2006.

Tyler, Tom R., and Jeffrey Fagan. "Legitimacy and Cooperation: Why Do People Help the Police Fight Crime in Their Communities." *Ohio State Journal of Criminal Law* 6 (2008): 231–275.

Union, Gabrielle. *We're Going to Need More Wine: Stories That Are Funny, Complicated, and True.* HarperCollins, 2017.

United States Army. *Field Manual 3–24: Counterinsurgency.* Washington, DC: Department of the Army, 2006.

United States Bureau of Labor Statistics. "Injuries, Illnesses, and Fatalities: Fact Sheet: Workplace Homicides from Shootings." 2013. www.bls.gov /iif/oshwc/cfoi/osar0016.htm (accessed May 30, 2017).

———. "Occupational Employment Statistics." 2010. www.bls.gov/oes /tables.htm (accessed May 30, 2017).

United States Department of Justice. "Attorney General Eric Holder Addresses the NAACP Annual Convention." *Justice News.* July 16, 2013. https://www.justice.gov/opa/speech/attorney-general-eric-holder -addresses-naacp-annual-convention (accessed July 23, 2017).

———. "Investigation of the Ferguson Police Department." Civil Rights Division, Washington, DC, 2015a.

————. *Report Regarding the Criminal Investigation into the Shooting Death of Michael Brown by Ferguson, Missouri Police Officer Darren Wilson.* Memorandum. Washington, DC: United States Department of Justice, 2015b.

United States Environmental Protection Agency. *Mortality Risk Valuation.* 2017. https://www.epa.gov/environmental-economics/mortality-risk -valuation (accessed January 30, 2018).

United States Federal Bureau of Investigation. "Officers Feloniously Killed." *2015 Law Enforcement Officers Killed and Assaulted.* 2015. https://ucr.fbi .gov/leoka/2015/officers-feloniously-killed/felonious_topic_page_-2015 (accessed September 17, 2017).

United States Government Accountability Office. "Death Penalty Sentencing: Research Indicates Pattern of Racial Disparities." 1990. https:// www.gao.gov/products/GGD-90-57 (accessed January 16, 2019).

United States Kerner Commission. *Report of the National Advisory Commission on Civil Disorders.* Washington, DC: US Government Printing Office, 1968.

University at Albany. *Sourcebook of Criminal Justice Statistics.* Hindelang Criminal Justice Research Center. 2013. https://www.albany.edu/source book/(accessed January 16, 2018).

Wagner, Peter. "Incarceration Is Not an Equal Opportunity Punishment." *Prison Policy Initiative.* August 28, 2012. https://www.prisonpolicy.org /articles/notequal.html (accessed August 10, 2014).

Walen, Alec. "Retributive Justice." *The Stanford Encyclopedia of Philosophy (Winter 2016 Edition).* Edited by Edward N. Zalta. 2016. https://plato .stanford.edu/entries/justice-retributive/(accessed January 17, 2018).

Walmsley, Roy. *World Prison Population List.* 9th ed. Essex: International Centre for Prison Studies, 2011.

————. *World Prison Population List.* 10th ed. Essex: International Centre for Prison Studies, 2013.

Wang, Vivian. "Video Shows Daniel Shaver Pleading for His Life before Being Shot by Officer." *New York Times,* December 9, 2017.

Washington, Booker T. "My View of Segregation Laws." *New Republic.* December 3, 1915. https://newrepublic.com/article/103513/my-view-seg regation-laws (accessed October 12, 2018).

Washington Post. "Fatal Force." 2017. https://www.washingtonpost.com /graphics/national/police-shootings-2017/(accessed September 23, 2017).

Waytz, Adam, Kelly Marie Hoffman, and Sophie Trawalter. "A Superhuman-ization Bias in Whites' Perceptions of Blacks." *Social Psychological and Personality Science* 6, no. 3 (2015): 352–359.

Weiner, David A., Byron F. Lutz, and Jens Ludwig. "The Effects of School Desegregation on Crime." National Bureau of Economic Research Working Paper No. w15380. 2009.

Weisburd, David, Alese Wooditch, Sarit Weisburd, and Sue-Ming Yang. "Do Stop, Question, and Frisk Practices Deter Crime?" *Criminology & Public Policy* 15, no. 1 (2016): 31–56.

Wellford, Charles, and James Cronin. *An Analysis of Variables Affecting the Detection of Homicides: A Multivariate Study.* Washington, DC: Justice Research Statistics Association, 1999.

Wells-Barnett, Ida B. *Mob Rule in New Orleans: Robert Charles and His Fight to Death, the Story of His Life, Burning Human Beings Alive, Other Lynching Statistics.* Chicago, IL: Ida B. Wells-Barnett, 1900.

———. *A Red Record: Tabulated Statistics and Alleged Causes of Lynchings in the United States.* Donohue & Henneberry, 1894.

Wenzel, Michael, Farid Anvari, Melissa de Vel-Palumbo, and Simon M. Bury. "Collective Apology, Hope, and Forgiveness." *Journal of Experimental Social Psychology* 72 (2017): 75–87.

Wexler, Chuck, ed. *Re-engineering Training on Police Use of Force.* Washington, DC: Police Executive Research Forum, 2015.

White, Steven. "The Heterogeneity of Southern White Distinctiveness." *American Politics Research* 42, no. 4 (2013): 551–578.

Wible, Pamela. "Her Story Went Viral. But She Is Not The Only Black Doctor Ignored In An Airplane Emergency." *Washington Post*, October 20, 2016.

Wideman, J. Edgar. "The Seat Not Taken." *New York Times*, October 6, 2010.

Will, George. "Repeal the Second Amendment." *The Dispatch*, March 20, 1991.

Williams, Lauren. "Hands Up, Don't Shoot." *Vox*, August 13, 2014. https://www.vox.com/2014/8/13/5998591/hands-up-dont-shoot-photos-ferguson-michael-brown (accessed August 3, 2017).

Williams, Morgan. "Gun Violence in Black and White: Evidence from Policy Reform in Missouri." Working Paper, MIT. 2017.

Wingo, Ajume. "Human Dignity and Modern Democracies." Edited by Danielle Allen and Rohini Somanathan. *Difference without Domination: Pursuing Justice in Diverse Democracies.* Chicago: University of Chicago Press, in press.

Wittes, Benjamin. "Ditch the Second Amendment." March 19, 2007. https://www.brookings.edu/opinions/ditch-the-second-amendment/(accessed January 30, 2018).

Wolf, Z. Byron. "CNN / ORC Poll Finds Racial Divide on Police, Justice System." *CNN Politics,* December 22, 2014. http://www.cnn.com/2014/12/22/politics/cnn-poll-racial-divide-justice/index.html (accessed January 22, 2018).

Wood, Elisabeth Jean. "Rape as a Practice of War: Toward a Typology of Political Violence." *Politics & Society* 46, no. 4 (2018):513–537.

Wright, Richard T., and Scott H. Decker. *Armed Robbers in Action: Stickups and Street Culture.* Boston: Northeastern University Press, 1997.

Zimring, Franklin E. *The City That Became Safe: New York's Lessons for Urban Crime and Its Control.* Oxford: Oxford University Press, 2012.

———. *When Police Kill.* Cambridge, MA: Harvard University Press, 2017.

Acknowledgments

This book was first conceived more than a decade ago, and we have many people to thank for their support, encouragement, and feedback over the years.

We are especially grateful to Danielle Allen, Sam Bowles, Glenn Loury, Paul Seabright, and Elisabeth Wood. Sam, Glenn, and Paul read through an earlier version of the manuscript with great care and helped us improve our logic and exposition. Glenn also engaged us in lively debate—via email, in person, and on his *blogginheads* show—always compelling us to clarify and sharpen our arguments. Danielle, working jointly with Rohini Somanathan, convened a series of workshops at Harvard's Safra Center for Ethics, where we had the opportunity to present some of our ideas in preliminary form to an extraordinary set of participants spanning many different disciplines. Libby invited us to present our chapters on the use of force at the Political Violence and Its Legacies workshop at Yale, where again we received enormously useful feedback from a very interesting and interdisciplinary group. She also sent us a steady stream of relevant stories and articles, many of which helped us refine and illustrate our arguments.

Before he passed away, Robert Curvin helped develop our ideas about Newark, 1967, and justice in general. Many others provided helpful suggestions and guides to relevant literature in conversations and written exchanges. We are especially thankful to David Allison, Marcellus Andrews, Mahzarin Banaji, Jenna Bednar, Sian Beilock, Carroll Bogert, Wendy Carlin, Daniel Chen, Don Davis, Crystal Feimster, Kai Friese, Heather Gerken, David Glasner, Daniel

Hirschel-Burns, Johannes Horner, Regina Waynes Joseph, Willemien Kets, Do-Yeong Kim, Philip Kitcher, Calvin Lai, Louisa Lombard, John Miller, Faith Miller-Sethi, Michelle Moody-Adams, José Moya, José Luis Montiel Olea, Atul Nerkar, Scott Page, John Pfaff, Steven Raphael, Mara Revkin, Shiva Sethi, Rohini Somanathan, Lisa Son, Sarah Thomas, Miday Wilkey, Archibald Williams, and Morgan Williams Jr.

Sixteen Barnard College students read early versions of several chapters in the seminar Stereotypes, Crime, and Justice in the fall of 2017. The lively discussions in this course helped us think through and clarify many ideas, and we would like to thank these students: Shumaisa Ahmed, Nergiz De Baere, Stephanie Ching, Melisa Hipolito, Tian Yi Huang, Charlotte Hughes, Fahmida Hussain, Rebecca Jedwab, Poonam Lakhani, Evie McCorkle, Mikala Merey, Roxanne Padilla, Jessica Reich, Zoë Ryan, Sin Wan Ada Tam, and Tian Weinberg.

Our students in the courses Urban Economics and the Economics of Race also had to endure preliminary versions of many of the ideas in this book, and we are grateful to them too. The students in the spring 2017 Economics and Philosophy seminar along with Philip Kitcher, who co-taught the course, also sharpened our ideas and discovered many connections that we had not previously seen.

We received early encouragement to write this book from Tim Sullivan, Seth Ditchik, Margo Fleming, and—at a crucial and ultimately decisive time—Ian Malcolm of Harvard University Press. Our manuscript editor Louise Robbins, production editor Sherry Gerstein, and copy editor Liz Schueler made the book more readable than it otherwise would have been.

We wrote parts of the manuscript at the Santa Fe Institute, an ideal environment for interdisciplinary research. We are grateful to the Institute, as well as our home institutions—Barnard College and Columbia University—for supporting our research. We also thank our research assistants—Arina Balako, Chloe Dennison, Julia Hewitt, Olivia Hartzel, Rebecca Jedwab, Natalie Kozlova, Fu Jin Ariel Leachman, Sophie Rothman, Sophia Seidenberg, and Pratyush Tiwari—for their effort and care.

Members of the Newark Police Department have tutored us through the years. We are grateful to Hubert Williams, Charles Knox, Joseph Santiago, Garry McCarthy, John Dough, and Megan Ambrosio. We also thank Rachel Morgan, a statistician at the Bureau of Justice Statistics, who provided us with data from the National Crime Victimization Survey and helped us understand these data better.

We presented an earlier version of Chapter 8 at a forum on the fiftieth anniversary of the Kerner Commission report at the Union Theological Seminary, sponsored by the Institute for New Economic Thinking and the Eisenhower Foundation. We received helpful comments there from Jeff Fagan, Amanda Geller, Arpit Gupta, and Darrick Hamilton, and are very grateful to them all.

Our greatest debt is to our families. Mohini and Manmohan Sethi, Faith Miller-Sethi, Shiva Michael Sethi, and Mary P. Gallagher—ably assisted by Niamh N. Gallagher and Nelly B. O'Flaherty—supported us throughout the endeavor and excused our inattention generously.

We apologize for any errors remaining in the book, including the unintentional omission in these acknowledgments of people who have helped us along the way. Our debt to you is even greater for not being properly acknowledged.

We dedicate this book to two parents-in-law—a white man and a black woman—who lived in very different social worlds but whose paths may well have crossed in Brooklyn many decades ago.

Marjorie Woods was born in a North Carolina sharecropping community in 1935. She moved to New York shortly after graduating from high school with hopes of becoming a nurse, but this path was largely closed to black women at the time. She found work as a nurse's aide at Kings County Hospital in East Flatbush, where she met and married Gerald Miller, one of the few black firefighters in the New York City Fire Department during his years of service. She completed an undergraduate degree after the birth of her third child, then two graduate degrees, and was a special education teacher in Suffolk County until her retirement. She was a striver, a survivor, an avid reader, and an inspiration to all who knew her.

Pat Gallagher was born in East Flatbush in 1929 and grew up there. He excelled as a student at Brooklyn Prep and was offered a scholarship at Notre Dame, but stayed in Brooklyn and went to Fordham College at night so he could support his parents and brothers. During the Korean War he served in Japan, and he married Mary Furey a few days before he shipped out. He joined the New York City Police Department upon his return and eventually worked his way up to lieutenant. During his entire tenure as a police officer, he never discharged his gun, except on the firing range, and his stories about his time on the force recalled buying meals for panhandlers. Pat too loved books and read voraciously, and he dreamed of opening his own small bookstore. Instead, his retirement was taken up watching out for his grandchildren and neighbors. He was a wise man and a good cop.

Index

INDEX

INDEX